Stan Brakhage: Interviews

Conversations with Filmmakers Series
Gerald Peary, General Editor

Stan Brakhage
INTERVIEWS

Edited by Suranjan Ganguly

University Press of Mississippi / Jackson

www.upress.state.ms.us

The University Press of Mississippi is a member of the
Association of American University Presses.

Copyright © 2017 by University Press of Mississippi
All rights reserved

First printing 2017

∞

Library of Congress Cataloging-in-Publication Data

Names: Brakhage, Stan author. | Ganguly, Suranjan, 1958– editor.
Title: Stan Brakhage : interviews / edited by Suranjan Ganguly.
Description: Jackson : University Press of Mississippi, 2017. | Series: Conversations with filmmakers series | Includes bibliographical references and index. | Includes filmography.
Identifiers: LCCN 2016051214 (print) | LCCN 2017005524 (ebook) | ISBN 9781496810694 (hardcover : alk. paper) | ISBN 9781496810700 (epub single) | ISBN 9781496810717 (epub institutional) | ISBN 9781496810724 (pdf single) | ISBN 9781496810731 (pdf institutional)
Subjects: LCSH: Brakhage, Stan—Interviews. | Motion picture producers and directors—United States—Interviews.
Classification: LCC PN1998.3.B74 A5 2017 (print) | LCC PN1998.3.B74 (ebook) | DDC 791.4302/33092—dc23
LC record available at https://lccn.loc.gov/2016051214

British Library Cataloging-in-Publication Data available

Stan Brakhage
INTERVIEWS

Edited by Suranjan Ganguly

University Press of Mississippi / Jackson

www.upress.state.ms.us

The University Press of Mississippi is a member of the
Association of American University Presses.

Copyright © 2017 by University Press of Mississippi
All rights reserved

First printing 2017

∞

Library of Congress Cataloging-in-Publication Data

Names: Brakhage, Stan author. | Ganguly, Suranjan, 1958– editor.
Title: Stan Brakhage : interviews / edited by Suranjan Ganguly.
Description: Jackson : University Press of Mississippi, 2017. | Series:
   Conversations with filmmakers series | Includes bibliographical references
   and index. | Includes filmography.
Identifiers: LCCN 2016051214 (print) | LCCN 2017005524 (ebook) | ISBN
   9781496810694 (hardcover : alk. paper) | ISBN 9781496810700 (epub single)
   | ISBN 9781496810717 (epub institutional) | ISBN 9781496810724 (pdf
   single) | ISBN 9781496810731 (pdf institutional)
Subjects: LCSH: Brakhage, Stan—Interviews. | Motion picture producers and
   directors—United States—Interviews.
Classification: LCC PN1998.3.B74 A5 2017 (print) | LCC PN1998.3.B74 (ebook) |
   DDC 791.4302/33092—dc23
LC record available at https://lccn.loc.gov/2016051214

British Library Cataloging-in-Publication Data available

To Don Yannacito
and in loving memory of Phil Rowe and Forrest Williams

Contents

Introduction   ix

Chronology   xiv

Selected Filmography   xvii

Interview with Stan Brakhage   3
    P. Adams Sitney / 1963

Stan and Jane Brakhage, Talking   29
    Hollis Frampton / 1973

On Filming Light   51
    Forrest Williams / 1974

All That Is Light: Brakhage at 60   66
    Suranjan Ganguly / 1992–1993

Stan Brakhage: The 60th Birthday Interview   76
    Suranjan Ganguly / 1992–1993

Stan Brakhage   96
    Scott MacDonald / 1996–2002

Another Way of Looking at the Universe   124
    Ronald Johnson (with Jim Shedden) / 1997

With Stan Brakhage   130
    Philip Taaffe / 1997

Interview with Stan Brakhage   145
    Pip Chodorov / 2003

Additional Resources   160

Index   164

Introduction

This has been a personal project from the outset—in fact, a labor of love in honor of a great friend, colleague, and mentor whom I had the privilege of knowing for twelve years before his death in 2003. It also gives me great pleasure to complete this book after assuming the directorship of the Brakhage Center, which is actively engaged in keeping alive the filmmaker's legacy.

When I began teaching in the Film Studies program at CU–Boulder, Brakhage was in his late fifties, famous and prolific, often making two to three films a month, a formidable creative presence in our midst. And then there was Stan with his Santa Claus laugh and bone-crushing bear hugs, whose explosive energy, bonhomie, and warmth became indispensable to our lives. His uniqueness as an individual encompassed both selves—something I've kept in mind while selecting the nine interviews in this book. Anecdotes, stories, jokes, and the occasional invective mingle freely with some of his most profound articulations. Stan sings, recites poetry, laughs uproariously, sighs deeply while speaking on a variety of subjects dear to him but, above all, on the art of film, his life-long obsession.

Stan always gave himself freely to those who sought him out, which explains the large number of interviews that exist in print and on audio and video tape. He was fond of company and rarely turned anybody away. And he was extraordinarily patient since most people asked the same questions and desired the same clarifications. I can testify to this myself because, shortly after we became colleagues and close friends, I began videotaping what was going to be an informal interview, lasting no more than two hours. I was then in the process of discovering his work during his Sunday salons, which took place on campus or in his living room and which a select few were invited to attend. Our interview eventually went on sporadically for several months, largely at Stan's initiative, generating a one-hundred-page transcript. I subsequently published two excerpts from it, which are included here. In retrospect, I realize how naïve and simplistic some of my queries—those of a young initiate—must have sounded, but Stan never displayed a trace of irritability. On the other hand, he was eager to open up, and spoke expansively and eloquently about his work. The experience deepened our friendship.

Given the large amount of material available to the Brakhage scholar and the many overlaps in content, making the final selection was not easy. Eventually, I chose those interviews that are fairly diverse in subject matter, provide a broad-based framework to his cinema and are conducted by people with various specialties. Thus along with such notable film scholars as P. Adams Sitney and Scott MacDonald, the book features the poet Ronald Johnson, filmmaker Hollis Frampton, painter Philip Taaffe, philosophy professor Forrest Williams, and the writer and filmmaker Pip Chodorov.

Adams Sitney's 1963 interview, with which this book opens, is arguably Stan's first major interview, at a very important time in his life when he was still editing *Dog Star Man*. Stan defines the contexts that shaped this seminal film and discusses in depth the key films that preceded it: *Anticipation of the Night*, *Cat's Cradle*, *Wedlock House: An Intercourse*, *Window Water Baby Moving*, *The Dead*, and *Sirius Remembered*. He also speaks of wife Jane's role as collaborator, especially in relation to *Window Water Baby Moving* and *Dog Star Man*—a subject that recurs in these interviews but often from shifting perspectives. He also alludes to a collaboration that verges on the mystical—a visitation by three mysterious "personages" in the dead of night while he was editing *Sirius Remembered*. The "power that was helping me from the inside out" anticipates his subsequent descriptions of the muse and her influence on him.

The conversation with Hollis Frampton and Jane is perhaps the most informal and lively. Tape Two features a deeply moving, poetic rendition of light and its specific qualities: "I see light that appears to pool. It appears to be a glow that's as if it had weight and liquid substance.... There's also a quality of light that streams over the ground ... running absolutely counter to the blow of the wind.... It looks very much like a mountain stream." And Stan talks of searching for "equivalents" since the camera is incapable of capturing what his eye reveals to him. Michael McClure's concept of "elfskin" is invoked along with Johannes Scotus Erigena's "All things that are, are light," which Stan loved to quote in different versions. Tape Two also features Jane's riposte—"He just uses me"—when Stan and Hollis discuss Stan's attempts to make a portrait of her. This, of course, generates a spirited debate with Jane claiming that such a portrait is essentially a self-portrait of Stan's.

"On Filming Light," which comes appropriately right after Stan's meditations on light, focuses to a large extent on his experience of filming *Deus Ex* under the artificial lights of an operating theater in Pittsburgh. Forrest Williams, the interviewer, was a CU philosophy professor and a distinguished Merleau-Ponty scholar. He starts off by making a crucial distinction between "radiant" light and "luminescent" light that dominates much of the conversation in the first half of the interview. Later, Stan talks about his use of light in *Anticipation of the Night*, *The Text of Light*, and *Sexual Meditations*. Williams, predictably, gives the interview a philosophical basis, alluding to Plato's Allegory of the Cave and Merleau-Ponty's concept of "profane vision." He concludes with the hope articulated in *Phenomenology of Perception* that we can somehow foil the "ruse" of vision that condemns us to "the oblivion of objects." Stan, in his own unique way, offers the same hope at the beginning of *Metaphors on Vision*.

My two interviews in *Sight and Sound* and *Film Culture* respectively allude to Stan's sixtieth birthday, which provided the context for their publication. They cover the fundamental aspects of his cinema, focusing on his theories of vision (especially closed-eye or hypnagogic vision and moving visual thinking), the predisposition of film as a medium to embody different forms of seeing, the ongoing search for equivalents and the adoption of non-filmic modes such as scratching and painting on film, the general absence of sound from his work and the occasional exception, his relationships with specific composers and musicians, and his concept of visual music. Both publications refer to the films of the late eighties and early nineties during which his hand-painted work had gained prominence. This new commitment to abstraction results in a repudiation of all previous modes of filmmaking. As he puts it, "I feel an increasing need to make something that has no title, that has no subject matter, that doesn't consciously draw on any of the other arts or even on the cells of the brain and the optic system...." And he reasserts the importance of film as song, a belief that sustained him all his life:

> I believe in song. That's what I wanted to do and I did it quite selfishly, out of my own need to come through to a voice that is comparable with song and related to all animal life on earth. I believe in the beauty of the singing of the whale; I am moved deeply at the whole range of song that the wolf makes when the moon appears, or neighborhood dogs make—that they make their song, and this is the wonder of life on earth, and I in great humility wish to join this.

Scott MacDonald's "Stan Brakhage" is a compilation of conversations from 1996 to 2002 (with a few gaps in chronology), constituting perhaps the most definitive Brakhage interview. In print it is eighty-five pages in length and indispensable to scholars who wish to study contexts, histories, influences, and the underlying thought process of most of Stan's major films. It deserves to be included in its entirety but I've had to limit myself to only a few excerpts.

Given Stan's lifelong passion for poetry (he often called himself "a failed poet") and his friendships with many eminent poets, I chose to include a short interview conducted by Ronald Johnson (with Jim Shedden, the Canadian filmmaker who made *Brakhage* in 1998). At one point, the conversation shifts to William Carlos Williams's famous formulation, "No ideas but in things," which Stan rejects, claiming that he works with ephemera and that cinema by nature is to be "fleeting and moving on." Johnson counters with "when you get the specific things, that's where poetry is alive," but for Stan the danger lies in film becoming "picture or illustration." The way out is to "lift these specifics so they can be made to reverberate," to create inferences since "the eye is always roving."

Along with poets, Stan's fondness for visual artists, especially painters, made me seek out Philip Taaffe's 1997 conversation with him, which is reproduced in full in his book *Composite Nature*. The two range back and forth over a wide range of topics, often returning to the subject of aesthetics. One humorous exchange alludes to the arboreal world. Taaffe asks, "What is this fear of fern forests, Stan; can we get to the bottom of this?" Stan's response "that they're too much the same on one side as the other, though they're not identical" subsequently provokes a critique of the geometric in art which he points out doesn't exist in nature or anywhere on earth but is a "late human idea." Earlier, he makes a strong case against symmetry, which he finds positively "dangerous" and best to be avoided. Another exchange revolves around the word "image," which Stan is reluctant to define. Instead, he voices his preference for "visual" and then attempts to describe "envisionment": "I suppose that means after the continuities of time, and out of all that vision, what reverberates as meaning—the composition of the whole of it." Considering that Stan likes to employ this complex term quite often, this is perhaps the best explanation he offers.

The last conversation in this book is between Stan and Pip Chodorov, based on audio recordings made for a fifteen-minute portrait film, two months before Stan's death in Victoria, Canada. His cancer was then at an advanced stage and he was on morphine. He was worried that he would ramble on camera—as he told me over the phone—but he is remarkably focused and lucid for the most part. The interview begins with an exegesis of the opening lines from *Metaphors on Vision* and ends with Stan singing, "I can't give you anything but love, baby!"(when asked what holds his disparate films together). During most of the conversation, Stan revisits some of his favorite subjects such as the distinction between prose and poetry in relation to cinema, film's relationship to music, and the uniqueness of the artist, and pays an extended homage to Gertrude Stein, one of his beloved mentors, by providing a fascinating reading of her legendary "rose is a rose is a rose is a rose." He also talks about *Chinese Series*, his final film, which he made by moistening a strip of 35mm film with his spittle and scratching on its surface with his fingernails. Near the end of the interview, he speaks with genuine humility of how he sees himself as "leaving a snail's trail in the moonlight than of someone sitting and consciously making an art," which acquires a special poignancy in the context of his illness and approaching death, a valedictory reaffirmation of a great artist's sense of self and legacy.

I owe a big debt of gratitude to Marilyn Brakhage, who has been an extraordinary source of help with this project. I especially wish to thank her for alerting me to certain interviews I would have otherwise missed and for meticulously revising the filmography and chronology. I also wish to sincerely thank Kalpana Subramanian for her painstaking research in preparing the first drafts of both documents. I am very grateful to my colleagues Don Yannacito, Phil Solomon, and David Gatten who generously provided wise counsel and moral support. I am also most thankful to Joel Haertling, Emilie Vergé, Jane Wodening, and Brad Arnold for answering some complicated questions and drawing my attention to key resources. Finally, a big thank you to Leila Salisbury, Valerie Jones, and Lisa McMurtray of the University Press of Mississippi for their patience and flexibility, and their assistance at every stage of the production of this book.

SG

Chronology

1933   Born Robert Sanders on January 14 in an orphanage in Kansas City and adopted by Ludwig and Clara Brakhage.

1940   Parents separate. Moves to Denver with Clara.

1941   Boy soprano in the junior choir at St. John's cathedral.

1948   Enrolls at South High School. Along with Larry Jordan, Ramiro Cortez, Robert Benson, Gordon Rosenblum, Stan Phillips, and others, forms the Gadflies.

1951   Finishes school. Awarded a scholarship to Dartmouth College.

1952   Leaves Dartmouth and buys filmmaking equipment with remaining college funds. Makes *Interim*, his debut film, in Denver, at the age of nineteen, with soundtrack by James Tenney.

1953   Spends most of the year in San Francisco. Attends the California School of Arts (now the San Francisco Art Institute) for a few months. Through Robert Duncan and Jess Collins comes in contact with Kenneth Rexroth and James Broughton. Makes *Unglassed Windows Cast a Terrible Reflection* in Nevadaville, Colorado, in summer.

1954   Works at various jobs in San Francisco, including commercial freelance 16mm photography and editing. Makes *Desistfilm* and *The Way to Shadow Garden*. Moves to New York in August.

1955   Makes *Reflections on Black* and completes *In Between*, his first color film with music by John Cage. During his stay in New York, meets Maya Deren, Marie Menken, Willard Maas, Jonas Mekas, and Adolfas Mekas. His first silent film, *The Wonder Ring*, is commissioned by Joseph Cornell. Awarded a Fulbright scholarship to study in Rome, which he eventually declines.

1957   Marries Mary Jane Collom.

1958   Lives in Princeton. Completes *Anticipation of the Night*. Wins the Brussels World Fair Protest Award. Films Jane giving birth to daughter, Myrrena, for *Window Water Baby Moving*, released in 1959. Myrenna is the first of five children from his first marriage.

1959   Moves back to Colorado. Completes *Sirius Remembered*, *Wedlock House: An Intercourse*, and *Cat's Cradle*, shot while living east.

1960	Birth of daughter Crystal.
1961	Begins work on *Dog Star Man*. Films the birth of his third child, Neowyn, for *Thigh Line Lyre Triangular*.
1963	Publication of *Metaphors on Vision*. Makes *Mothlight*. Birth of son Bearthm.
1964	Begins work on *Songs*, shot in 8mm, which will include *23rd Psalm Branch* (1966–1967). Completes *Dog Star Man*. Birth of son Rarc.
1967	Wins a Rockefeller Grant that enables him to start shooting the four-part *Scenes from Under Childhood* in 16mm.
1969	Starts teaching film history and aesthetics at the School of the Art Institute of Chicago (until 1981), traveling from Colorado every other week.
1971	Completes *Eyes*, *Deus Ex*, and *The Act of Seeing with One's Own Eyes*, collectively known as the Pittsburgh Trilogy or the Pittsburgh Documents. First retrospective at the Museum of Modern Art, New York. Publication of *A Moving Picture Giving and Taking Book*.
1972	Completes the six-part *Sexual Meditations*. Publication of *The Brakhage Lectures*.
1973	Receives the Brandeis University Creative Arts Award Citation.
1974	Makes *The Text of Light*. Receives the Colorado Governor's Award for the Arts and Humanities.
1977	Publication of *Film Biographies*.
1978	Receives a Guggenheim Fellowship.
1979	Receives the Jimmy Ryan Morris Memorial Foundation Award.
1980	Completes the *Sincerity* and *Duplicity* film cycles.
1981	Receives the Telluride Film Festival Medallion. Begins teaching in the Film Studies program at the University of Colorado, Boulder. Honorary Doctorate from the San Francisco Art Institute.
1982	Publication of *Brakhage Scrapbook*.
1984	Makes *Tortured Dust*.
1986	Maya Deren Award for Independent Film and Video Artists. Separates from Jane. Begins work on the four-part *FaustFilm* cycle.
1987	Completes *The Dante Quartet*. End of his marriage to Jane.
1988	Makes *I Dreaming* with music by Joel Haertling and Stephen Foster. Receives the Denver International Film Festival Award for Outstanding Achievement in the Art of Film. Awarded the University of Colorado Medal. Publication of *I . . . Sleeping*.
1989	Marries Marilyn Jull. Completes the first film in the *Babylon Series* as well as the first two parts of the *Visions in Meditation* cycle. Publication of *Film at Wit's End*. Receives the MacDowell Colony Medal. Birth of son Anton.

1990	Makes *Passage Through: A Ritual* with music by Philip Corner. Begins work on the Vancouver Island films.
1991	Completes *Christ Mass Sex Dance*, set to music by James Tenney. Birth of son Vaughn.
1992	The Library of Congress selects *Dog Star Man* for inclusion in the National Film Registry.
1994	Collaborates with Phil Solomon on the hand-painted and step-printed film *Elementary Phrases*, the first of three collaborations. Receives an honorary degree from the California Institute of the Arts.
1996	Surgery for bladder cancer.
1997	Makes *Yggdrasill: Whose Roots Are Stars in the Human Mind*.
1999	Jim Shedden's film *Brakhage* is released in the US.
2000	Receives an honorary degree from Bard College.
2001	Publication of *Essential Brakhage*. Completes *The Persian Series*.
2002	Retires from teaching as Distinguished Professor. Moves to Victoria, British Columbia, Canada.
2003	Dies on March 9 in Victoria at the age of seventy. His last film, *Chinese Series*, is made by scratching on a strip of 35mm film with his fingernails. Publication of *Telling Time: Essays of a Visionary Filmmaker*. The Criterion Collection releases *By Brakhage, An Anthology, volume 1*, a 2-disc DVD set. Volume 2 is released in 2010.

Selected Filmography

INTERIM (1952)
16mm, 24 minutes, black and white, sound (music by James Tenney)

DESISTFILM (1954)
16mm, 6 minutes 48 seconds, black and white, sound

THE WAY TO SHADOW GARDEN (1954)
16mm, 10 minutes 54 seconds, black and white, sound

IN BETWEEN (1955)
16mm, 9 minutes 20 seconds, color, sound (music by John Cage)

REFLECTIONS ON BLACK (1955)
16mm, 11 minutes 8 seconds, black and white, sound

THE WONDER RING (1955)
16mm, 5 minutes 34 seconds, color, silent

FLESH OF MORNING (1956)
16mm, 20 minutes 53 seconds, black and white, sound

NIGHTCATS (1956)
16mm, 8 minutes 33 seconds, color, silent

DAYBREAK AND WHITEYE (1957)
16mm, 9½ minutes, black and white, sound

LOVING (1957)
16mm, 3 minutes 51 seconds, color, silent

ANTICIPATION OF THE NIGHT (1958)
16mm, 39 minutes 53 seconds, color, silent

SELECTED FILMOGRAPHY

CAT'S CRADLE (1959)
16mm, 6 minutes 16 seconds, color, silent

SIRIUS REMEMBERED (1959)
16mm, 10 minutes 35 seconds, color, silent

WEDLOCK HOUSE: AN INTERCOURSE (1959)
16mm, 10 minutes 47 seconds, black and white, silent

WINDOW WATER BABY MOVING (1959)
16mm, 12 minutes 11 seconds, color, silent

THE DEAD (1960)
16mm, 10 minutes 21 seconds, black and white and color, silent

THIGH LINE LYRE TRIANGULAR (1961)
16mm, 5 minutes 56 seconds, color, silent

BLUE MOSES (1962)
16mm, 10 minutes 25 seconds, black and white, sound

MOTHLIGHT (1963)
16mm, 3 minutes 13 seconds, color, silent

DOG STAR MAN (1961–1964)
16mm, 74 minutes 34 seconds, color, silent
Dog Star Man: Prelude, 1961, 16mm, 24 minutes 42 seconds, color, silent
Dog Star Man: Part 1, 1962, 16mm, 30 minutes 35 seconds, color, silent
Dog Star Man: Part 2, 1963, 16mm, 5 minutes 17 seconds, color, silent
Dog Star Man: Part 3, 1964, 16mm, 7 minutes 30 seconds, color, silent
Dog Star Man: Part 4, 1964, 16mm, 5 minutes 56 seconds, color, silent

THE ART OF VISION (1961–1965)
16mm, approximately 260 minutes, color, silent

FIRE OF WATERS (1965)
16mm, 6 minutes 21 seconds, black and white, sound

TWO: CREELEY/MCCLURE (1965)
16mm, 3 minutes 11 seconds, color, silent

EYE MYTH (1967)
16mm and 35mm, 8 seconds, color, silent

THE HORSEMAN, THE WOMAN, AND THE MOTH (1968)
16mm, 18 minutes 30 seconds, color, silent

SONGS (1964–1969)
Song 1, 1964, 8mm, 2 minutes 46 seconds, color, silent
Song 2 and Song 3, 1964, 8mm, 4 minutes, color, silent
Song 4, 1964, 8mm, 3 minutes 2 seconds, color, silent
Song 5, 1964, 8mm, 3 minutes 20 seconds, color, silent
Song 6 and Song 7, 1964, 8mm, 4 minutes, color, silent
Songs 1–7, reissued in 1980 in 16mm, 17½ minutes, color, silent
Song 8, 1964, 8mm, 2 minutes 42 seconds, color, silent
Song 9 and Song 10, 1965, 8mm, 6 minutes, color, silent
Song 11, 1965, 8mm, 3 minutes 4 seconds, color, silent
Song 12, 1965, 8mm, 2 minutes 58 seconds, black and white, silent
Song 13, 1965, 8mm, 2 minutes 27 seconds, color, silent
Song 14, 1965, 8mm, 1 minute 59 seconds, color, silent
Songs 8–14, reissued in 1980 in 16mm, 19½ minutes, color, silent
15 Song Traits, 1965, 8mm, 28 minutes 47 seconds, color, silent,
15 Song Traits, reissued in 1981 in 16mm, 28 minutes 47 seconds, color, silent
Song 16, 1965, 8mm, 4 minutes 25 seconds, color, silent
Songs 17 and 18, 1965, 8mm, 5 minutes, color, silent
Songs 19 and 20, 1965, 8mm, 8 1/2 minutes, color, silent
Songs 21 and 22, 1965, 8mm, 6 minutes, color, silent
Songs 16–22, reissued in 1983 in 16mm, 24 minutes, color, silent
23rd Psalm Branch, 1966–1967, 8mm, 63 minutes 42 seconds, black and white & color, silent
23rd Psalm Branch, reissued in 1979–1980 in 16mm, 63 minutes, 42 seconds, black and white and color, silent
Songs 24 and 25, 1968, 8mm, 6 minutes, color, silent
Song 26, 1968, 8mm, 4 minutes 48 seconds, color, silent
Songs 24–26, reissued in 1984 in 16mm, 11 minutes, color, silent
My Mountain, Song 27, 1968, 8mm, 17 minutes 23 seconds, color, silent
My Mountain, Song 27, reissued in 1987 in 16mm, 17 minutes 23 seconds, color, silent
Song 27, Part 2: Rivers, 1969, 8mm, 24 minutes 31 seconds, color, silent,
Song 27, Part 2: Rivers, reissued in 1988 in 16mm, 24 minutes 31 seconds, color, silent

Song 28, 1969, 8mm, 2 minutes 47 seconds, color, silent
Song 29, 1969, 8mm, 1 minute 37 seconds, color, silent
Songs 28–29, reissued in 1985 in 16mm, 4 1/2 minutes, color, silent
American 30's Song, 1969, 8mm, 18 minutes 32 seconds, color, silent

SCENES FROM UNDER CHILDHOOD (1967–1970)
Scenes from Under Childhood (Section One), 1967, 16mm, 23 minutes 46 seconds, color, silent or sound
Scenes from Under Childhood (Section Two), 1969, 16mm, 39 minutes 54 seconds, color, silent
Scenes from Under Childhood (Section Three), 1969, 16mm, 27 minutes 33 seconds, color, silent
Scenes from Under Childhood (Section Four), 1970, 16mm, 44 minutes 57 seconds, color, silent

THE WEIR-FALCON SAGA (1970)
16mm, 28 minutes 42 seconds, color, silent

THE MACHINE OF EDEN (1970)
16mm, 10 minutes 45 seconds, color, silent

THE ANIMALS OF EDEN AND AFTER (1970)
16mm, 35 minutes 27 seconds, color, silent

THE PITTSBURGH TRILOGY/THE PITTSBURGH DOCUMENTS (1971)
Eyes, 1971, 16mm, 35 minutes 12 seconds, color, silent
Deus Ex, 1971, 16mm, 32 minutes 18 seconds, color, silent
The Act of Seeing with One's Own Eyes, 1971, 16mm, 31 minutes 50 seconds, color, silent

THE PEACEABLE KINGDOM (1971)
16mm, 7 minutes 39 seconds, color, silent

SEXUAL MEDITATIONS (1970–1972)
Sexual Meditations #1: Motel, 1970, 8mm, 5 minutes 7 seconds, color, silent
Sexual Meditations #1: Motel, reissued in 1980 in 16mm, 5 minutes 7 seconds, color, silent
Sexual Meditation: Room with View, 1971, 16mm, 2 minutes 58 seconds, color, silent
Sexual Meditation: Faun's Room, Yale, 1972, 16mm, 1 minute 49 seconds, color, silent

Sexual Meditation: Office Suite, 1972, 16mm, 2 minutes 37 seconds, color, silent
Sexual Meditation: Hotel, 1972, 16mm, 5 minutes 36 seconds, color, silent
Sexual Meditation: Open Field, 1972, 16mm, 5 minutes 42 seconds, color, silent

THE PROCESS (1972)
16mm, 8 minutes 1 second, color, silent

THE RIDDLE OF LUMEN (1972)
16mm, 13 minutes 22 seconds, color, silent

THE SHORES OF PHOS: A FABLE (1972)
16mm, 9 minutes 47 seconds, color, silent

THE WOLD SHADOW (1972)
16mm, 2 minutes 24 seconds, color, silent

CLANCY (1974)
16mm, 3 minutes 56 seconds, color, silent

DOMINION (1974)
16mm, 3 minutes 55 seconds, color, silent

"HE WAS BORN, HE SUFFERED, HE DIED" (1974)
16mm, 7 minutes 14 seconds, color, silent

HYMN TO HER (1974)
16mm, 2 minutes 19 seconds, color, silent

STAR GARDEN (1974)
16mm, 20 minutes 58 seconds, color, silent

THE TEXT OF LIGHT (1974)
16mm, 67 minutes 12 seconds, color, silent

THE STARS ARE BEAUTIFUL (1974)
16mm, 18 minutes 28 seconds, color, sound

SHORT FILMS: 1975 (1975)
16mm, 36 minutes 31seconds, color, silent

SHORT FILMS: 1976 (1976)
16mm, 19 minutes 47 seconds, color, silent

THE GOVERNOR (1977)
16mm, approximately 54 minutes, color, silent

BURIAL PATH (1978)
16mm, 8 minutes 2 seconds, color, silent

NIGHTMARE SERIES (1978)
16mm, 19 minutes 28 seconds, color, silent

PURITY AND AFTER (1978)
16mm, 3 minutes 55 seconds, color, silent

THOT-FAL'N (1978)
16mm, 10 minutes 26 seconds, color, silent

CREATION (1979)
16mm, 15 minutes 49 seconds, color, silent

SINCERITY (1973–1980)
Sincerity, 1973, 16mm, 26 minutes 48 seconds, color, silent
Sincerity II, 1975, 16mm, 37 minutes, color, silent
Sincerity III, 1978, 16mm, 34 minutes 57 seconds, color, silent
Sincerity IV, 1980, 16mm, 36 minutes 1 second, color, silent
Sincerity V, 1980, 16mm, 38 minutes 58 seconds, color, silent

DUPLICITY (1978-80)
Duplicity, 1978, 16mm, 21 minutes 17 seconds, color, silent
Duplicity II, 1978, 16mm, 14 minutes 23 seconds, color, silent
Duplicity III, 1980, 16mm, 22 minutes 18 seconds, color, silent

THE ROMAN NUMERAL SERIES (1979–1980)
I, 1979, 16mm, 4 minutes 50 seconds, color, silent
II, 1979, 16mm, 6 minutes 38 seconds, color, silent
III, 1979, 16mm, 1 minute 33 seconds, color, silent
IV, 1979, 16mm, 1 minute 37 seconds, color, silent
V, 1979, 16mm, 2 minutes 12 seconds, color, silent
VI, 1980, 16mm, 8 minutes 58 seconds, color, silent

VII, 1980, 16mm, 3 minutes 51 seconds, color, silent
VIII, 1981, 16mm, 2 minutes 56 seconds, color, silent
IX, 1981, 16mm, 1 minute 47 seconds, color, silent

MADE MANIFEST (1980)
16mm, 10 minutes 18 seconds, color, silent

MURDER PSALM (1981)
16mm, 16 minutes 32 seconds, color, silent

THE GARDEN OF EARTHLY DELIGHTS (1981)
16mm and 35mm, 1 minute 43 seconds, color, silent

NODES (1981)
16mm, 2 minutes 43 seconds, color, silent

THE ARABIC NUMERAL SERIES (1980–1982)
1, 1980, 16mm, 2 minutes 27 seconds, color, silent
2, 1980, 16mm, 3 minutes 28 seconds, color, silent
3, 1980, 16mm, 5 minutes 53 seconds, color, silent
4, 1981, 16mm, 5 minutes 36 seconds, color, silent
5, 1981, 16mm, 2 minutes 24 seconds, color, silent
6, 1981, 16mm, 6 minutes 47 seconds, color, silent
7, 1981, 16mm, 6 minutes 57 seconds, color, silent
8, 1981, 16mm, 3 minutes 34 seconds, color, silent
9, 1981, 16mm, 7 minutes 41 seconds, color, silent
0 + 10, 1981, 16mm, 20 minutes 37 seconds, color, silent
11, 1981, 16mm, 6 minutes 1 second, color, silent
12, 1981, 16mm, 17 minutes 2 seconds, color, silent
13, 1981, 16mm, 2 minutes 17 seconds, color, silent
14, 1982, 16mm, 2 minutes 55 seconds, color, silent
15, 1982, 16mm, 4 minutes 19 seconds, color, silent
16, 1982, 16mm, 5 minutes 4 seconds, color, silent
17, 1982, 16mm, 5 minutes 54 seconds, color, silent
18, 1982, 16mm, 5 minutes 43 seconds, color, silent
19, 1982, 16mm, 7 minutes 27 seconds, color, silent

UNCONSCIOUS LONDON STRATA (1982)
16mm, 22 minutes 15 seconds, color, silent

EGYPTIAN SERIES (1984)
16mm, 18 minutes, color, silent

TORTURED DUST (1984)
16mm, 88 minutes 9 seconds, color, silent

JANE (1985)
16mm, 13 minutes, color, silent

FIRELOOP (1986)
16mm, 2 minutes 12 seconds, color, sound (by Joel Haertling)

THE CASWALLON TRILOGY (1986)
16mm, 8 minutes 40 seconds, color, sound

CONFESSION (1986)
16mm, 22 minutes 15 seconds, color, silent

THE LOOM (1986)
16mm, 42 minutes 29 seconds, color, silent

THE DANTE QUARTET (1987)
16mm or 35 mm, 6 minutes 3 seconds, color, silent

KINDERING (1987)
16mm, 2 minutes 51 seconds, color, sound (music by Architects Office).

I DREAMING (1988)
16mm, 6 minutes 35 seconds, color, sound (music by Joel Haertling and Stephen Foster)

MARILYN'S WINDOW (1988)
16mm, 7 minutes 42 seconds, color, silent

MATINS (1988)
16mm, 2 minutes 15 seconds, color, silent

FAUSTFILM (1987–1989)
FaustFilm: An Opera, 1987, 16mm, 42 minutes 20 seconds, color, sound (voice-over by Stan Brakhage, music by Rick Corrigan)

Faust's Other: An Idyll, 1988, 16mm, 40 minutes 23 seconds, color, sound (voice-over by Stan Brakhage, sound by Joel Haertling)
Faust 3: Candida Albacore, 1988, 16mm, 25 minutes 16 seconds, color, sound (music by Rick Corrigan and Doll Parts)
Faust 4, 1989, 16mm, approximately 38 minutes, color, sound (voice-over by Stan Brakhage, music by Rick Corrigan)

VISIONS IN MEDITATION (1989–1990)
Visions in Meditation, 1989, 16mm, 16 minutes 19 seconds, color, silent
Visions in Meditation #2: Mesa Verde, 1989, 16mm, 16 minutes 9 seconds, color, silent
Visions in Meditation #3: Plato's Cave, 1990, 16mm, 16 minutes 36 seconds, color, sound (music by Rick Corrigan)
Visions in Meditation #4: D. H. Lawrence, 1990, 16mm, 17 minutes 41 seconds, color, silent

BABYLON SERIES (1989–1990)
Babylon Series, 1989, 16mm, 4 minutes 45 seconds, color, silent
Babylon Series #2, 1990, 16mm, 2 minutes 9 seconds, color, silent
Babylon Series #3, 1990, 16mm, 4 minutes 48 seconds, color, silent

CITY STREAMING (1990)
16mm, 18 minutes 18 seconds, color, silent

PASSAGE THROUGH: A RITUAL (1990)
16mm, 49 minutes, color, sound (music by Philip Corner)

DELICACIES OF MOLTEN HORROR SYNAPSE (1990)
16mm, 8 minutes 16 seconds, color, silent

A CHILD'S GARDEN AND THE SERIOUS SEA (1991)
16mm, 70 minutes 39 seconds, color, silent

CHRIST MASS SEX DANCE (1991)
16mm, 3 minutes 48 seconds, color, sound (music by James Tenney)

INTERPOLATIONS 1–5 (1992)
35mm, 12 minutes, color, silent

UNTITLED (FOR MARILYN) (1992)
16mm, 10 minutes 27 seconds, color, silent

BOULDER BLUES AND PEARLS AND . . . (1992)
16mm, 22 minutes 24 seconds, color, sound (music by Rick Corrigan)

CANNOT EXIST (1994)
16mm, 1 minute 15 seconds, color, silent

CANNOT NOT EXIST (1994)
16mm, 7 minutes 57 seconds, color, silent

CHARTRES SERIES (1994)
16mm, 8 minutes 35 seconds, color, silent

THE MAMMALS OF VICTORIA (1994)
16mm, 34 minutes 9 seconds, color, silent

NAUGHTS (1994)
16mm, 5 minutes 3 seconds, color, silent

TRILOGY (1995)
I Take These Truths, 1995, 16mm, 17 minutes 44 seconds, color, silent
We Hold These, 1995, 16mm, 11 minutes 35 seconds, color, silent
I . . . , 1995, 16mm, 27 minutes 6 seconds, color, silent

THE "b" SERIES (1995)
16mm, approximately 12 minutes, color, silent

. . . (PRELUDES) (1995–1996)
. . . *(Preludes)* 1–6, 1995, 16mm, 10 minutes 23 seconds, color, silent
. . . *(Preludes)* 7–12, 1996, 16mm, 15 minutes 30 seconds, color, silent
. . . *(Preludes)* 13–18, 1996, 16mm, 9 minutes 9 seconds, color, silent
. . . *(Preludes)* 19–24, 1996, 16mm, 8 minutes 50 seconds, color, silent

COMMINGLED CONTAINERS (1996)
16mm, 2 minutes 42 seconds, color, silent

LAST HYMN TO THE NIGHT—NOVALIS (1997)
16mm, 17 minutes 18 seconds, color, silent

SELF SONG & DEATH SONG (1997)
16mm, 3 minutes 45 seconds, color, silent

YGGDRASILL: WHOSE ROOTS ARE STARS IN THE HUMAN MIND (1997)
16mm, 16 minutes 58 seconds, color, silent

COUPLING (1999)
16mm, 4 minutes 35 seconds, color, silent

THE GOD OF DAY HAD GONE DOWN UPON HIM (2000)
16mm, 47 minutes 52 seconds, color, silent

WATER FOR MAYA (2000)
16mm, 2 minutes 25 seconds, color, silent

THE JESUS TRILOGY AND CODA (2000)
16mm, 20 minutes 15 seconds, color, silent

THE PERSIAN SERIES (1999–2001)
Persians 1–5, 1999, 16mm, 15 minutes 40 seconds, color, silent
Persians 6–12, 2000, 16mm, 25 minutes, color, silent
Persians 13–18, 2001, 16mm, 8 minutes 35 seconds, color, silent

OCCAM'S THREAD (2001)
16mm, 6 minutes 47 seconds, color, silent

RESURRECTUS EST (2002)
16mm, 7 minutes 51 seconds, color, silent

PANELS FOR THE WALLS OF HEAVEN (2002)
16mm, approximately 35 minutes, color, silent

CHINESE SERIES (2003)
2003, 16mm or 35mm, 2 minutes 18 seconds, black and white and color, silent

Stan Brakhage: Interviews

Interview with Stan Brakhage

P. Adams Sitney / 1963

From *Film Culture*, no. 30 (Fall 1963): n.p. Reprinted by permission.

Stan Brakhage: I can remember when I got married, many of my friends who had been waiting for me to transform into a homosexual were bitterly disappointed, frustrated, and considered that, by their mythos of what the artist was, I was completely through. It wasn't all just their personal wants, but it was in respect to the mythos. A married artist was an incomprehensible thing to many friends, artists working in film and other mediums. They were referring to a whole mythos that passes most clearly through Jean Cocteau in *Orpheus*, that is, that moment where the whole film unreels itself and Orpheus is cast back into the arms of Eurydice, and he himself as poet, deeper than social-conscious poet, is completely destroyed. That mythos has been one of the most dominant this century, and I had to cope with that at a time when the total form structure of my work had changed completely when *Anticipation of the Night* was made. That was, in one sense, to be my last film. I had seen myself, cast before where I was as a human being, as leading to inevitable suicide through another contemporary myth. Certainly by the age of twenty-six, I was getting too old to still be alive and around and fulfilling the myth of myself. *Anticipation of the Night* was the vehicle out.

P. Adams Sitney: Do you mean you were actually going to kill yourself at the completion of the film?
SB: I didn't think this through consciously. Occurrences that happened afterwards made it clear that's what I'd intended. For months, I'd been getting more and more ill with neurotic diseases, some of them, like asthma, which had a long history in my life, and others that were completely new. At that time the fourth and fifth fingers of my left hand, that is the marriage and death fingers, were completely crippled with arthritis; I couldn't move them, I was practically on a cane (at the age of twenty-six, mind), I was defeated in all searches of love, trying to reach out of myself, except in relation to film. Even the drama structures of film were

collapsing around me, like old walls that I could no longer inhabit. There was a reach out, but when those walls fell, it seemed as if there was nothing but night out there, and I then thought of all my life as being in anticipation of that night. That night could only cast one shadow for me, could form itself into one black shape, and that was the hanged man. That is the shadow seen on the wall at the end of *Anticipation of the Night*. On the one hand, I was hyperediting the film, that is, pitching more of the forming into the editing process than any film I had made up to that time. On the other hand, I was saying, "When I come to the hanged man sequence, I'll shoot it spontaneously. I will go out and put a rope around my neck and photograph as the feelings arrive and just attach that section on to the end of the film." I didn't really become aware of what I had intended until months after our marriage.

PAS: Did you get married while the film was still being made?
SB: I was still editing the film, specifically the birth-of-the-child sequence in which the child is made out of abstractions, that is, water abstracted, the rose as a concept of prismatic light breakings, etc.; in other words, the child is formed completely out of mythic elements. Right at that moment something, physically in myself, was wrenching out to another being, Jane, at a moment when she, for similar reasons in her own life, was completely open-ended; that is, ready for suicide. She reached to me, and we had a beginning, finding expression in immediate sex love, but with enough power open-ended re: sex-death, that Spanish tradition, that we had something to go on with. The conscious mind wasn't aware of this for some time.

A month after we were married, I was out on the front lawn with Jane, whom I wasn't yet seeing deeply beyond sex desire, and I was putting a rope around my neck and standing up on a kitchen chair in a suburb of Denver with all the neighbors gathering on porches to wonder what that madman was up to now. Those neighbors had seen me set a rosebush on fire and photograph it with upside-down camera. (The image was too myth-structured, too unreal to me, to be used in *Anticipation of the Night*: It had to be made more out of eye sources.)

Anyway, neighbors were gathering, watching me putting rope around my neck and photographing my shadow against a wall. There was no need for the kitchen chair: My shadow was never seen below the waist. And out of my non-recognition of where I actually was as a total being, I was trying to re-enact, dramatize, or, in some sense, fulfill my own prophesy that I must die by hanging, and I was trying to realize what I had intended.

So there I was on a chair with rope around neck photographing and, then, fortunately a friend dropped by and was also watching the process, and I handed the camera to Jane and said, "Well, that's that," meaning I'm finished, and without realizing or remembering that the rope was around my neck, stepped off the chair and swung in midair for a few seconds, was grabbed by the friend, put back up on the chair, and suddenly had the full realization of what had been intended. I was sure that I had intended for months to finish the editing of *Anticipation of the Night* up to that point, go out into the yard, climb up on a chair camera in hand, jump off the chair, and while hanging run out as much film as I could, leaving a note saying, "Attach this to the end of *Anticipation of the Night*."

I had to re-enact some semblance of this intention. This is particularly appropriate to my idea (as expressed in *Dog Star Man: Part I*) of the rhythm of life being such that you could paraphrase it in two steps forward and one back. That instant, when I didn't realize where I actually was in relationship to Jane, and where we were going with new form, was the back step. I had to step back, that is, take my fall—rope around neck and all, and pitch myself into a close proximity with death, to realize what had been intended. At that point, I was not really seeing Jane or what we had, the strength of love, and what it could build: She was the person who received the camera when I said, "Well, that's that!" Or the person who was thought of as just doing the housework or as only in bed with sex the touchstone of something flowering between us that would be the growth up and out; but everywhere else we could not see each other, and this non-seeing, which many share during the first months of marriage, became so crucial that I felt out of absolute necessity we had to film.

One day in midst of a quarrel, I felt the necessity to take the camera and photograph her again and again. I grabbed the lights and began letting her face emerge in and out of black and white flashes in order that as much as I could see be immediately pitched into expression. I moved the light with one hand—painting her image as it moved over her and away into darkness—and photographed her with the other hand.

PAS: Was *Wedlock House: An Intercourse* the film being made?
SB: Yes. At a crucial moment out of some graciousness that I did not fully comprehend (I kept feeling a little guilty wondering what Jane's view of me would be). I sensed that my view, or what I would cast upon her, was becoming too dominant. So I handed her the camera, and she took it very quickly. We were trying to reenact the quarrel, trying to comprehend it.

PAS: You were acting?
SB: We started by acting but, as we began passing the camera back and forth, the quarrel was pitched onto a visual level. Jane didn't have much technical knowledge of the camera, but enough to make it possible for her to control it out of her anger and determination to grasp those images, that is, her view of me, and retain them

for me to look at later. Her images came out of such a quality that they could actually cut back and forth with mine. She too grabbed the light, as I had done, and began taking up the same form of painting-in my image with moving light source; she automatically grasped what my style was on a feeling level, and went right on with her version of it. This was the first time we were both photographing; I photographing her, she me, but in relation to the form that was springing out of me. We got glimpses of each other, in flashes of moving light, as if emerging out of long hallways in sheer darkness. All the quarrels we were having at that time became pitched on that visual level. You do not need to know this, of course, to see *Wedlock House: An Intercourse*.

It is extremely interesting to Jane and me that her face changes so much through that film, and it changes always in reference to women I had known previously. At certain moments, she looks like the girl in *Interim*; at certain moments, like the girl in *Desistfilm*; at certain moments, like girls that weren't in any of these films; and, at some moments (shudder), like my mother (bless her). The amazing thing was that, without will, and with the light being moved interpretively faster than the brain could move, I was capable of forcing, by those movements, her face into a variety of contexts, which were actually what was standing between me and my being able to see her as she was then. Her pictures of me related to pictures of her brother and other men that she had known. As a matter of fact, I was wearing a cast-off Army shirt of her brother's. This was one of her strongest images of him in that film. She was not conscious of this. The viewer, not having known, would not realize this by looking at the film and those images. But this is how we were astonished and kept tabs of the formal integrity that was passing between us. The next step was to take this material and edit it.

We were so shocked by seeing the footage that we suddenly had an intense realization of what we had to cope with as human beings to make our love grow together and be more than something that could flower in a dark bed where nothing more than body material was accessible for its pure sensual growth. That's what I mean when I say sex is a touchstone, but not a foundation. The crudity of trying to make sex a foundation would be like trying to take the Blarney stone and make it the foundation for Babylon; you know, horrible. Foundation has to spring new at each moment from each happening. Cornerstone of any foundation or structure always, whether it's for one person, or two people, has to be supporting where they are at each moment. So we had to keep "making it new" in the pitched structure we had in mind as to where we were going. That it always be new, with its cornerstone supporting the moment where we were, however hard it was to make it tangential to that moment and where we thought we were going. I started editing *Wedlock House* months later. We had moved from Denver to Princeton, NJ, and it took me months to accept that footage as being material for a balanced work of art.

Looking at the images and getting only horror, I was afraid of editing, afraid that I would be performing some black-magic act, cursing what little chance we had for making a love structure out of our life together. For months, I resisted, resisted. I struggled with that footage trying to edit it, you know, trying to get it balanced. Finally, I gave up and said, "If horror is what it is, then I will go straight into it." It was like breaking through a sound barrier: Suddenly, the total beauty of what happened to us right straight off the battle ground of our lives was what was structured and made true scenes in these flashes.

The last shots give a clear sense of where we were when I was editing that film. I had been capable of editing all those images so they expressed, first Jane's parental love, then her romantic relations, then her sex relations, and my own also, and interrelated them and finally brought those image-material faces, hers and mine, to the point where it was close to the way we saw each other when I was editing the film, which was months after it was shot. Jane was involved in the editing, too: I would ask specific questions as to what she saw in this facial feature of mine, always referring her to my images, not to my view of hers. I drew statements out of her that structured the work so that the quarrel would be totally fair. Then comes the finished work, which, in photography and in spirit, is so dependent on her view of me and the things she said about my images that it was something like a collaboration; that is, her view of me and mine of her finally meshed so carefully and so closely together that it does tend to be a balance, not collaborative, but true.

PAS: The film ends with an intercourse scene. How does that fit in?

SB: That was the whole other level of it. There were the faces, the movements through the hallways, the dramatic action, the quarrel and the coffee-cup scene, and then always interspersed and intercut with this was *Intercourse*, that being to me the course, the way of the course; intercourse. Sex, which was the thread that seemed to hold the whole tapestry together, was always weaving in and out. It held together precisely to the extent that all intercourse scenes remained distinct from dramatic scenes. It became like warp or woof. You can call intercourse warp or woof, whichever you like, but whatever it is, the dramatic scenes are the other. The beauty of the ending is that, previously, every moment the film moves out of intercourse scenes into drama scenes or quarrels, or searches, etc.; it does so by plastic cutting on a single part of the body, but, at the end of the film, Jane's face goes to pure white, and the intercourse emerges out of white, making the most total plastic cut in the film.

PAS: Your next film was *Cat's Cradle*, wasn't it?

SB: *Cat's Cradle* was next shot, but not next edited. The next edited was *Window*

Water Baby Moving. Cat's Cradle presented a crucial problem because then, Jane, like most young people, had an image of what marriage was, which was very uninteresting to her. I had a concept of what marriage was that was struck off of the marriage of two close friends of mine, James Tenney and Carolee Schneemann, who had married shortly after the making of *Loving*, in which I had seen them as ideal lovers. So they were heavily involved in the mythos of filmmaking by way of *Loving*, and the love they had found for each other and the marriage they had made was an idealized one. Fool that I was, like many young husbands are, I felt an urgency to take Jane into a relationship with them, that is, went to visit them in Vermont and stayed two very disturbing weeks with them; where naturally Jane, not sharing my mythos of marriage, and certainly not by way of another man and woman, resisted all of that concept tremendously. I was trying to take an ideal form and strike a marriage thereof, like taking a cookie shape and making cookies.

There was a fantastic level of sarcasm, particularly between the two women. Women are always great in this area, you know, resisting each other by way of fantastic allusions, of which men, if they don't listen carefully, are never aware. And I was trying so hard to relate to Jim as man that there are images in *Cat's Cradle* in which you can't tell whether it's Jim or myself you are looking at, even though he had a beard and I didn't. How do you explain that kind of visual magic? I was trying to superimpose Jane in relationship to Carolee Schneemann and failing miserably on all counts: The touchstone of this seemed to be that the cat belonging to Jim and Carolee happened to come into heat after we arrived and shockingly enough remained in heat all the time we were there. So the cat became the source of sex objectivity, and I didn't see it symbolically any more. I didn't have time to fool around with symbols, and I didn't have enough film to waste trying to create symbolic structures. I had to move right into the shape form of what was developing straight off the cat. That cat became a source of hyperforms and a touchstone visually and formally of everything else that happens in the film. Since I did not have time to bother about casting dramas, I began shooting very short shots, which interrelated total scenes. I had to get an image, an *idée fixe*, out of the way so I could see what was not on the surface, and so we could go on. Then Jim and Carolee could go on unhindered by the myth, and we could all be friends; but there was a tremendous battle that had to take place first.

PAS: But the film itself doesn't express very much of the battle. I mean I didn't see it in the film.
SB: Well, you see, that would be hard for me to disengage myself from, I am so aware of the battle that was struck off from it. But people tell me that it is very lyrical, and I think it is probably a song that uses all this material that was so painful to deal with at the time for making a tone poem that struggles to contain

a sense of separation. A key phrase to it, which I discovered later, was Freud's quotation that Durrell uses in the preface to *Justine*. Freud wrote in a letter, "I am accustoming myself to the idea of regarding every sexual act as a process in which four persons are involved." So, all sex within *Cat's Cradle* tends to be interrelated; that is, there is no sex that does not involve four people with the cat seen as a visual medium of heat. Sometimes it is hard to tell whether there are four people in it, or three or two. One person even though it was a portrait of a single person. And some only see the cat. Well, this is fine, on whatever level you want to look at it, it still contains that lyric song, if not of struggle, then of love and its complications creating possibilities of marriage. That's the play in there; *Cat's Cradle* relates to the game children used to play. The cat is like the cradled center, like "the cradle of civilization" or "cat's cradle," the string game. I mean it is that complex . . . two hands and a string; but at a certain point two hands are not enough to play the game and you need four hands; you need two external hands to come in and move the string around to make "the cat's cradle."

PAS: And then *Window Water Baby Moving*?
SB: In that film, Jane was so busy fighting the battle to destroy my myth of what ideal marriage was, in order that we might be free, that she was not actively involved in the filming except as . . . Look at the source of inspiration she was providing for me at each and every shot, as she resisted the domination of anyone else's ideally formed life. By the time of *Window Water Baby Moving*, Jane and I were so separate that we were in a position to come together.

PAS: You were in Brussels during part of the time of Jane's pregnancy, weren't you?
SB: I went to Brussels for a month to attend the Exposition of Experimental Film. This was early in the pregnancy. Then I went to Geneva to do work on a commercial job. That was during the seventh to eighth month of pregnancy. I became involved with death. This was when I shot the material for *The Dead*, which was edited three years later. Also there was one aspect of childbirth that was very dangerous to me. Again I, still subconsciously carrying the weight of my pitched suicide, and casting it forward, had the notion that my child might take my place in life and leave me free to die. That idea became more and more intense the closer we got to the actual birth. There were two things that held me back in terms of this mythos: 1) Would it be a boy or a girl? If it were a boy, it would be a better stand-in for me. (This was all subconscious, but later figured out re: what I did in filmic expression.) 2) Jane had had German measles at three months, and we had one in so many chances of a monster-birth. Jane became more and more concerned with the birth and more and more removed from aesthetic concern, and certainly removed from death

wishes. Except she was so deeply aware of the dangers of my problem that she told me afterwards that, even though she wanted a boy, she hoped it would be a girl because she had some sense that that would be less dangerous to me. She became involved in her own bodily processes, reaching out, and finally in giving birth to the child. Everything to me was on the perceptual level . . . I desired that it be cast into a form that was neither home movie nor medical film, but that it contain the total reason for having the child, including any subconscious death wishes and our sense of love, starting right with the body, and all that we know of marriage by this time.

PAS: Did she mind your filming the birth?
SB: No. She realized that was how I could be most there. That is why we struggled so hard and managed to have the child born in our home. It was more crucial to Jane than to me that I be there when the child was born. So the Excuse Form for doing this was to make a film as she was giving birth.

At that moment when the woman goes into second stage and is pushing the baby out, many women begin cursing their husbands, about whom they otherwise say very beautiful things; and, at the very least, most women have no patience with any fumbling whatsoever, and men at that moment tend to become very ineffectual. While Jane did say "I love you" (which was a great joy to me), it was immediately followed by "Please leave me alone," and then with "Are you filming?" Her concern was that I be there but not bothering, or impinging on her. A woman at that stage can often have a good relationship with the doctor, because he is capable of receiving the child, and helping it out. But a husband is too emotionally involved at a moment like this. I literally could not have watched that birth if I had not been working. I'm sure I would have passed out, but since I was working and intensively involved with my own concerns, Jane and I could be together in the most clear sense.

PAS: Who photographed you?
SB: She did right after Myrrena was born. She had said a long time before, "I want a picture of you then, too" (we had pictures of me from before the childbirth, of Jane and I kissing, of my hand) and "Don't you want a picture of yourself? You must have it." And I said, "Well, who will take it?" She said, "I will." So I said, "All right," but I never expected that she'd have the strength. Sure enough, it was the first thing she thought of after Myrrena was born. She said, "Give me the camera." I, hardly knowing what I was doing, just handed it to her. She photographed all those images of my face. I grew prouder and prouder of her, of the baby, of having made it; I was out of my head. And she, just having given birth to the child, was recording my face. Do you see what the process was there?

PAS: And what did you do after *Window Water Baby Moving*?
SB: The next film that I edited was *Cat's Cradle*. We moved from Princeton back into the mountains of Boulder, Colorado, where I began working on *Cat's Cradle*. We lived in Silver Spruce then, the same place that we lived during the whole shooting of *Dog Star Man*. Right before I started shooting *Dog Star Man*, I edited *Cat's Cradle*.

PAS: Did you have any idea of what *Dog Star Man* would be?
SB: No. At least all the ideas I had subsequently proved to be irrelevant.

PAS: Then the next film to discuss would be the *Prelude* to *Dog Star Man* itself.
SB: There were other works in the way; for instance, I had shot *Sirius Remembered* after I photographed the childbirth film, and it was edited right after *Cat's Cradle*.

PAS: Now *Sirius Remembered* is another death poem.
SB: Another death poem.

PAS: How would you relate it to your general psychology of death, then?
SB: I had photographed the material for *The Dead*, but I didn't edit it. I let it wait for two years before I edited it. In the meanwhile a dog of ours, named Sirius, that we cared very much about, was hit by a car and killed. We laid him out above the ground because of Jane's ideals about death. She said how beautiful and natural it is to find the bones of dead animals in the forest. She, from psychological needs of her own, did not like the sense of burying anything. It was midwinter, and the ground was hard, so I went along with her, and we laid him out underneath a tree in a little field that we called Happy Valley. Every time thereafter that I went out in back of my house in Princeton, I saw that body, which did not begin to decompose. It was midwinter, and it remained frozen solid. Every time I'd see it, I'd break into what were to me incomprehensible tears. Suddenly, I was faced, in the center of my life, with the death of a loved being, which tended to undermine all my abstract thoughts of death.

I remember one marvelous time, which gave me the sense of how others could avoid it. Parker Tyler and Charles Boultenhouse came to visit us, and Charles wanted to go out into the fields "to gather a little nature," as he put it. "Nature" was such a crisis to me at this time that I was shocked at that statement. Charles made some martinis, handed me one; and Parker, Charles, and I all went out into Happy Valley where they toasted the new buds of spring that were beginning to come up, etc., and marched right straight past the body of Sirius either without seeing it at all (any more than they can see my film *Sirius Remembered*) or else they saw it and refused to recognize it. Charles was envaled in the ideal of toasting the budding spring and here was this decaying, stinking corpse right beside the path where we had to walk, and he literally did not, could not, or would not see it. All three attitudes, I think, arise from the same source.

PAS: When did you decide to film the body?
SB: I filmed it all during that winter and did the last photography the day after Parker and Charles visited. At that time, the corpse was all torn up. I, sobbing each time, went out alone with camera and photographed it. Jane said something, after watching me photograph it, that made me realize the deep form taking place. She knew dogs. She told me that every time I went to photograph that body: 1) I was trying to bring it back to life by putting it in movement again; 2) I was uprighting it by taking the camera at an angle that tended to make the dog's image upright on the screen; 3) (which was really significant) Jane had often watched dogs do a strange dance around dead bodies not only of their own species but of others (it's like a round dance: The dogs, individually or in a pack, often will circle a dead body and then rub the neck very sensually all along the corpse perfuming themselves from the stench of decomposition). Those were literally the kinds of movements with which I was involved in making *Sirius Remembered* without realizing it. Jane threw open the whole animal world; that is, the animal parts of myself that were, at that moment, engaged in filming the body.

PAS: I also find two intellectual parts: 1) the influence of very tight, formal music—possibly Webern—and 2) Gertrude Stein, who has always influenced you. Now, where were you in relationship to the musical forms?
SB: At this moment, I was coming to terms with the decay of a dead thing and the decay of the memories of a loved being that had died, and it was undermining all abstract concepts of death. The form was being cast out of probably the same physical need that makes dogs dance and howl in rhythm around a corpse. I was taking song as my source of inspiration for the rhythm structure, just as dogs prancing around a corpse, and howling in rhythm structures or rhythm intervals might be considered like the birth of some kind of song. I won't try to guess out of what urgency.

PAS: But was not Webern an influence?
SB: Not at this point. I had been through Webern's influence. Webern and Bach were strong influences on *Anticipation of the Night*. But the structure that was dominating rhythmically would be like jazz . . . no, not jazz . . . it would be like song, simple song, plain song—plainsong, that's what it was clearly—Gregorian chant! That kind of howling would be the rhythm structure that was dominating *Sirius Remembered*.

PAS: Where were you in terms of perceiving Gertrude Stein?
SB: I would say the greatest influence that she had on *Sirius Remembered* was by way of my realization that there is no repetition, that, every time a word is "repeated," it is a new word by virtue of what word precedes it and follows it, etc. This freed me to "repeat" the same kind of movements. So I could literally move back and forth over the animal in repeated patterns. There are three parts to the film: First, there is the animal seen in the fall as just having died; second, there are the winter shots, in which he's become a statue covered with snow; and, third, there's the thaw and decay. That third section is all remembered, where his members are put together again. All previous periods of his existence as a corpse, in the fall, the snow, and the thaw, are gone back and forth over, recapitulated and interrelated. Gertrude Stein gave me the courage to let images recur in this fashion and in such a manner that there was no sense of repetition.

PAS: You've spoken before of effects of snow and whiteness. This was the time before *Prelude*, while you were making *The Dead*. You've spoken before of the power of whiteness, and you have images of snow in *Sirius Remembered*. Can you see how this would be a motif?
SB: Yes, there are certain motifs that emerge through all my work but some of them come together most clearly in *Sirius Remembered*. One example would be "the tree." Over and over again, the camera pans from the corpse up a tree. I had no sense of why I was doing that at the time, but now I realize I was planting the first seeds of my concern with the image of the white tree, which dominates *Dog Star Man*; and remember the dog star is Sirius. So there for the first time, the dog star is emerging, and then man's relation with dog or my pitching my sense of self into the dog corpse. My abstract senses of death were conflicting with the actual decay of a corpse. First, when it wouldn't decay and turn into clean white bones and, then, when it did. What we finally had to face in terms of those bones was ironic.

We had already gotten a new dog called "The Brown Dog." We wanted him to be the opposite of what Sirius was. He was a bum that we saved from death in the dog pound. He was deliberately not given a fancy name but continually referred to as "The Brown Dog," as if having no life of his own. The events that made the last shooting of *Sirius Remembered* possible were as follows: The stench of decomposition that was so strong in the valley began coming into the house and we couldn't locate it. First of all, we didn't know what it was. We thought a rat had died in the wall somewhere. Then we began wondering if it were blowing through the windows from Happy Valley, which was half a block away from the house. The next night, we smelled it coming straight off "The Brown Dog," and then we knew that he was perfuming himself off that corpse. We tried to joke about it; we called it "sheep-shit smell." We tried to call it "cheese"; we tried to call it anything rather than recognize what it was. The next day, I had to see for myself, and I forced Jane to come with me. We found that the corpse in the field was being eaten and that what was eating it was our current family dog. As we walked into that field, he demonstrated for us by sitting down innocently and beginning to tear off and devour a leg bone. Suddenly, we had the realization of what made clean bones: they were picked clean. The psychological implications of how the family dog had to demonstrate to us how he was appropriating the powers of Sirius struck us. It is significant to us that "The Brown Dog" became the dog star of *Dog Star Man*. Jane broke into tears as the idea of death as a happening in life became clearer and clearer.

We began questioning why dogs perfume themselves that way. I recalled Baudelaire's poem, where he speaks with disgust of the populace for being like his dog who hates the smell of perfume but likes to come in covered with shit. Well, Baudelaire had not smelled deeply enough. I became capable of smelling that stench at the center of all meat eaten. In the bacon for breakfast was the stench that was coming out of Happy Valley. I also began smelling it in ladies' perfumes: The center of most perfumes is a decayed matter very comparable to the stench of the dead dog. Every time I sat down to edit *Sirius Remembered*, I began having diarrhea. It was as if to unload the decay somehow. Every time I'd go into an intensive editing process on that film, I'd have it. By way of that film, other visions began emerging with extreme intensity, which were relevant to *Dog Star Man*. One night, after Jane had excused herself early and gone to bed, I was working. It got to be about two o'clock in the morning, and, suddenly, I sensed Jane behind me. She handed me a small dried-up plant, which I put on the table. She was always bringing me little things from the forest. I noticed the plant began to move. Every time I looked at it, it would be pointing in a different direction. Then I noticed that I was making a lot of wind and motion with my arms, and it was flipping and turning. It was a talisman hardened with its own death. I watched it closely, and it became a source of inspiration. In the morning, Jane had no memory of having brought me that plant.

Then, other weird things began happening. One night, I was stuck on a splice when I was dealing with decay. Decay is a long-term process of things pulling apart, transforming slowly, and producing heat. Where the decay was most intense on the inside, it would melt the snow on the outside of the body. I was concerned with how to edit that, how to cast such a slow process into a form that would be hard. The form would have to be as hard as the stone image of Sirius covered with white, as if he were a statue. I was having trouble with a splice at three o'clock in the morning, at which time I had a clear sense of three personages looking over my shoulder. As I started to turn around, something seemed to pass through me. The phrase came to me, "He thinks we have *something* to do with what he's doing," as if said very sarcastically. I was immediately depressed with an emotional despair. I have no intellectual explanation of where those words came from. That phrase seemed to cut across all the lines of my thought at the moment, as if it was laid down there or strummed. Imagine all the rest of my thoughts as strings moving out from a center of consciousness. Suddenly, from some subconsciousness so strong that it seemed coming from elsewhere, came this damning phrase that struck off all of my sensibilities and cast me, in a second, into the most horrible gloom I've ever had. I stopped work. I was like a destroyed man. A split second later, I had an all-encompassing circular sense that seemed to surround me as if I were inside a globe. That globe rang again with words heard from the inside out as if of my own thinking; yet alien to it: "They think we have *nothing* to do with what he's doing."

PAS: Who is the "we"?

SB: The "we" had referred to the voice that was speaking and the three entities that had spoken before. It was clear to my mind in an instant. I was overjoyed. And I began reaching to make that splice. Instantly, there was a large jelly sensation in the air as if this all-encompassing force had stopped and turned to a mass of jelly. The nearest approximation I could give, but it would be like a cartoon of the feeling, was like a Buddha, like a giant baby Buddha sensation, all jellied and fat and enormous. It was a chaotic force to me, oriental or foreign, as if dribbling out the phrase "He" (referring to the last voice speaking) "thinks we" (referring to all voices that had spoken) "have *something* to do with what he" (meaning me) "was doing." Again I was cast into an intensive and horrible gloom such as I had never had before. This was immediately superseded by yet another voice sensation from the mind inside out that was all-encompassing and came with a sense of finality. And it said "He" (referring to the last voice speaking) "thinks we" (meaning all the voices having spoken) "have *nothing* to do with what he" (meaning me) "is doing." It was as if there were some power that was helping me from the inside out, which freed me to go on to work beautifully the rest of that night, and the film was finished two days later.

PAS: How do you explain the voices?

SB: I have no explanation of the voices other than as I've given to you.

PAS: Do you believe this was a vision?

SB: I don't know. The only visual senses I have of what might have spoken are crude cartoons. The first was Greek-like—it suggested a sense of Greek religion. But that would be a cartoon of what I sensed. It was like three Greek women or three Greek men, I don't know which. Probably men, or hermaphrodites. The second voice was like a circle. The third voice was like a Buddha or like a giant, bubbling, jellied baby. The fourth voice was so encompassing that I have no picture for it at all.

PAS: Do you often have voices?
SB: Yes, often, but never before anything that incredible. That was so incredible but real that it immediately gave me the free power to go on and finish that film. When I was involved in editing the decay process, Jane looked at the footage and immediately reacted. She began cleaning the sink and cleaning, cleaning, cleaning all over the house. She said, rather mysteriously, "I can't talk about it," and, "I'm too busy." I said "What's the matter?" and she said, "Well, I feel dirty." Suddenly, I had a sense she'd been engaged by that section of the film, and that was the first time I realized that I wanted an enclosed form, which would not engage people. That decay section should be edited so finely and structured so beautifully that one would not have to get rid of the dirt.

PAS: Then do you believe all good art is unengaging?
SB: Yes, I do. From that moment on, I was completely convinced Jane was the source of inspiration even there.

PAS: Your early films try to engage though?
SB: Yes, surely, but I honor that in my early films which is the least engaging now. That's the only thing I've been able to look at over and over again for years and still learn from. Everything in my early works that was of engagement bores me now. I'm no longer there; I'm not concerned with previous engagements. These days, my struggle is to make each work complete unto itself. I began having ways to create an unengaging form by watching her reaction, re-action. Then, for the first time, my central concern in working was the necessity arising from both Jane and me, not just from myself. It was like being able to pitch the center of a working process between the two of us. In some way, this working process that began developing between Jane and me was dependent on the necessity out of which our drives emerge and is cast out not between us but in some space that is the shape of both of us, and yet doesn't . . . enclose us. Terms like *in between* and *interim* and all those "ins" or all those "outs" like *re-flections*, and re-this and re-that, re-placement, ceased to exist; and we began living in direct relationship to a larger concern than each other or these dichotomies. We inhabit a world of which the Orient gives us some sense by way of Zen, where good and bad, yes and no, cease to exist as opposites and become one thing. The perfect symbol for this is the yin and yang enclosed within the one circle. The form springs directly from the separation line between the two, which contains all the sensuality of that

meeting. I don't know how to put it, but when a man and woman have this, and they give birth to a child, that child is not a thing enclosed between them. They don't fight over him or smother him. In that sense, the work of art arising from such a process out of the total needs Jane and I share is like a child arising out of that kind of love and is then free of each of us.

PAS: May we get back to the film's progression now? We're getting off on a series of abstractions.
SB: No, I think we're getting off concretely when we talk about what arises from life's necessities rather than aesthetics. Talking about total forms without containing a sense of how they arise out of immediate life-experiences is terribly abstract.

PAS: Can you get on with *The Dead* now?
SB: By the time I began editing *The Dead*, I had shot most of the material for *Dog Star Man*. Jane and I went out onto the mountain where she shot all the images of me and, without being directed, cast them easily and quickly into the forms with which I was concerned; that is, our shared necessity was so close we wouldn't even have to exchange directions. She would be out there, and I might gesture wildly, and she would get it that quickly and photograph some image or myself in relationship to an image structure in just the way I wanted.

PAS: You said you had shot all of *Dog Star Man*. Do you mean all of *Part I* and *Prelude*?
SB: No. I mean all of the material for *Dog Star Man*.

PAS: That was going into all four parts?
SB: Yes, I thought I had all the material at that time; now I realize I needed more. At the time, I was convinced I had all I needed for what I thought would be roughly a four-and-one-half hour work. Now I'm confused on that subject. I'm not even sure I'll be able to finish that film. First of all, whenever I had to be photographed from any distance Jane would have to do it. Then, at times, she went out with the camera to get things that I had some sense she could photograph better than I and with more total clarity. Once, when I was ill and couldn't get out to shoot as the sun was setting and the sky was meaning what I sensed was needed at a certain moment in the film, Jane rushed out to get it, bringing back even more than what I had hoped for. So I tended more and more to give her any chance to add her view to mine for a more total view.

Certain crises were presented to me, in the shooting of *Dog Star Man*, of which I was not consciously aware. I didn't really stop to think why I, attempting to show a man's life work in terms of one simple action encompassed in a day, should choose that that man be a woodsman. I didn't even know why I had let my hair and beard grow that long. I had done it to give it a try and suddenly it became crucial to the film.

PAS: How long were they?
SB: My hair was down below my shoulders, and my beard was halfway down my chest. It was a hard thing to live with. I mean to walk down the streets of Boulder, Colorado, carrying that kind of an image, but I was aware that somehow I needed it. I cast myself as a woodsman with an ax and started climbing the hill. The dog was always following me and getting in the way of the photography. I began to accept this and realized the need for the woodsman to have a dog. Increasingly, I began to be amazed at the amount of footage we were shooting at each and every sight impingement. I saw the whole forest in relation to the history of architecture, particularly religious architecture, at least in the Western world. Sensing structure, architecture, history of the world as emerging, I began seeing prismatic happenings through snow falling, etc., and in relation to stained glass windows, for one example. This was not when I started photographing, but often through unexpected things that came through Jane's photography.

Without realizing why, I dragged a white tree up two thirds of a mountain, replanted it at a certain point, then struggled with it, and pushed it over. As if battling with myself, some other man, or a monster, I struggled with that white tree, threw it over, then chopped it up. When I did that and sat down to think about it later, I began realizing why I was having asthma attacks again. The greatest clarity about why I was having attacks at this time came to me from reading a book on idiotoxic disorders by Dr. Freeman. He nailed down the foremost dream images that affect idiotoxically disordered people, that is to say, people with migraine, asthma, epilepsy, etc. That dream contains the elements of a man fighting with himself, with some beast, a dog, a serpent, a cat, or with his twin brother, or with another man. He fights naked in front of a dead white tree (usually sitting far in the background) while a woman, three women, or nine women, watch this battle. This is a standard symbol you can find stamped on Cretan coins such as the one on the frontispiece of Robert Graves's *The Greek Myths*.

PAS: Is the white tree also on the Cretan coin?
SB: The tree is there also. It's a living tree, and it's not white. A white tree is most immediately a dead tree. There are other kinds of white trees (there can be a silver tree), but if it's a white tree, then, in the mind, it's a dead tree. The question that any white tree raises is, "Does it have the potentiality for new life?" that is, "Is it white because it's lifeless, or is it white because it's that kind of tree?" I began

having daily asthma attacks and was terribly concerned with whether I was going to die. (By this time, we had the second child, another girl. All the material of the filming of her birth was to be going into *Dog Star Man*.) I was again faced with death as a concept; not watching death as physical decay, or dealing with the pain of the death of a loved one, but with the concept of death as something that man casts into the future by asking, "What is death like?" And the limitation of finding the images for a concept of death only in life itself is a terrible torture, that is, Wittgenstein's *Tractatus Logico-Philosophicus*, 6.4311: "Death is not an event of life. Death is not lived through. If by eternity is understood not endless temporal duration but timelessness, then he lives eternally who lives in the present. Our life is endless in the way that our visual field is without limit." In Freeman's book, there is a painting by a woman patient of what she saw in a dream while having asthma attacks. The white tree is there, the woman, the man fighting with a beast. That fight may represent Saint George slaying the dragon; it is any man coping with his beast nature or, as he may find that beast in his twin brother, his Doppelgänger, or his opposite, as Dionysius's Hercules. I had to cope with that material just as Jane had to cope with each asthma attack and my postulating the death wish again in the center of our marriage, which could destroy our future.

Right at that moment, I put *Dog Star Man* in cans, stuffed it away, and began editing *The Dead*. As I edited *The Dead*, I worked my way out of the crisis in which I was dying.

PAS: Did the old material from 1958 come to you in a flash?
SB: I always had it there waiting for the time when the necessity would make it that vital that I could begin to work with it.

PAS: In that film why did you use material shot only in Paris?
SB: I used material shot only in Paris because that was a total world of something that, if I'd leave it long enough until it impinged on me directly in life, would have a total form of its own.

PAS: Did your death wish emerge from that political mix up at the Brussels Experimental Film Exposition in which you didn't receive the money you hoped to get?
SB: I would say that would be material for it, not cause of it. Money is always for us one way in which we comprehend the form of what we want. It's very important to us. I mean, as in a fairy tale, you always have to get the treasure to get the princess and live happily ever after. I mean the hero has to kill the beast to get the treasure to get the princess to go off to the castle in the glass mountain and live (question mark) happily ever after. That's the form; and money is always part of

the equation. I take that as an equation that is so strong in our consciousness that wherever money arises as a problem, as it always does in an artist's life, it needs to be wrenched awry by an aesthetic $E = mc^2$.

PAS: You edited *The Dead* then?

SB: Yes. *The Dead* was the work most clearly removed from my direct relationship to Jane. She had to keep out of it. She always insisted on keeping out of asthma attacks, that is, she would not become my mother. She kept absolutely clear, and sometimes it was very painful. But she had the integrity, which I little understood at the time, and particularly in the middle of an asthma attack, to keep absolutely out of my express death wishes and even desperately try not to recognize them. *The Dead* was shot when I was away from Jane for a month and a half; and it was edited when she was avoiding me most of the daytime to keep out of the whole asthma destructive force that was operative through me. I had to find, realize re: *The Dead* that somehow all images of death or all concepts of it are structured here in life. Then I knew as to why I'd shot in the same day, and out of the same needs, material in the graveyard of Père Lachaise and on the Seine. And even then, I knew somehow that they were going to go together. But how together? That became clear at the time of editing.

PAS: And shots of Kenneth Anger in a cafe?

SB: I had no idea at the time of shooting that Kenneth Anger, as an image, would be used in *The Dead*. I was running out the end of a reel, which I wanted to get out of the camera so I could put in the color film for doing the shots of the Seine. So I said, "Well, I have no picture of you, still or otherwise." We were sitting in a cafe; so I took the image of Kenneth. It was only when I relooked at that footage that I realized that *that* one level of what I meant by *The Dead* was how I saw Kenneth and what he was encased in I saw him as a concept. Seeing him as one of the dead, I had great concern and care and love for him at that moment. He was years without working, trapped by concepts of the nineteenth century with no way to break out, almost a destroyed man, and yet still living . . . that was the important thing. All the rest of the people in *The Dead are* dead. They're the walking dead; but he was a living dead. So he became my double in a sense—my "stand-in," one might say. He was the image that was most immediately available for me to cast out there as statement: "Do you want this? . . . Do you want to be trapped by all those symbols? . . . Do you want to be trapped six ways sideways by concepts that are ahead of where you actually are?" And then my answer was: "No!" Then I could structure *The Dead* by way of the concept of the future as that through which we can't live. When we're living through it, it's different from the concept of it. It's comparable to how you can't live through death. So the question becomes one of all that is pitched out of life; how the walking dead come to be that; and how what is sculpted in stone becomes concept of what is sculpted *out* of stone; and how the living people do relate to that, and how even trees, shaped that way and so ordered and structured, become living dead and like the walking dead, who are people so dead on their feet that you can't even use the word "living" in relationship to them . . . well, not Kenneth. He was shining with all that beauty and concern with life; and yet he was trapped six ways sideways by forms he had pitched ahead of himself—all that he wanted to do (such as film *Maldoror*) and could not find the means or the money to do. This was intensely painful to me. I would have given anything to have found a way for him to do what he wanted, not only to see *Maldoror* done by Kenneth Anger, or maybe not even foremost for that reason, but to let Kenneth have a way to accomplish it so that he could have gotten through it and could have gone on. He was ultimately defeated. There's new hope for Kenneth now, because he did escape from that trap that *Maldoror* posed for him, and he is back in the United States and has a new film in progress. Europe, weighted down so much with that past, was *The Dead*. I was always Tourist there; I couldn't live in it. The graveyard could stand for all my view of Europe, for all the concerns with past art, for all involvement with symbol. *The Dead* became my first work in which things that might very easily be taken as symbols were so photographed as to destroy all their symbolic potential. The action of making *The Dead* kept me alive.

PAS: How did you go about editing *Prelude*; and what do you mean by the Freudian dream aspect of it?
SB: Right from the start I had some sense, and I don't quite know where it came from, that the work would be in four parts with a prelude. Once Jane and I had gone through the whole gathering process to get that total world and had survived the sense of death that was postured by collecting the material, the next step was to get a sense of the form of the film. At first, I could only think of that large a work in symbolic terms. I thought, for instance, that the man climbs the mountain out of winter and night into the dawn, up through spring and early morning to midsummer and high noon, to where he chops down the tree . . . then I don't know what: But I know there's a Fall—and the fall back to somewhere, midwinter—my idea of what that fall will be still remains nebulous. I thought of *Dog Star Man* as seasonally structured that way; but also, while it encompasses a year and the history of man in terms of the image material (for example, trees become architecture for a whole history of religious monuments, or violence becomes the development of war), I thought it should be contained within a single day. Then I thought about what any day's form-structure touches off. One thing I knew for sure (from my own dreaming) was that what one dreams just before waking structures the following day. That dream material is gathered from the previous

day and, therefore, is a gathering of all previous days, *ergo* contains the structure of all history, of all Man. I hadn't been involved directly with Freudian concepts, or even psychology, since I'd departed from drama as major structurer of my work; but suddenly drama, and psychodrama, therefore, became pertinent to me in a new way. The first step in recognition of this was that I began rereading Freud intensively to learn those early structures of dream experience. I had the sense that I could make a prelude before creating any of the rest of the work. Generally in the history of art, preludes are composed of parts and bits from the work to follow. Now I wanted to compose the prelude first, rather than last (as is usual), so that the rest of the work would spring out of the prelude. I had only a vague concept of the four parts that would follow. So I realized that whatever happened within this prelude would determine what was to come; and, in that sense, I wanted it to be as real from the very beginning as life happening. I wanted *Prelude* to be a created dream for the work that follows rather than Surrealism, which takes its inspiration from dream. I stayed close to practical usage of dream material, in terms of learning and studying, for a while before editing. At this time, I left strict myth considerations out of my study process as much as possible.

PAS: But there is much myth in it, isn't there?
SB: Naturally, there's much myth in it. But that was not the primary concern at this time. Myth became important later in terms of sensing the overall structure. Once I had wanted very much to make a film, called *Freudfilm*, that would illustrate the process of dream development and would show how a dream evolves out of the parts we don't remember into those we do. In *Prelude*, I wanted to make a film that would swing on those transformations of unacceptable to acceptable images. And, finally, I wanted that to be the determining editing factor on the cutting table, and it did become that. I had to start with material that was incomprehensible and work my way backwards. For a long time of editing I was crossbreeding surrealistic concerns with, say, John Cage's sense of form through various chance operations. And then I would go over and over that material and restructure it; and finally ended up with one strip of film the length of *Prelude* as you find it now.

The hand-painting was always in direct relationship to the particular kind of "closed-eye vision" that comes only in dreams. The commonest type of "closed-eye vision" is what we get when we close our eyes in daylight and watch the moving of shapes and forms through the red pattern of the eyelid. Since *Prelude* was based on dream vision, as I remembered it, it had to include "closed-eye vision." Painting was the closest approximation to it; so I painted, throwing down patterns and controlling them in various ways. Shapes emerge out of that kind of eye-nerve action and reaction. The next step, once I had one whole strip of film, was to start with the second, the superimposition strip. One can have three, four, or more strips the full length of the film and superimpose one image on another wherever one wants. I took the strip that was largely determined by chance and surrealistic operations and began editing a second strip to it. From this point on, everything that I laid down was hyperconscious. I would go back and change shots to alter the form in strip number one as the need would arise in the developing form of strip number two. Strip two always developed out of what was on strip one to structure it and to transform it into something that would be comparable to what could be remembered when one awoke in the morning. On one hand, there was that incomprehensible mass of material arising out of surrealistic and chance-operation concerns, which I called the "chaos" roll; on the other hand, there was the "structured" roll, which represented the dream transformed and made accessible for conscious memory in the morning. By the time I got through, there were no chance operations left in the film.

PAS: How was Jane effective in this?
SB: Jane had little or nothing to do with the development of the "chaos" roll. That was edited very quickly; I was pulling down shots and splicing them in faster than I could possibly think about it. Jane was always looking at them. At times, I would alter the form by feeling some emanation from her as she'd stand in the room. I would feel: This is not right; this is not working. We wouldn't work faster than feeling, you know. Other times, she'd sit down and we'd talk together for a long time; and then I would go back and rip up whole sections of the film. Other times, we'd be immediately clear about the quality of a series of splices. Still other times, after I'd finished making a section, we'd look at them together, then go sit down, talk, have coffee, rehearse a Gertrude Stein play, or play with the children, or whatever, and see what kind of clarity emerged.

PAS: How many children were there then?
SB: By this time, there were two. Crystal was born in the middle of the shooting of the *Dog Star Man* material.

PAS: Did you shoot *Prelude* material separately?
SB: No. I pulled material, willy-nilly, as it seemed to me most chaotic. Two things determined what I pulled out of that mass of material to go into *Prelude*. One was that material be incomprehensible to me. That would be comparable to Buñuel's statement about *Andalusian Dog*, in which he said that he and Dali could not understand why in the world they were shooting those things that they did shoot. I was playing that surrealist game. The other reason for pulling specific material was that the symbols be directly relevant to the Cretan coin as an image of the creation mythology. That image, traditionally, comes to us through Adam and

Eve, you know, the man, the tree, the snake, all distorted and changed because of the Hebraic tendency to build up such a damned patriarchy. If you check it back through Graves's *The White Goddess*, and read the original version rather than the reader's digest King James version, you get a much clearer image. Most cultures have a similar creation myth, which contains these elements in one form or another. These elements are related to the dream of those suffering from idiotoxic disorders. Collecting those symbols was one problem; getting them all clear and in a pattern in that work was another. Those were the two factors that determined what I pulled out and began to work with.

PAS: The next film was *Thigh Line Lyre Triangular*, if I'm not mistaken?
SB: That was the next film photographed, but *Films by Stan Brakhage* was the next completed. As soon as *Prelude* was finished, Neowyn was born and I photographed the material for *Thigh Line Lyre Triangular*.

PAS: How was *Thigh Line Lyre Triangular* different, when it was finally edited, from *Window Water Baby Moving*, the earlier birth film?
SB: The main difference is the painting on film in *Thigh Line Lyre Triangular*. Only at a crisis, do I see both the scene as I've been trained to see it—that is, with Renaissance perspective, three dimensional logic, colors as we've been trained to call a color a color, and so forth—and patterns that move straight out from the inside of the mind through the optic nerves. In other words, an intensive crisis I can see from the inside out and the outside in.

PAS: You mean double exposure?
SB: I see patterns moving that are the same patterns I see when I close my eyes, and I can also see the same kind of scene I see when my eyes are open.

PAS: You mean you see color spots before your eyes?
SB: Right—spots before my eyes, so to speak . . . and it's a very intensive, disturbing, but joyful experience. I've seen that every time a child was born. Notice I use the word "crisis." I don't mean crisis as a bad thing. At an extremely intensive moment, I can see from the inside out and the outside in. Now none of that was in *Window Water Baby Moving*; and I wanted a childbirth film that expressed all my seeing at such a time.

PAS: And you added shots of animals, too?
SB: That was because, at moments like that, I get flashes of what I call "brain movies." I'm taking Michael McClure's term—he said, "When you get a solid structure image that you know is not out there, but is being recalled so intensively that you

literally see it in a flash, that's a "brain movie." Most people only get them with their eyes closed. They close their eyes, and they see, in a flash, something from their childhood, or some person remembered, or something; and that should also be in the film experience. What I was seeing at the birth of Neowyn most clearly, in terms of this "brain movie" recall process, were symbolic structures of an animal nature. This struck me as odd because I was working six ways sideways, day and night, to avoid symbolism. It was as if something had gotten backed up in my mind, so that it could release symbolic terms at me as soon as it had a crisis. Curiously enough, those animal symbols were easily represented by taking material only out of *Anticipation of the Night*.

PAS: Why are you never seen as father in this film?
SB: That's because I centered the occasion in my own eyes.

PAS: Then from that you went on to *Films by Stan Brakhage*. How was Jane effective in this?
SB: *Films by Stan Brakhage* emerged because certain people concern me with engagements from time to time. For instance, I've been asked for years, "Why don't you make a home movie of your children?" Actually, I've taken a lot of pictures of the children, of Jane and our life, and of places we've moved to, you know: Home movies, in a very simple sense . . . like recording something. I had always done this; but I had never edited any of the material. People kept asking, "Why don't you make a film out of this material?" It seemed to me like a challenge; but I was also concerned that I not make something of engagement, and that the source material or records be transformed into a work of art, if possible. I had a camera with which I could make multiple superimpositions spontaneously. It had been lent to me for week. I was also given a couple of rolls of color film which had been through an intensive fire. The chance that the film would not record any image at all left me free to experiment and to try to create the sense of the daily world in which we live, and what it meant to me. I wanted to record our home, and, yet, deal with it as being that area from which films by Stan Brakhage arise, and to try to make one arise at the same time.

PAS: And Jane was photographing all the shots of you?
SB: Yes, we worked together on it.

PAS: There are intercourse scenes in that film. How were they photographed?
SB: I was free to try to be as tricky as I could possibly be because I actually didn't have any hope that the images were going to come out at all; so I set the camera up and backwound it. While I was making this film, I thought I was rehearsing

for making a film later with fresh film stock. Much to my surprise, delight, and joy, the fire had cast that film into an intensely blue field. It was not like a filtered blue because pure colors could still come through the center of it. It was a weird thing what that fire had done. Now I wish I knew at what temperature that film had been cooked.

PAS: Getting back to your method of photography . . .

SB: I set the camera up, flipped the switch, and threw myself where Jane was, in front of the lens, and eventually the camera ran down. Then I backwound and added superimpositions of the children. I was using a Cine Special; and I could go back to the precise place I wanted, I didn't want a film that would require much editing. I wanted it to be on an immediate level, like a sketch. And somehow the film turned out to be madly and wonderfully and incredibly much more than I had ever expected. I joke about it. I call it an "avant-garde home movie" because I don't think it's a major work like *Prelude* or like any of the *Dog Star Man*, for that matter. I'm not really satisfied with what I got there, but it certainly turned out to be more than I ever expected.

PAS: And then came *Dog Star Man: Part I*. Will you discuss how Jane worked with you on this?

SB: In the editing of that film, we worked together to the greatest extent we ever have. From the moment I began work on it, I kept saying, "I think it's going to be something like a Noh drama in slow motion." I didn't know why I said Noh drama, because I had never been concerned with it. I hadn't really studied any form of the Noh drama except what came to me by way of Ezra Pound. As I subsequently found out, that was precisely what I was concerned with: what Ezra Pound got from the Noh drama, which structured his concept of Imagism and later of Vorticism, when he added comments onto Gaudier-Brzeska's book. That was the literal structural sense that I was inspired by for the total form of *Part I*. And yet, I had to get the mind disengaged. In the first place, I had to leave room for Jane to come in to sit with me and view each stage of editing so that I might be emotionally open to everything that she said and did. I had to engage my mind in some area that would leave the rest of me free for the extension of love; and my trick for doing it was to question whether I could make the form grow stronger through chance operations than through a conscious decision (it wasn't any more serious than that). I forced myself to adhere to a conscious decision, never allowing a piece to go in by sheer chance and never allowing a decision that was weaker than a chance operation. I wanted *Part I* to be the opposite in rhythm from *Prelude*. I wanted it to be slow, drawn out, extended to the greatest possible tension that the material could contain. And I insisted to myself that was why I made each and every splice be completely enigmatic as a conscious thing. A splice had to be made simply, because that and only that was the thing that worked visually. Sometimes, it would take a week to make ten permanent splices. I would slowly, torturously, and laboriously try this, try that, break it apart and try something else. Sometimes, I would chew up the whole previous shot by tearing off one piece of film after another that I'd spliced and have to start with the shot previous, etc. After I had a certain path or direction started by a series of splices, Jane and I would look at it together; and we would begin talking deeply about the film on many levels.

PAS: Was it a work print you were looking at?
SB: No, original. I always work with original. I can't afford a work print; so I'm used to working under those terms. Jane and I would talk for hours about ten splices that went together. It was as if we were making a path that could contain the deep concerns of both of us. I would lay down paths that would be perfectly fine for my sense of it; and all the splices would work in this deep, enigmatic way and carry through metaphysical concerns. But it would not contain her vision. Sometimes, I would get too influenced by what she'd say; and I'd lay down a path in which she would be comfortable, but which would not contain my direction. We were not making compromises, rather we were finding the one right path that would contain the total view that would be an opening to something new. That slow, laborious, and torturous process is why it took us a year and a half to finish editing *Part I*. Meanwhile, anytime the mind would start intruding, I would somehow tie it up into John's Cage. John's Cage was marvelously used in the making of this film in the sense that, at any moment, I could reach over and grab it and, as a threat, clap the possibility of chance operations over all brain dominance.

PAS: Are the "silences" in the film the Silence of John Cageism?
SB: No, I wouldn't think they'd have any relevance at all there; because the visual "silences" meant to me that out of which something was becoming . . . you see, I really love John Cage's music even though I only used his aesthetics to tie up my brain with. I do love the occasions in his music, but more particularly in the music of Morton Feldman, of sound occurring and there then being a silence that's just long enough to sustain *that* sound before the occurrence of the next sound. But the visual silences, or lapses, in *Part I* were more directed by thoughts of the emergence of images out of either black or white. And my thoughts were directed by a feeling for destroying the dichotomy of blacks and whites as extremes. My tendency was to shape the whole work in such a way that there are no distinctions between black and white.

PAS: Then let me ask one question that concerns all your work. You talked about your own dog, you've talked about your family and so on. Aren't some critics in a way justified when they say that this is, not quite narcissistic, but very limited in scope as opposed to Eisenstein who posits his personal drama in historical context in *Ivan the Terrible* or in comparison to von Stroheim, or someone who works in a more objective form?

SB: In the first place, I hope I would not say "my own dog." The minute "own" comes into it, dog would become property; the same for "my own children" or anything like that. They're mine to care for now. And so to get rid of that part of it.

I would say I grew very quickly as a film artist once I got rid of drama as prime source of inspiration. I began to feel that all history, all life, all that I would have as material with which to work, would have to come from the inside of me out rather than as some form imposed from the outside in. I had the concept of everything radiating out of me, and that the more personal or egocentric I would become, the deeper I would reach and the more I could touch those universal concerns that would involve all man. What seems to have happened since marriage is that I no longer sense ego as the greatest source for what can touch on the universal. I now feel that there is some other concrete center where love from one person to another meets; and that the more total view arises from there. . . . First, I had the sense of the center radiating out. Now, I have become concerned with the rays. You follow? It's in the action of moving out that the great concerns can be struck off continually. Now the films are being struck off, not in the gesture, but in the very real action of moving out. Where I take action strongest and most immediately is in reaching through the power of all that love toward my wife (and she toward me), and somewhere where those actions meet and cross, and bring forth children and films and inspire concerns with plants and rocks and all sights seen, a new center, composed of action, is made. The best reference I can give you for the definition of soul-in-action, rather than at-center, is Charles Olson's *Proprioception*.

Stan and Jane Brakhage, Talking

Hollis Frampton / 1973

From *Artforum* 11, no. 4 (January 1973): 72–79. ©*Artforum*, January 1973, "Stan and Jane Brakhage (and Hollis Frampton) Talking." Reprinted by permission.

Tape One

Hollis Frampton: Last night you said you would like to make something beautiful . . . and get away with it.
Stan Brakhage: What does one mean by "get away with it?"

HF: Things that are beautiful are seductive, are they not?
SB: Ah, yes, you've worried me for some time by saying that *The Riddle of Lumen* was the least seductive film I'd ever made . . . until I realized that you meant I'd gotten away with it. Seduction is what the people who steal beauty use it for. What I mean in getting away with it is that I want to be able to get all the excitement, the absolute ecstasy at times . . . and I feel confronted by anything that I've photographed or even been moved to begin to think of photographing . . . get all that excitement and intensity all the way over into whatever I make. That's what I meant by getting away with it.

Maybe that's too simple. Let's think of it a minute in terms of something somebody else got away with. Sergei Eisenstein got away with the short cut. He used every trick in the bag to get away with it. For instance, the machine-gunner. There was a reason for the short-cut: it was approximating the machine-gun. Bullshit. That was the excuse whereby he could get away with a quality of vision that was closer to the ecstasy of what his own eyesight must normally have been. Similarly, in that same shot, not only did he have the machine-gun as a context to lean on, but he was intercutting two or three distinct scenes. He kept repeating—I can't even remember exactly—do they repeat exactly: 1, 2, 3; 1, 2, 3 or do they go 1, 3, 2; 1, 3, 2?

HF: No, there's a transposition.

SB: If there is, then he's really getting away with something. Because there is no reason there should be. So he was confuting reason. What he was relying on was that the normal sequence of pictures is 1, 2, 3—a scene following a scene and so on. He was relying on repetition, and relying on that to make motion, the trickery of motion. We have a repetition of cuts, every single sixteenth of a second; and every shot encounters something almost like itself. All he did was to space two or three scenes apart from each other. So he got away with expressing something that was normal to his vision. And how do we know it was normal to his vision? Because of the *persistence* with which he expressed this thing, and because of the lengths he went to make it acceptable. Even socially acceptable: look at all the words he wrote about it.

With every artist it's a case of trying to get something of what's really intrinsic to his being, and separable from all social senses of what other human beings are, out into the general air. I can't beat, as a basic maxim, Robert Duncan's statement: I exercise my faculties at large. In the same way other men make war, some make love; I make poetry—to exercise my faculties at large. It's like hoity-toity the way it's put. Really what it means is that young men and women are faced with an impossible contradiction between their own intrinsic loneliness, and their own absolute dependence upon others. To make themselves *imaginable* within the general airs of all the other imaginations that others have accepted of themselves—they're forced to accept an equivalent. It's either that, or madness, or death, or total withdrawal, or a bitter eccentricity... and all the various other alternatives every artist toys with.

When I was a certain age, and when the glasses and the fat of me were a solid manifestation of my own removal from everything around me that I was so dependent on, I lost weight and threw away the glasses. When I threw away the glasses I literally could not see to cross the street safely. That meant I had accepted other persons' sense of sight—it didn't mean I couldn't see. I mean the ways in which I was seeing weren't acceptable, and therefore they weren't acceptable to me. I had no other equivalent for any of them in any of the books or pictures. Everyone else had an easy referential relationship with Renaissance perspective.

HF: You're saying that the spectacles designed to give you corrected perspective were, as we say, rose-colored glasses?

SB: If they had *worked*, they would have been. But they didn't work. The assumption that anything mechanical like that will work, is based on the idea that seeing is mechanical and other people are trying to see according to those glasses. Why I couldn't cross the street safely, was that no one had given me the idea that there were ways in which I could make myself safe in crossing the street, just as surely as that shared, "acceptable" form of making yourself safe.

HF: That you could see with the eyes you had?
SB: Yes, perfectly well. The one place where I did see in relationship to all other people's seeing was the movie house, from the beginning, glasses or no.

HF: Did you take off your glasses when you went to the movies?
SB: Yes, but when I first took them off, the screen was just muggy shapes and blurs. I was struggling to re-see. But people in the movie house, with or without glasses, are on a much closer plane than in the general phenomenal world, because there is a system for sight that even with glasses, apparently, I could accept. In fact, it's a system that's more suited to someone with glasses than not because it's a system that passes through lenses.

HF: Now, you're at this end of twenty years of work which pretty well does establish the primacy of a vision of your own. You have survived the necessity to get something out....
Jane Brakhage: There's the need to make more, each year....
SB: Well, people have also made a large case for beauty as terror. Assuredly the dragon must look beautiful to St. George when he finds it, because he's there to do it in. And he dances with it in so doing. But he can only dance with it if he kills it... and that sense of beauty hangs like a very dark shadow over at least the first half of the twentieth century. And I think my growing disinterest in that sense of beauty has a lot to do with why I'm embracing so many aspects of the nineteenth century, over the last several years. In the nineteenth century there was a much more direct relationship with beauty, and it became *fearful*. One wonders why. Certainly we understand why, socially. It's just as simple as this: no honest, decent, socially involved man is going to sit around painting roses while an obvious misery is destroying the world in front of his eyes. It's impossible. He either puts on blinders, or removes himself to a garden; or he becomes essentially a social artist. And to the extent that he's unable, because of his obsession and his own primary needs, to become a social artist, he immediately opts for discovering the beauty of the monster that confronts him. Not an unworthy task, in fact one of the more favored in Western history, is the confrontation with the dragon—to be slain. But what interests me now is that I envision a way in which that dragon can be confronted, and danced with, without killing it. Everybody deeply involved in the social scene jumps all over me (and everybody else that says any such thing) because they think that we mean to get along with the Devil, or to help the dragon slay people, and that's not what I mean at all.

JB: What's the dragon?
SB: Well, the dragon is the ashcan of the Ashcan School of painting. The dragon is the tortured and screaming faces of Germans in German Expressionist painting. The dragon is the waste of city landscape.

JB: So you're not doing in the dragon?
SB: Well, I think in a way I am. I think going to Pittsburgh was confronting the dragon in his den. I didn't go to Pittsburgh to photograph the city as the Emerald City of Oz, or to make a cathedral of it like Feininger. I walked straight into a police car, and then a hospital, and then a morgue. And this had to do with the city as an image of death, or as a vast graveyard of sensibility.

HF: The dragon has often been emblematic of what is unwarranted and surprising, and thus undesirable, in perception and in imagination.
SB: Kenneth Anger embraces the dragon, except that he has made it, as he's said, just a maligned god. I mean if Lucifer is to be taken as a dragon as most people would, then Kenneth would say, no, no, this is the god. It's Jehovah who's a dragon. Certainly one of the first things you can say about Kenneth Anger's films is that they are *beautiful*. They are unashamedly beautiful; and when they are terribly frightening, or awe-full, they are so because they exist in the lavish beauty of Kodachrome, used in its most unembarrassed fashion.

Every artist, in some way, is trying to get around this dilemma, which really is a nineteenth-century dilemma. What did Eisenstein have to start with, to celebrate? Heroics! He was confronted by a mass of people, which for most of the history of the world is a pretty ugly apparition in any form in which it occurs. He made *this* the hero. He strung people out in the most incredible patterns, across vast landscapes and around city streets, in order to create an image of the heroic mass. *There's* a contradiction!

Another question the artist runs up against—the prime one—is to find a way to make manifest to the general air his own socially unacceptable particularities. Then the artist starts confronting ways in which his culture is unacceptable. By "his" culture, I mean, say, the culture of Lump Gulch, which I have so far found no way to transport to New York or San Francisco. And by this I'm not just meaning to be able to give that vision to others, or not even primarily that. I've found no way yet to reconcile my living *here*, in relationship to my dreams of the city; not those dreams in relationship to the cities as they *are*, those specific cities I've known in New York, San Francisco, and, of late, Pittsburgh.

So there's Eisenstein (who presumably, if you look at those young pictures of him, had a normal bourgeois upbringing) confronted with the ordinary nineteenth-century leanings toward the dramatic-heroic, forced to use as his material, first of all by his own decision and then later by the decision of the Politburo, the ordinary mass. That's something he had to reconcile. He had irreconcilable elements enough to tear a man apart, if he can't forget them. His only means of having both these elements in the same air with himself and his proclivities was to *make an image*. That was probably, on his part, very much a *conscious* collective image. So there actually is the artist working for the state. But obviously he couldn't do it if he wasn't on the goddamn spot himself.

HF: The spot being the problem of reconciling his own particularities with what had been presented to him as how one was supposed to be?

SB: It's *two* how you are supposed to be's. One, the primary one, is from his childhood. Then there's his own personal revolt, which puts him in the way of being representative of the other. I think anytime any artist is working, he's working with material that's so disturbing to him, it's just like a scientist picking up pieces one of which might be distilled radium. Haven't you had that sense when you're putting two pieces of film together, that it might burn you to a crisp?

HF: Absolutely.

SB: That sounds too much, though, like the condition is heroic. I'm always in terror that I'll never be permitted to make another film. You know, the *real* danger is that I'll start believing the role I've created for myself, or that others have created for me, and that this will become such a viable and totally acceptable role in the world that I'll start living it, and then there'll be no need to create anymore. Why should there? I mean then I'll have a place in the world, like everybody else. The trouble is that if that had happened to me just naturally between the ages of one and six, or even by the time I was eighteen, I probably wouldn't be an artist. I'd be going around in the world fulfilling my role. But it *didn't*. The film is a by-product . . . and a very useful by-product. Hopefully, if it is an art, then it's a useful by-product in the sense that I can use it again and again to re-experience.

HF: As a magical amulet to hang around your neck, to ward off evil?

SB: I don't know. Maybe people who make objects feel that way about it. But how can you feel that way about film, which is a continuity art? In film, the closest metaphor is the *thought process*, so "remind myself" would be the most correct way to put it, because film has the ability to be closest to thought process in its continuities.

HF: Just by virtue of its being continuous?

SB: Yes. I do think that the way people name it has a lot to do with it. I think that *kino* has a lot to do with Russian cinema.

HF: The name means *move*, it means movies.

SB: *Cinema* means something a little different, it has that tendency, in the world-language, to be going on to imply *cinematographer* which means *writer* of movement. And I think that kind of distinction, while it's small, grows from its small acorn across the span of fifty years and takes a very strong effect. *Film* is our word. That's how independent makers distinguish themselves from the pros, who make movies. So it's ghosts we're after, as a group, although every single one of us is changing that continually, and at some point it will be so thoroughly changed that the word "film" won't be used anymore, or it will be changed after twenty-five years or we'll drop that word.

Again, it's a question of "making place." And then there's this aspect of it that I begin to be aware of. I become aware, at a very early age that I'm not sharing the world of vision that I'm supposed to in order to exist in the general air with all the people around me. What a terrifying situation! What to do? O.K. then twenty years later I begin to be perfectly aware that the place I'd made for myself, and the altering of sight that occurs absolutely contingent with that, is similarly embarrassing young kids all over the world and just those I would most sympathize with.

Well, I've brooded on this on dark nights. I can never quite bring myself to say, "Ah, fuck it, that's their problem" . . . which is the extent to which I am "social" . . . and it worries me.

HF: That's because it *has been* your problem.

SB: So an awful lot of this talk we do, and a lot of the writing and the teaching, and an awful lot of study, has been trying to find some way to slip this goddamn knot altogether. There is the kind of man that goes out to level all the buildings that interfere with the new landscape, that he and some few others envision. Eisenstein had a lot of that fire in him too. I feel him trembling at times, always on the edge of wanting to cut the Gordian knot. He was stubborn. He was a good stubborn man. It all holds together once you begin to see him as human. He's also very toughened by the time the Politburo is telling him how to live. He's used to evading that since he was six or so . . . people were telling him how to live or fuck or whatever so he's toughened. And that's another thing all artists seem to share—something has toughened them. Usually it's that they don't accept it, so they're in a tough spot. Right from scratch. Then, something that they've embraced in their not fitting not only doesn't fit with the society around them but is obviously enough to get their heads cut off. If everyone realized what is perfectly true, that they *don't* fit . . . if each person realized how distinct and unique he or she is, well, then, art would become normal everyday expression. And people would swap their artifacts or works of art or their words as naturally as they now swap slogans that are handed to them by the State. Art is personal in the making and it is personal in the appreciation. All that I try to do in my lectures, and when I teach in Chicago, is demonstrate my personal appreciation. The outside social hope is that it will inspire others to demonstrate theirs, or at least to *have* theirs. That if I can do it, then anyone else can make up his own Eisenstein. I made up my Eisenstein, or at least the Eisenstein that was real to me at the time of writing that essay on Eisenstein ["Sergei Eisenstein," *The Brakhage Lectures*, Chicago, 1972]. Having done that, anyone else can. Mine is certainly unique and personal . . . which is why it gets attacked. Consider the level of the argument against it—that I am in it, that I am visible in it. Ken Kelman said, about the essays in general, that I had done a good job of fitting into the shoes of other filmmakers, but that always a big Brakhage toe sticks out!

HF: Let's extend this a bit. If everyone is free to make up his own Eisenstein, then everyone's likewise free to make up his own Stan Brakhage.
SB: Right. Absolutely right.

HF: In this case we have a little help from Stan Brakhage?
SB: Now there's the trouble with artists being living. That's why people so much prefer for artists to be dead, because anybody free to make up his own Stan Brakhage can give me the feeling that I have not found any kind of place in the world. Having done that I will naturally explode or fight back or argue or scream or cry or do something embarrassing.

HF: You're saying that there are thousands of Stan Brakhages, but they're all in other people's heads . . . which leaves you in an embarrassing position.
SB: It may be so, that's preferable to everybody agreeing on who Stan Brakhage is, and then beating Stan Brakhage over the heads of the coming generation, which is the thing normally that's done. I had my own head beaten bloody by Sergei Eisenstein, whose work I loved, and whose tradition I was working, absolutely lineally, to spring my own traps. And the horror that is happening now, with my work, to another generation of people, really sits heavily on my sore head.

HF: It has also been used, for as long as I've known your work to beat you yourself over the head. After *Anticipation of the Night* you were beaten over the head with the psychodramas.
SB: Well, that's always very confusing too. Here again we have Eisenstein and the Politburo. I guess he never lived down *Battleship Potemkin*. What to do about that? It happens because people have such a narrow view of person, because most people are trapped in a narrow view of themselves, which they've been forced into by social expediency. *Not* by social necessity. I do not subscribe to the despair of

the old Sigmund Freud, in *Civilization and its Discontents*, for instance. But it is *expedient* to regard anything narrowly.

To put it simply: in the name of "progress," an *extensive* view of human personality has been almost destroyed as a possibility of consideration for most people. There's really no problem in seeing that the same man who made *Anticipation of the Night* then made *Dog Star Man*, then made *Scenes from Under Childhood*, and is now doing the films I'm doing. There's really no problem with that at all, because you have one absolute surety to go on, and that's *style*. I had thought to emphasize that by *signing* those works. It takes me hours to scratch on film: By Brakhage. Certainly since *Desistfilm* that's been there as a possibility for most of my films. If I can sign checks while leaning on a steering wheel, while sitting at my desk, while I'm raging, while I'm sad, while I'm happy, while I'm writing quickly, while I'm working slow . . . and all these checks obviously bear the signature of Stan Brakhage, which is absolutely defensible in a court of law by a handwriting analyst, and is immediately obvious to most people on sight, then why is it that most people have so much difficulty recognizing style in art?

HF: I think it has to do with a constricted definition of style that has arisen particularly with regard to plastic arts, in the last twenty years or so: that it is not something that can be as *various* as the signature of one person, but that it is as *fixed* as the same signature repeated exactly by a forger.

SB: What you're saying is that there's such a degree of forgery in the world that it has made style suspect.

HF: I wrote recently that style is the adoption of a fixed perceptual distance from the object. That was in connection with nineteenth-century photography, and I used Julia Margaret Cameron as an example but I had very much in mind any number of painters of my own generation, who are very careful to demonstrate constantly a step-by-step continuity in their development, from one work to the next.

SB: That's interesting to me because I used to know my continuities like the alphabet. I knew not only the orders of the films made, but I knew almost to the month and certainly the year when each film was completed, when the shooting was done, or editing or whatever. Since we've moved here, to this location in the mountains, that's ceased to be so. I can tell you when the first two or three films were made when we came here; and I can tell you the order and the months of the last six months. But I cannot really differentiate any of the rest. That's interesting. So I'm thinking that for a while there was that determination to hold each step in mind and build a progression, as if I were making a ladder.

HF: Is it something that happened in your work because you came here? Or was it simply because of the time in your life?
SB: I think both. For many years I was thinking I was getting *out* of something. There were steps in the direction of finding my place in the world. This place, after all, carries the exactitude that we have lived here eight years now. That length of time I never lived anywhere else on earth or anywhere near it. So that I've found my place in the literal physical sense.

And I've become aware that I'll *never* find my place in the world . . . and that all that I can do is keep making elbow room in the general air. I can toss out some metaphor for *this* aspect of myself and some metaphor for *that*, but it's unending.

But that hasn't anything to do with the creative act. What I mean is, that I feel as if the creative powers *use* my social embarrassment, and whatever else is useful, to permit the making of the work; and I feel that in an equal degree while I'm working on something, making place for the particularities of my vision, and my thought processes, my own physiology, in the world. So that's an absolutely poised shared experience: a dance, you could say, between my sense of myself and something that I don't know anything about . . . or a mystery.

HF: That verb *make* comes up again and again—*make* place, *make* sense, *make* a work of art, *make* love—with two implications I think. First, as taking an active posture toward something. And second, with an implication that things that must be *made* have a kind of half-life, that unless they're continuously restored and regenerated, we run out. Why do we say *make* love for instance? Suggesting that it has to be remade . . .
JB: Maybe it does.
SB: I completely believe that.

HF: Like a radioactive substance that gives out energy and is diminished and needs to be augmented.
JB: Making your image!
SB: Yes, which is always very important to me; after all that's how I got into this in the first place. That's how they, if there is any they, dragged me into this. Well, there *is* a *"they."* I just don't know if this unnamable likes to be referred to as a "they." I am very clear that I receive instructions from the outside. I have had no question about this since I was editing *Cat's Cradle*; and certainly since *Sirius Remembered* I have had no questions about it. At times I have questioned it—but I have had no questions *about* it. It's made me think about younger artists a lot; and I think the young depend very much, not only on a lot of instructions, but depend on *drama*. As I get older, I don't depend on *drama*.

In fact, I begin to have a sense that I understand something of what it is to be an old artist. And it's something so simply wonderful as being granted a responsibility for what's been given you to do . . . as distinct from being charged continually with forces you have absolutely no control over. I've seen many artists begin to make this transition. I'm watching Paul Sharits begin to make it, for instance. Actually in *S:TREAM:SS:ECTION:S:ECTION:S:SECTIONED*, Sharits presented us with the voices of the Muses, literally on the sound track. Having done that, he had certainly a more comfortable relationship with them. The relationship, in getting older, is a less dramatic relationship with what some men call the Muses, and much more. . . .

HF: What we used to call intercourse, in politer days?
SB: Yes, I think so. A shared responsibility, maybe. Do you know the story about Paul, and how he came to that sound track on *S:TREAM:SS:ECTION:S:ECTION:S:SECTIONED*? That was the sound he heard while working on some film—not, I believe, this one—when he was sitting late at night in his little room in Baltimore. And he couldn't *stop* the sound, it kept coming back. There are infuriating aspects to the voices of the Muses which were captured beautifully for us by Rameau in that piece called *The Conversation of the Muses*. In fact, people should really listen both to the sound track on *S:TREAM:SS:ECTION:S:ECTION:S:SECTIONED* and that piece by Rameau. There can be no question, while we may not know what it is we're talking about—"Muse" may be only a very inferior term—that there is *something* that artists share. Some refer to them as whisperings, some as outright visions, some as sounds, or ways in which sounds in the surrounding atmosphere gang up and produce effects on their nervous systems. It's a pity no one ever thought, to ask, say, Eisenstein about it.

HF: He would have felt constrained not to answer.
SB: Yes, he probably would have. But, it's surprising. You'd think that certain men would never give any answer in relationship to anything that is the contemporary experience of something. And then they surprise you. For instance, I can believe that Eisenstein might somewhere have left some such statement, because I have seen D. W. Griffith's statement (and I am paraphrasing it, but I am very close): all that I really want to do is to make you see. Now, that's about the last statement in the world that I ever would have expected to share with Griffith. And the only change I would make in it is the obvious one: I would change the word *make*. But he was, after all, very involved with social drama . . . he wanted to *make* people see. And, look, in the very beginning we have the implication of Muses in film—in Méliès's work, in no uncertain terms, however humorous the context.

But, of course, people really *haven't* accepted film as an art form yet. And until that becomes a general assumption, we're certainly asking too much to expect people to consider how the Muses operate in relationship to the creative act in film. But actually, in the twentieth century, it's embarrassing to mention these things, because everybody's so concerned with the social usability of art; there's nothing very usable about what most people would regard as madness. Thinking over how I work today, and how I used to work, and what slight difference there is . . . it goes along with the whole change in my life. When I was younger, I really couldn't find much significance except in a dramatic confrontation. It isn't an older person's sense of living to be dependent on drama. As you get older you see the damage that it does, for one thing, and you *feel* it more. Then, the minute you begin giving up pieces of that form of knowledge, then you discover so many others. I shouldn't say *you*, that means I'm not quite sure what I'm trying to say. I discover many other ways to be informed, and many other ways to elbow myself, my physiology, a little place in the world, than through dramatic confrontation. And as I do so my whole life changes incredibly. The work process doesn't depend on dramatic confrontation. This is why it isn't important to me anymore to know which film came when.

Again, some men were not permitted that. We were talking about style earlier, and you said there have been so many forgeries in the world that people are no longer cashing esthetic checks on the basis of style. Consider this though. Who are the forgers of Méliès? What are their names? When you say Méliès you get, right away, a sense of style. Now tell me, who's forged that style? We're not talking about the grammar he's left, or the things he's given socially; we're talking about *style*. Come on, give up! No one has!

HF: I do. You're right.
SB: The closest you come . . . and you have to leap all the way . . . is Jean Cocteau. And I certainly wouldn't call him a forger of Méliès. He's just the only one who picked up on Méliès's style sufficiently to let it quiver in his work every now and again.

HF: I heard a demurrer from you, Jane.
JB: I don't think he forged Méliès at all.
SB: No, I didn't mean that he did. I only meant that he was sufficiently aware of Méliès's style.
JB: You shouldn't have said that he did.
SB: All right, let's take another one. Let's take the big chief in the line-up, Sergei Eisenstein. Who forged his stuff? Same thing: no one. Now let's cap it. Who's

forged Stan Brakhage's style? O.K., a lot of names come suddenly to mind as possibilities. But I'm sure they did with each of these men, in their time, because at the time something is being made, the style is not seen or perceived clearly enough to distinguish the forgeries.

In fact, we know that there were many forgers of Méliès. And there were forgeries upon forgeries, and the forgers became much more successful than Méliès, and that's how he was beat out. We know that . . . but where are they? Nobody could ever bear to look at them twenty years later, or we'd have a few of them around.

HF: What a paradox this is: the Master ends up in the candy store and the forgers go into oblivion!

SB: And we know people's sensibilities change incredibly. For instance, Edison lined up a string quartet on the Carnegie Hall stage, in front of a supposedly experienced audience, and had fake strings on all their instruments, and fooled the audience with a cylinder recording of a quartet played while they went through the motions. No one could pull that stuff today.

HF: But then it also seems unthinkable that people in France and the Soviet Union ran around behind the screen to look for the actors in the Lumière films. They were *black and white*, for God's sake.

SB: And people recognized themselves in Méliès's *The Dreyfus Affair*—people who'd been to the trial took it as a newsreel footage and recognized themselves among what was actually a crew of actors. That's the whole basic trick . . . which brings us to another interesting point. We *are* in a continuum. Now that we see that forgery only operates within a time-bound context, and therefore can't be anything more than a brief distraction from what an art is—or from what the style of the man who made it is—then we come to the question: what about a lineal tradition?

My big problem has been, all these years, that no one has recognized that I (and all my contemporaries) are working in a lineal tradition of Méliès, Griffith, Dreyer, Eisenstein, and all the other classically accepted filmmakers. Why not? Why are they unable to recognize that? I took my first cues for fast cuts from Eisenstein, and I took my first senses of parallel cutting from Griffith, and I took my first senses of the individual frame life of a film from Méliès, and so on. Why has it taken so long for anyone to recognize this as a lineal tradition? Why did we all have to go through that terrible embarrassment of the late sixties when we were presented to the world as though we sprang full-blown, completely new, from an LSD dream? Why is it that those men who studied grammar, even of Griffith and Eisenstein, were so slow in recognizing that? In fact, most of them still don't and would rather curl up like the Wicked Witch of the . . . North?

JB: West!
SB: . . . in a pool of black smoke, than acknowledge that lineal tradition.

HF: We live in a "heroic" culture. We live in the midst of "masterpieces."
SB: *Do* we?

HF: Well, we certainly don't.
SB: I think maybe there's a simpler explanation: that they never were really looking at the person or the personal style of Eisenstein.

HF: Which is to say, they never looked at the films.
SB: Exactly. They never looked at the art of the films.
JB: What were they looking at?
SB: The trickery. And the "social significance," as it's called. Well, to be graceful about it, maybe this is the only use most people have for art. In fact, one could let them have it that way, if they weren't so mean about it. I don't particularly care, for instance, if people *really* don't want to interest themselves in obsession or vision.

I used to care a lot. But I guess I was beaten in my arguments with P. Adams Sitney, years ago. He just simply did *not* want to close his eyes and see hypnagogically, so that he would have some sense why I was hand-painting film a frame at a time. Finally, I've made peace with that. Why should he, if he doesn't want to? But on the other hand, as long as he and many others busy themselves with pronouncing to the world what we are, what the artist is, then there's bound to be a continual fuss in the relationship between us.

Tape Two

SB: It's my problem, at the moment, that I am once again, or let's say especially for the first time, trying to make a portrait of Jane. This is after years and years of Jane's image being central to film after film after film. And this is weighted with the problem that every now and again Jane will say, well, you've never gotten an image of *me*. *So* here I go for the first time—again.

HF: Why is it that he can't make a portrait of you Jane?
JB: He just uses me.
SB: Oh, boy, now I'm in trouble! The whole women's lib movement at this instant descends on me like a puddle of Harpies!
JB: I've just been doing something like having a baby, or minding the kids, or standing around or something. And he just photographs a woman having a baby,

sweeping the floor, or making a bed. It's the making of the bed or whatever *Jane* does with it.

HF: Jane, you have to realize that, from the outside, you are presumably the most profoundly differentiated and individuated woman in the history of film—and, probably, one of the most completely differentiated *persons* in the history of art.
JB: Hmm. You really think so?

HF: You can look it up in the goddamned library, Jane. Of course you are!
JB: Where? Who said that?

HF: I said it. Then you cut your long hair off and fucked it up.
JB: There, that's just what I mean. . . .
SB: I think that's probably why she cut off her hair.
JB: That's *right!*

HF: You felt, then, that you had no life outside your cinematic myth, that you were becoming a movie star, in fact, that kind of object.
JB: Yes, an appendage.
SB: I'm sure Saskia must have felt similarly, Saskia who was asked to dress in all those fancy costumes so that Rembrandt could paint her as this, that and the other. He used himself in the same sense.
JB: I didn't resent it. I just feel that's the case, that's how it is.
SB: I'll be the first to say bullshit.
JB: That was years ago that I did care, and now I don't, and now you can make the goddamn film because I don't give a shit.

HF: I'd like to remind both of you that I am the interviewer here.
JB: What kind of rights do you have here?
SB: Why don't you whip your camera out and make another film, *Bride of Critical Mass*? No, let me finish what I was going to say. I think actually what it is—I think everybody will recognize this as a truth—is that you just want *more*. And that's perfectly reasonable, and I am willing to comply . . .
JB: I *don't* want anymore.
SB: . . . because I have that *necessity*. I have never been able to make anything for you or for anyone else, actually. I've tried to make children's films for the children. At times I've really felt I would swap everything else I've accomplished to be the Hans Christian Anderson of film. But I cannot commission a children's film from myself. I've tried to make films for Jane, and they always fail very

quickly and I throw them away. In fact, they've never been seen. But she, rightfully, always wants more and more. This really is her inspiring function in the creative process.

HF: Do you feel this way about his portraits of other people, Jane?
JB: *Scenes from Under Childhood* is maybe really a thorough thing. But that's the only thorough thing I can think of, unless the Pittsburgh films, which are documentary, and therefore more objective, so the cops can be seen as "out there." Most of his stuff is inward.

HF: You have always the feeling he's making a portrait of himself?
JB: Yes.
SB: I agree.

HF: That's why you say you're simply part of a pretext for that self-portrait. Has the case ever been otherwise for an artist?
JB: Yes, that's a good question.
SB: I can state it better than that. Has the case ever been otherwise for any human being, ever?
JB: So I quit complaining, because I felt that that was not something that he *could* do.
SB: You see, to accomplish that feeling that you designate as "out there," with relationship to the images of the police in *Eyes*, the clearest way to accomplish that is in drama. And drama is where the art completely and totally lies in order to state a truth. If we'd been making drama films all these years, and you were an actress, then there would be many images of you that would seem "out there" in the sense that the police do in that film.

HF: You do have a film between you which very precisely mimes the Aeschylean drama, and that's *Wedlock House: An Intercourse*, in which the camera is tossed back and forth like the stichomathy in Greek argument, and the camera is the impersonal messenger that brings everybody bad news.
JB: We did that in *Scenes from Under Childhood* too, in one of the last parts.
SB: We were "acting," as all people do when they quarrel. To the extent to which we act, we give the appearance of being "out there." The Pittsburgh police were, surely, continually acting. In fact an enormous part of their job is to act; so it is with doctors, with all public servants.

HF: So it is with teachers. We know as teachers the classroom is a great theater.
SB: Certainly. So to the extent that we have ever been acting, there's a sense of a

presence "out there." But that to me is the same as what got me, and every other artist, into this in the first place. The *act*, the general shared public act, is, for some reason, not possible, to a man or a woman. And if that man or woman still chooses to attempt to relate to all these others in their social acts, he or she is then forced to make his or her *own* act, an act that will accommodate the necessities of the person. And there is a beginning of an art.

There are two interests in art. Robert Duncan is curiously always very dedicated to the theatrical act. This is why he was so fascinated with Ingmar Bergman, for instance. He was interested in that sense of making, that you "make it up," with all kinds of conscious trickery, into a vast lie which is then so removed from ordinary living experience that it serves as a truth, a truth which carries the feeling that it is "out there." I'm not against this way of creating. In fact I guess this is where I started—I started with drama. For instance Janis Hubka probably recognizes herself very much better in the first film I made, *Interim*, than you [Jane] ever have . . . because we've been so little involved in drama since we've known each other. There's no real sense of there being an "out there."
JB: I'm no kind of an actress.

HF: Hear, hear, bravo, encore!
JB: Gee, is it that bad?
SB: I have tremendous necessity to keep re-seeing Jane, and all my many ways of seeing are engaged with her continually. And of course some of them have never been used. And some of them are very habit-bound. And I shudder at the thought of those artists who continue to paint and repaint their loved ones in the same fashion, in the same situation.

HF: As if, by some kind of magic, to freeze them in a snapshot.
SB: To hold to the original vision. Yes, that's a good term for it—the snapshot approach to it. For one thing I'm fascinated right now to make a film bouncing the light off Jane, which is something I have never really done, and to make it a film that's totally about her, in the sense that all its considerations center on her. And *that* I've never done.

HF: Do you like to have light bouncing off you, Jane?
JB: I'm trying, I'm trying.
SB: Well, I said it wrongly. I don't bounce the light. I turn on a bulb, and don't have megalomaniac senses that I bounce the light in so doing—or I set up an elaborate lighting apparatus and aim it this way and that way. But I really *catch* the light. That's what it's all about.

HF: You catch what's leftover—after Jane is through with the light.
SB: O.K., let's get it straight, after Jane is through with the light I catch it. That's the normal condition of my life anyway, so that should work for something magnificent.
JB: What is your interest in light?
SB: I see so many qualities of light, so many things that seem to *be* light but aren't anywhere categorized as such or spoken of as such or referred to by other people as such. I always have, and as I get older I see more and more. I see so many qualities of light continually, every day constantly new ones and new aspects of old ones, that it's become a normal condition. At this time in my life it is the variety of the quality of light that I see, and live with daily, that removes me most from feeling I share sight with other people.

HF: And that leads you to the necessity of making something that will share that sight with other people?
SB: Yes.

HF: You've spent a lot of time attempting a very exact registration of the seeing process. But the prime condition of seeing, *at all*, is light, the carrier wave which makes everything visible, which visible things modulate, change and so forth. And that seems to be a very recent shift of focus in your interests.
SB: It's not recent, because it was a long time ago that I was startled by Scotus Erigena's, "All things that are, are light." Along with all the many gifts of Ezra Pound, this was certainly one of the most startling and immediately meaningful to me. Because even if it were, as it first sounded to me, an absurd statement in the face of my scientific prejudices, it still expressed beautifully the natural condition of the filmmaker at the moment of making. And of late that phrase has come back to me again in many forms—one of the most beautiful of which is Hugh Kenner's exposition of it (and all other aspects of light in Ezra Pound's work) in his book *The Pound Era*. It comes back to me at a time when I really *need* it because slowly and gradually over the years my attention to the world in relationship to light has increased my seeing of all kinds of things that other people either don't see, or don't admit they see . . . or don't have any *way* to admit they see. So now I take that statement very much more literally. One can make scientific arguments about it. So much of everything we know—and it's hard to think of anything for which this is not so—is, in its state, because of light. Let alone *whether* we see it or not. Year after year more and more things began to seem to me to *glow*. Having been raised by Germans in Kansas, and being fussy, I troubled myself to try to figure out if I was *superimposing* this glow upon things, in my mind's eye, or if things were

coming from some outside and pressing on my brain at the point where it surfaces as an eye. And finally, even through some experiments, I came to convince myself at least some of these extraordinary things were certainly coming from the outside and pressing in on me.

So far I'm just talking about an intrinsic light that seems to be emanating from all things. I wrote, when younger, about certain experiments that Jane and I made with qualities of light, like "elfskin," for instance, which term we got out of old Saxon by way of Michael McClure. That is, the quality of light that emanates from all beings. But that was too general a sight. Finally I found a way to make some equivalent of it by combining high contrast positive and negative film, slightly off register. That gave an approximate of that thing we were seeing, that we and Michael were calling "elfskin," and were presuming that maybe the Saxons did.

But now there are so many qualities, that that seems just one among hundreds. Other qualities of glow from . . . not only beings, but all objects.

Now let's take another sense of light. That light that we more normally refer to, light that comes from the sun and bounces around here on earth, by which we see. I suppose for a long time I had a normal relationship with *that* light, or thought I did. But one day I knew rain was coming. I asked myself how I knew. We get many scuttling clouds that go over and deposit nothing . . . but I knew rain was coming! And then I *saw* it. I saw streaks of whitish lines, almost as if drawn, or as if comic-strip drawn, very quickly coming down on a slant into the ground. There was a feeling that this was being *sucked* into the ground, that these were actually being pulled, as if by gravity. These lines were, in fact, a metaphor for rain. Very shortly thereafter rain began to fall. Because of my scientific upbringing I tested myself. Again and again, as I sat on the porch, I would ask myself, as one cloud or another looking promising passed over, is it going to rain or not? And I finally was producing a 100 percent record. Because before every actual rain there came this light manifestation. It looked like streaks of light, metaphors of the coming rain.

By now, I've seen so many other similar qualities of light that precede a material manifestation, that the question came to my mind: maybe everything that's taken shape on earth, had its shape defined for it by light, by some quality of light, before it came into existence. I even thought maybe that's what ghosts or spirits are, maybe that shape humans have taken was preceded by that which we call angels, or demons, or ghosts. I see them; and what am I to do with having seen them? The best that you can do, is to try to determine if you're making it up.

For instance, I have seen angels. That is, in the twentieth century, a rather embarrassing sort of thing to admit. I have seen figures, usually with wings or something like wings, that are in a tradition of what we call "angels" when referring to painting or sculpture in Western art. After I'm through the experience of seeing them, then I rummage my mind, and this whole bag of books over here, to see if I can find an angel that's like the one I saw, or a composite of angels that would have made up mine. To try to figure out if my mind has taken many parts of angels out of the history of painting and projected one in front of me. I've never found anything at all like what I *saw*. Angels are quite a tradition, you know. It doesn't begin with Christianity. Just one sculpture that shows that angels aren't Christian is the *Victory of Samothrace*. East and West there is a tradition of angels, which have been expressed in various forms of art.

These visions occur, these days, normally, and just as something passing. They don't occur in any way that would be particularly dramatic, helpful, or useful. And so with the qualities of light. I see light that appears to pool. It appears to be a glow that's as if it had weight and liquid substance. It doesn't pool in holes in the ground, necessarily, or any depression. But it pools *as if* there were some hole there. And it is of a glow that's all of what we call light, as we extend that term to phosphorescence. It happens quite normally. And there's also a quality of light that streams over the ground; and I've seen it running absolutely counter to the blow of the wind. Just streaming, in all senses as if it were a charged or phosphorescent mass of floating liquid. In fact, it looks very much like a mountain stream, only it's a slight differentiation of qualities of light coming from the sun, and bouncing in the ordinary ways that we recognize and refer to.

Now if there's no other value in all this, there is at least this specifically for me at this time—that I can't photograph it. The materials of film are too clearly attuned to some other quality of light, or too gross or too inferior or whatever to be receptive to these qualities of light. I find myself in the position of having to search out an equivalent. So I am back in the same spot I was when I realized that I couldn't photograph closed-eye vision. I could not get a camera inside my head so I painted on film to get as near an equivalent I could of things. I was, yes, seeing, but had no way to photograph. Here again I cannot photograph so I have to search for equivalents that will give something of the quality of what I'm seeing. Well, that takes me back to the absolute beginning—because, all along, all I or anybody else have been able to do, is create by whatever means—film or any other art—an *equivalent* of what we were seeing.

HF: That's a classic definition of the artist's problem.
JB: It's a weird thing to do in the first place.
SB: Yes, it is, isn't it? But if you think about it, it's so beautiful, because only by doing such a weird thing could you actually get involved in trying to create an equivalent for something that most people *weren't* already seeing. I mean you begin trying to get an equivalent that's rather close cousin to whatever anybody else is seeing.

And this is the value of the classics and of the other artists that the young man adores and worships. His life depends on them, because they have, through their personal needs, taken a thing so far and then here comes . . . myself as a young man, and I know that my eyes are doing this and that and the other and suddenly Eisenstein is giving me a beginning of an equivalent to do something that *I'm* doing. And this isn't really taking something *further*; the process here is the adjusting of my equivalents to his.

HF: So you find you are not, after all, so very particular, that there are needs you share with others?

SB: It's more that, if nothing else that the works that I make can be close to his. If I can't live reasonably in a world of standard cliché visions, at least my films can live in a world of developing visions along with his. I don't really feel that I could actually get along with Sergei Eisenstein any easier than I might with my mother. But I can sense that the *works* can share a world. Presumably, then, later, other people will share something, such as is useful to them. I'm trying to find a way not to put down the normal decision of most people to accept a limited vision in order to communicate with each other. That's their business, if they want to do that. I would probably do it too, if it were possible.

JB: Why do we have to communicate with each other?

HF: I don't really think there's any question about having to; we simple *do* it. That's Ray Birdwhistell's paean to inevitability.

SB: Let's be careful of the word communication though, to absolutely distinguish it from, say, Stan VanDerBeek's sense of the word communication. I think that's a very dangerous word. I don't really mean that I want to communicate with other people in that sense of getting my message all the way over, or I'd have maybe tried to become a politician. That's what makes certainly a dictator—that absolute insistence on total communication. In my case it had to do with the eyes. I wanted to share a sight. That's not the same as telling "them" about that sight. I wanted to feel like I lived in the same world with other people. That's not the same as communicating. My primary necessity was not that they understand me, or obviously I'd never have become an artist. My primary need was that, at some point, I share a sight with them. Is that fair and clear? Does that make sense? I want to say it right?

JB: It's *you* you're talking about.

SB: If I had needed to show them "sights," then presumably I'd have gone to Hollywood.

JB: You can see how that doesn't necessarily have to be a very widespread need.

SB: To tell you the truth I don't even think it's very important. I don't think it has much to do with the creative act. We're back again to talking about what creative forces use, in people, to prompt a man or a woman to lend themselves to creativity. You know one of the nicest simple social definitions of an art that I have ever heard came from the brother of Robert Oppenheimer, Frank Oppenheimer. He is a very nervous scientist, who's suffered particularly because of the things that happened to his brother, and a very attenuated man. And one day he simply said, "I always think that an art just says: now see this, now hear this."

HF: But you imply an extended and intensified sense of "see" and "hear," do you not? You have talked about seeing as a registration of the whole electromagnetic spectrum. When you speak about seeing as a metaphoric precedent for coming rain, you extend the sense of seeing to include anything that is light.

SB: But would people say that you *could* call this light? What about what it is that I see as a pool? What about the streams I see move along the ground, contrary to the wind? What about those things that Wilhelm Reich suggested . . . that I have seen? He sees a certain quality of movement of a glowing particle in the air, billions of glowing particles, that make a little half-spiral. And he called this orgone energy, and he tried to use it to cure cancer . . . or at least he tried to see whatever curative effect there might be in it. He's the only person who referred in writing to something that I was seeing.

Among these particles there's another quality that looks like light, like a light particle that has a particular movement. I can see it with my eyes open, and with my eyes closed. I see it very intensely in the blue sky when I relax my eyes. It fills that blue with golden movement, and I see the sky as gold. I have performed one of his experiments, that proved to me satisfactorily that it was "out there," because it would magnify through closed eyes. Now, he refers to it as blue, I do yellow. That's no problem, blue and yellow being so interchangeable on the optic nerve level. I'm sure, by a simple shift of attention, I could see the blue. I *prefer* to see them yellow. And at that point people can rush in and say, well, so you prefer to see them yellow, you prefer to see them. You create them, you invent them. But I was seeing them for a long time before I ever read anything by Wilhelm Reich, so here was another voice that sustained me. Someone else was seeing something of some such thing, to put it in a nice Gertrude Stein phrase.

What I ponder on, and what I suppose I'm going to think more about as I get older and older is, can't I just make films and stop talking about it? I would be horrified by people who would insist on this system of qualities of light, and derive it from me, and apply it to my films. . . . I would be as horrified by that as I was by P. Adams Sitney's absolute refusal to close his eyes and see if he couldn't see something that was related to the painting on my film. He made a very strong refusal. It was Jane who put me at peace with that. She said, leave him alone, why does he have to do that? And in the long run that's safer . . . because the other way leads to a religion. They'll make a religion out of it.

HF: If your own eye insists upon your absolute right to feel different, then it must also confirm the absolute right of others to feel different.
SB: That's right. Then, the minute P. Adams refused to search for his own hypnagogic vision, we had our next quarrel, which sprang up when I said I am the most thorough documentary filmmaker in the world because I document the act of seeing as well as everything that the light brings me. And he said nonsense, of course, because he had no fix on the extent to which I was *documenting*. He and many others are still trying to view me as an imaginative filmmaker, as an inventor of fantasies or metaphors.

HF: You are saying, along with Confucius: "I have added nothing."
SB: Yes, I have added nothing. I've just been trying to see and make a place for my seeing in the world at large, that's all. And I've been permitting myself to be used by some forces that are totally mysterious to me, to accomplish something that satisfies me more than what I *thought* I was setting out to do.

Art is the reaching out to this phenomenon or light or moving creatures around us—I don't even know what the hell to call it. I have no name for it. And the extent to which different societies at different times have decided that everyone shares this or that relationship with the world is all some social usage of art, long after the fact of its creating and usually after the fact of the artist's living. People finally decided, all of them, to see sunsets. Well, what have we left out?
JB: All the rest.
SB: There's not too much about specific films. I don't know that it's even appropriate to talk about them.
JB: The list is too long.
SB: I don't feel that way about them anymore. It doesn't seem to make much sense.

On Filming Light

Forrest Williams / 1974

From *The Structurist*, no. 13/14 (1973–74): 90–100. Reprinted by permission of *The Structurist* and with agreement of the estate of Forrest Williams.

NB: The following discussion is an abridged version of a conversation that took place in Denver, Colorado, on February 9, 1974. Some rephrasing and editing has been employed for the sake of continuity. We would like to thank Gordon S. Rosenblum for his kind hospitality which made the occasion possible. The visually important distinction made between "radiant" light and "luminescent" light makes no attempt to follow scientific nomenclature rather than ordinary parlance. As should be clear in the various contexts, the distinction is essentially *the humanly significant* (as compared to scientifically useful) contrast between sun-like light, including the incandescent bulb, which we commonly experience as light that radiates beams, and luminescent or phosphorescent light (e.g., neon fluorescence caused by electrical excitation of gas particles) which is not at all sun-like. —FW

Stan Brakhage: Maybe I should just describe briefly what we're both looking at. It's a photograph by Michael Chikiris of myself filming open-heart surgery. As still photography, it would be regarded as a typical documentary shot. You see most of the room. You see clearly that man, in this case myself, is filming. It's quite obvious that people are gathered around engaged in a surgical procedure.

Forrest Williams: I was interested in starting with this because the most conspicuous and unusual thing is that the light is wholly planned, and in a way that's never been done before in human history. This neutral, flat, shadowless light wasn't needed before and couldn't have been accomplished before our time.
SB: Yes, this is a situation in which we have a totally artificial light of a complex nature. One can regard anything that happens as natural, so the fact that man creates a light, as Edison did or as many others have done, is not necessarily artificial. What's particularly artificial about this image is that the qualities of light

created here are scientifically balanced, so that these people during the operation have an agreed-upon norm of light, particularly in terms of color. There is overhead neon lighting, which is luminescent light, but then, probably for purposes of color identification among themselves while looking at tissues, these people have a very balanced radiant light (the kettledrum overheads). They are trying to create as flat, as shadowless a light as possible. Now, I am standing off to the side, trying to utilize this light so it will leave a—hopefully creative—image along a line of a film that is itself balanced for particular coded recognition of color by spectators. I have a variety of films to choose from, but whichever one I load in that camera was both created by the Eastman Kodak Company and was processed by my laboratory to achieve a certain agreed-upon norm of what kind of color this hospital light has produced.

FW: So there are several norms already functioning before you even start to shoot. Making the film must have been a more-than-usual challenge.
SB: Yes, just as I'm more than usually challenged, as a patient, to stay alive in a hospital because of the deadly surroundings. It was a struggle just technically to get enough light in many places to make a film at all. Quite often I had to run the camera at slower speeds, and manipulate around that, in order to make a film impression of the halls. They seem to us maybe quite normal as we walk down them, but in the name of economy they are in fact quite dark. Luminescent light is not a very happy light in its amount, as well as in its colorations, for human beings. The challenge was to see what I could do with this light. I've nearly died in hospitals several times. Maybe, by the time I'm an old man, 90 percent of the people will die in a hospital, which is a terrible place to be. This presumably will be all the light that's left to me. I had to use five different kinds of film stock, with different filters for toning, for qualities of light that most people are insensitive to. For instance, neons produce a marked greenish or blueish cast, or in some cases a yellowish, yellow-greenish effect, particularly in their lighting of flesh. It's most noticeable in the shadowed areas. Most people aren't aware of it. But it's there, if they decide to look at it. Almost all flesh is lit in these institutions like German Expressionist painting. Sallow colors, traditionally not very interesting to us, colors that are disturbing. The effect is due to the overriding neons or luminescence which light the room, preparatory to an operation, or for the janitor to clean up by, or whatever. Those neon lights, that luminosity, because of its inexpensiveness, illuminate all the hallways and many of the rooms. Then there is the radiant light, installed for a particular flat, color-temperatured, balanced, focused illumination. It is used for a very strict definition. Then, there I am, using both kinds of light through various kinds of filters to make a statement which, when the film was finished, was maybe best described by its title, *Deus Ex*.

FW: You told me once it was a kind of pun.

SB: Yes, it suggests, of course, the phrase *deus ex machina*. The experience of making the film suggested to me that this hospital was a religious institution devoid of God. The "ex" is a pun in English, of course, upon the lack of Deus, but it also means to suggest the machine by allusion to the original phrase. Except that the machine, which the Greeks had as a stage device, we now have in such a front place that it's an assumption: there's no point in mentioning the machine because it's all machine. All the people are accredited to the extent that they do not behave personally. And yet there are two strange ironies. About thirty people are involved in this operation, in a kind of teamwork which has conditioned the light they're working under and all the machinery around them. And yet, they are also caught, as I saw them while filming, in a ritual that finally becomes quite personal: here is a man with his chest opened and his beating heart visible to them. It is something so religious and so personal—as one might regard Aztec sacrificial service with respect to either the priest and the people and/or the victim. The victim is always personal. Yet there is a complete institutionalization of the light illuminating the beating heart of a person whom I had in fact met the day before, who was of course quite frightened of the ordeal he was facing. And then one also has this man over in the left-hand corner, looking very ill at ease, dressed in surgical robes, with a camera, attempting through their battery of institutional lights and through the battery of norms that are established on the film surface to create a personal statement, which is what I believe an art to be. He can only be saved through this operation, by a thorough scientific agreement on practically everything. On the other hand, the artist is seen caught, as never before, in a set of values alien to his creative expectations. For instance, the static-free shoes they put on me were never designed to fit over the boots I wear. When I'm working, I'm dependent on sweat to know that I'm actually with it, but sweat creates problems in this room because it diffuses into moisture that can carry germs.

FW: What strikes me particularly is your phrase that the light is institutionalized. It's a social product of technology, geared to a specific kind of action, cooperative and institutionalized. Hardly ever, I think, has anyone tried to film in light like this. What happens then? How does one make a personal statement with respect to light, within these institutional ways of making the light itself?

SB: The patient, essentially, has the easiest job, he just lies there, anesthetized, while they either save him or not. And that I think is what might be called a metaphor for how most people utilize light. They just drift through it, and use it to see in the ways they were trained to see. I'm not going to do that, and not only find that unacceptable, but horrible. I'm continually trying to defeat any norm whatsoever, to make a track, a person. Now this doesn't mean eccentricity, but quite the opposite. It means that I'm in the service of whatever forces impel me to work, and will utilize anything to be true to those forces. Not that I'm trying, as some people think, to make a newness or be shockingly different, or do something eccentric to gain attention. Quite the opposite. It's just that I don't understand how there is anything but person. I do accept, as Charles Olson put it, that there is no such many as mass. And I absolutely understand Gertrude Stein when she said that everybody's heard the word "red," for example, in such a variety of ways, that no two people through experience can agree exactly on what it is. Now that is the light that's true. The fake we have put up to permit communication, which is to me another fake, is that there is a norm that can be agreed upon. People can be made to act as *if* they recognized each other's colors and each other's qualities of light, and somehow, in the mechanism of that behavior they can accomplish the engineering of open-heart surgery or any other kind of engineering. But to me the sacrifice is too great, albeit I am involved with it to the extent that the arts are. There are certain aesthetic trainings which every one of us inherits almost with mother's milk as unspoken assumptions, whereby we are able to communicate, as they say, with each other. But this is a play, far removed from life as it really presents itself to each individual person. The arts also have their trained assumptions, so that every artist is struggling along and inheriting a line of centuries of development at every move he makes. We do at least have a choice in the instant that we're living to insist on extending this tradition into the personal. Of course the result quickly gets academized and further generations learn it with mother's milk. Well, one would say, how can the world accommodate, I mean, obviously, how can the world accommodate all these individual and personal visions? And to that I say, how not?

FW: The technicians and the artist standing in the same room, the former operating and the latter filming, remind me of a statement my former teacher, the philosopher Maurice Merleau-Ponty, once made. He pointed out that what he called "profane vision" doesn't see light, doesn't see reflections in the objects, doesn't see shadows, doesn't see lighting. Rather, it sees *according* to all of these. Albert Hofstadter, in his remarkable book, *Truth and Art*, noted that our gaze follows light, and light thus becomes invisible. It's as if the medical personnel had to take "profane vision" to its limit, while for you the light, the reflections, the shadows, the lighting, their relative presence and absence, which they simply see according to, have to be an acute experience.

SB: If I hadn't been primarily involved in them as an artist, I probably would have passed out.

FW: You'd have been drawn into what they were doing, and you're not equipped emotionally or technically or intellectually to do anything useful in an operating room. So there you are, involved in something that they necessarily have to be as unaware of as possible, and vice versa. You picked a situation where most of the variety and richness of light, color, reflection, and so on have been eliminated.

SB: Yes, the task or challenge was to document as well as to be personal. As distinct from my other films, I didn't permit hypnogogic vision to affect me in this hospital environment. I didn't permit dreams or memory recall to find manifestation along the track of film, though they were, of course, influencing me. By contrast, for example, to *The Horseman, the Woman and the Moth*, where I was trying to create, by painting on film, the equivalent of hypnogogic vision. Of course, I had to paint on the film, because there's no way to photograph closed-eye vision. The primary thing people see when they close their eyes is a whirling, grainy moving of particles that, as in this picture, make shapes. I call them grains of sand, Helmholtz called them flying gnats. That's one of the special qualities of vision which is closed-eye. Later our interpretations will solidify and become part of memory-recall processes. For example, I can by act of will call up my grandmother's face, and her face will to some extent be made up in my image and be supported by these "phosphene" reactions which look like grainy moving particles. So closed-eye vision gets very much into what we call the personal for the simple reason that nobody has yet categorized it to an extent we might agree on. *Deus Ex* moves along the line of agreed-upon sight whereas *Horseman*, to most people, I'm sure, still looks like a mess, almost totally uninterpretable.

FW: How is it that you move along the line of agreed-upon sight in *Deus Ex*? The agreed norm is in the operating room, that which presented itself to your camera lens; then you, I take it, tried to remain somehow faithful to that in your personal statement, but it wasn't their agreed-upon norm any more.

SB: The struggle in *Deus Ex* is very intensively between the personal sight and the agreed-upon sight. What I've made most personal in *Deus Ex* are the color qualities of the light, which to me just means that I've manipulated the film to give an equivalent of what I actually see. I actually see the colors that neon gives off.

FW: You see the green in the faces, for example, the blueish tinges in the flesh?

SB: I think most people screen out color as they screen out most noise in order to survive. I was trying to take this luminescent coloration, which I also would so much like to screen out or be out of, and I was trying to work creatively with it, whereas in *Horseman* I was taking-making an equivalent of that work I see when my eyes are closed, and making a little story out of it. Every film I make is a crisis of one kind or another, either joy or sorrow or something, and I do believe that the light is what will save me. I believe I move toward the light, that I'm aware of its varieties. I don't move toward it just to make use of it to help me get around among objects, I really move directly toward the light. When I'm seeing, it's the light I want to be conscious of seeing, and all its varieties of play.

FW: That's such an ancient symbol in our philosophy, from Plato to Goethe and on, as you know.
SB: Yes, the cave.

FW: The freed prisoner moving toward the light. Plato doesn't presume that it's necessary to tell us why he moves toward the light at the end of the cave. When he gets into the world of light that the cave prisoners have never seen, he finally finds the sun to be beyond Being and beyond Truth: it's the source of both, neither something that itself exists nor something that is true. Light does have that elemental character: not a thing, not an object, but that by which all things are rendered visible.
SB: I hate such paranoia if it's unsubstantiated, but I really believe that although all of us move toward the light, most people are caught in tricks imposed by some very greedy people, so they move along certain channels of *prescribed* light. And the way they get tricked is that they don't look at the qualities and varieties of light. They're only trained to use it as something bouncing off objects, or papers, or signs; finally even the objects cease to exist. People are then just left primarily with signs. These signs are illuminated by manipulation within their academic and parental training. The only way to spring that trap, which is what art is constantly offering as one of its possibilities, to humanity, is to be aware of how the qualities and varieties of light illuminate shape. The more people can be confused in their seeing, the more easily they can be directed. Most academic training makes a very narrow cave for people's awareness. Of course, then when I show things outside the cave in my films—for example, the hand-painted worlds of *Horseman* that show people what every person has most readily available, the world of closed eyes—people are often very disturbed and frightened.

FW: The analogy to Plato's allegory holds there too. When Plato's freed cave-dweller returns and tries to tell people about the light, the objects, the reflections of a more liberated vision, they think he's crazy.
SB: I'm feeling that I am of that quality of craziness these days. The statement that should have busted all these objections wide open is Duns Scotus Erigena's "All that is, is light," which is so obvious. In *Anticipation of the Night*, there is an image of sunlight coming through a window, across the inside of a darkened space, which happens to be the living-room of the house I was living in. Starting from the upper right-hand corner we see a shadow of my hand. In the film the shadow of the

whole man passes back and forth across the field of window-light . . . The oldest autobiographic statement we have in the world is some caveman's hand which he traced on a wall; and I'm reminded that the symbol for daylight, morning, for the beginning of day for the Chinese is the hieroglyph of a window with a horizon line through it. That's one of the oldest concepts we have of the moving toward the light. I intuitively went for this notion at the very beginning of the film. The title is significant: I didn't expect to live much longer, and really didn't care to. I started the shooting in 1957, before I met Jane. It seemed to me my life was coming to an end because I had come to the view that all of childhood was just an anticipation of the night of adulthood, which I found myself inhabiting impossibly at the time. I think the condition I had got into is so much the normal condition of most people. Even for the ancient Chinese the sign of daylight was light coming through the window of the house, not the sun in its blazing glory but of the house, probably the oldest institution in the history of the world. When I made *Anticipation*, I was of course still sunk very much in metaphor. I still felt myself very close to literature, and with this film was trying to break out of that closeness. It is a series of metaphors that show the trapped (as I felt it) condition of person. The fact that we have to speak so much of our individuality and independence is a sure sign of the loss of person as a primary consideration. As Gertrude Stein said, there are two kinds of people in the world, dependent independents and independent dependents. That hand, dangling loosely, a part of the darkness that surrounds it, with only that window symbol of some light shining through—that was the condition of the person and the "cave."

FW: These are issues that are entangled in the differences between luminescence and radiance.
SB: Radiant light is much less efficient, so we can expect that all forms of luminescent light will take over, finally in our homes, as they have in all our institutions. This presents a terrifying possibility, when you consider that humans hardly ever saw that quality of illumination before our lifetime, or saw it only in occasional flickers, a gas, a chemical glow of decayed wood in a swamp. They were ephemeral and usually quite frightening images of luminescence.

FW: I was just fantasizing a history of man and cultures in terms of the history of light. Where the light remains natural, one could still do it. One could study the different qualities of natural light different peoples have lived with—an African jungle, the plains of North America, and so on—and then introduce the peculiar phenomenon of people today spending perhaps eight to twelve hours a day in luminescent light generated for narrowly defined purposes—for economy, for efficiency in typing. There's evidence that luminescent flickering affects brain waves and causes irritability. Groups that couldn't agree under luminescent light could come to a better understanding when provided with radiant light.

SB: I can believe it, because, without being speciously old-fashioned, the psychological qualities of luminescence can be said to be very unhappy for people generally. Maybe there will grow up a generation that knows essentially no other kind of light, and they might swim in it better than we do. But we do have a whole anthropological upbringing, however that's affected us, with radiance as the only illumination and as desperately important to humans. Edison just extended that possibility of radiance. As of the last twenty years we're experiencing a quality of light which Wilhelm Reich, for instance, found deadly, and called "dead light." There seems to be corroboration that it's harmful physiologically. Mice die in front of television. One may expect tremendous changes in people, whether for good or ill.

FW: People scoffed ten years ago when Bobby Fischer said he couldn't watch television because it emitted damaging rays. I saw him in his semi-final match, and the light he had specified was an immense bank of blueish-white lamps, which had to be radiant, not luminescent, and calculated to eliminate shadows from the chess-board. Under the extreme tension of championship play, he had to have perfect conditions. In *Deus Ex*, the luminescent light presented a kind of challenge to make something out of it for the movie screen. The light, in your case, became the chess match.

SB: The more we speak of it, the more disturbed I am about luminescence. It's in so many cases an example of the death of something. The rot of tiny sea creatures. The swamp. Radiance implies the transformation of something. The log that burns and turns into ashes and smoke. Whether this is "scientifically" accurate or not is another matter. But in human thinking . . . Now, the shadow figure made by me throughout *Anticipation* later moves out onto the lawn, dramatically, and struggles to inherit a world of light—not something at the end of Plato's cave, not something so conditioned, nor the play of fire-light at the near end. I don't like either end of that cave, actually.

FW: Which is ironic, since it's the first image in literature of a movie-house. Today Plato would place his prisoners before a movie screen, living in terms of the images, learning to predict which would follow which, and believing that to be knowledge for man.

SB: Yes, well, he was trying to spring the same trap I am. I spent an extraordinary amount of my childhood in movie-houses, and I'm out to spring the trap of the movies, the illusions. I'd be overjoyed if someone said as a result of seeing some film of mine that they'd never have to look at a film again. Because I really want to help people to see, to the extent I have any clear social function as an artist. Otherwise, I'm personally of course just trying to spring my own trap, or the trap that was imposed on me.

FW: Let's see, there are fifteen years between *Anticipation of the Night* and *The Text of Light*, that you're working on now. Do you think you're springing the same trap? I don't think so myself.

SB: I don't know that I've rid myself of things, but I have transformed them for myself along the line of filmmaking. *Anticipation* sprang for me and a great many other filmmakers the trap of narrative. We got that restricted sense of a beginning, middle, and end from Aristotle, didn't we? Somewhere in there I started listening to music more carefully and thoughtfully, for example, the overriding message of the Baroque, which is: "my beginning is my ending, my ending is my beginning." The simplest part was that my films were no longer dependent on stage drama. Then they were no longer dependent on the novel. Of course, you cannot ever finally escape narrative, a musical melody is a narrative in its way. Maybe all these struggles are just attempts at continually transforming things, not springing traps.

FW: How did you get to *The Text of Light* through your other films?

SB: Suddenly I was able to make a film called *The Process*. I was reading Hugh Kenner's *The Pound Era*. Aside from the anti-Semitism of the *Cantos*, which is a very sad inclusion in it, Pound's poem is at center a light poem. It deals with the recognition of light along the line of historical personages or persons. Suddenly I saw that light could be the *protagonist* of a film. Everything the film was made of, all the things that light had bounced off, to be channeled through the tunnel of the lens onto the film, and then to be re-projected onto a screen, would all be the protagonist. No divisiveness of characters whatsoever, though there would be characteristics of light, depending on what it bounced off. Oddly enough, the film is not at all what one would even loosely call "abstract." In almost every shot there are very definite and recognizable things. But they're so photographed that the light is what one is first aware of. The next film was *The Shores of Phos: A Fable*. I tried again to make light the protagonist, and tell a fable by the movement of it. I shot it through the back window of my house, onto the yard, where the goats and donkey walked back and forth. It started with the simplistic idea that in most fables someone really only walks back and forth. They're given something to do at the beginning, they go, they walk on a journey, they do it, then they come back.

FW: You mean, life is like that.
SB: Yes.

FW: You remember, at the beginning of the Book of Job, God calls to the Devil, wanting to speak with him about human life. He says, Where are you coming from? The Devil replies that he's been walking up and down, and going to and fro. I always thought the biblical author captured the whole of human agitation in that simple phrase.

SB: That's wonderful. That's really what *The Shores of Phos* is about. The walking variously interferes with and bounds the light, making the various movements of the light, which is the real protagonist. About which people know very little. If you ask someone where and how does light move, he'll probably say, Well, from there (pointing to the sun), down to here (maybe spreading his hands). But light is bouncing in a multiplicity of directions. Right now, there are things that appear to glow because they kick back the light subtly in terms of color. There's a yellow glow on the left of your face. There's a hard smack of light that comes from the metal at the back of you. There's the smack of light we're all so aware of that comes off the surface of the eyes, kicking back very hard (as one might loosely say) the play of light in this room. Then there are all the manifestations of light as color that comes from the degree to which light penetrates your face, the first or second layer. There's the extent to which you absorb color, so I see color which your face is rejecting. When I get involved in it, I see what looks to me like light-streams along the ground, horizontal, or pooling. Before it rains, there are what look to me to be almost cartoon-like streaks of light. And then, the reflection of light off the falling rain. There are so many of these qualities, and, of course, I have no way to photograph them, the emulsion isn't sensitive enough. I had to make equivalents, or emblems out of gross bounced light for these other qualities. An example from *Shores of Phos* is a yellow flower with a green edge to it, thrown totally out of focus, which makes visible a quality of light that isn't visible in a focused image. The normal assumption is that everything should be in focus in a film, or rather, that a film ought to be about just what is in focus in experience. The sad thing about this assumption is that in fact at any given instant most of what you're seeing is out of focus. So-called peripheral or soft-focus vision influences us as much as, in some cases more than, what we're focused on. Soft-focus makes a shape that's accommodating to the light, rather than to the context whereby we know the light as a sign. Most people see a picture of a flower as a sign, before anything else. But when they see a thing that has a shape that isn't read as a sign, then the involvement will be primarily with the quality of the light, which is pouring in and influencing us more than anything we're focused on.

FW: As I recall, you made some other departures from more or less conventional techniques, in *Sexual Meditation: Open Field*—again, because of your involvement with filming light. In this case, however, the innovation had to do with the method of printing more than with the filming process itself, didn't it?

SB: Yes, it's a printing method called "bi-packing," and it isn't novel as such. Used simply as a "trick" for getting what Hollywood and TV call "special effects," it's quite old. It consists of placing two filmstrips, which are filmed at separate times, together in the printer, so that the light of the printer shines through the double layer of film strips. The cigarette pack floating, say, between two lovers in a television commercial is a "special effect" that can be achieved that way. The thirties film *The Invisible Man* was done that way. However, in these familiar uses, bi-packing is combined with superimposition or the "matte" process. I don't think it has ever been used by itself and for the entire length of a film, in order to develop its possibilities on the screen.

FW: But there's no sense of "special effects" in *Open Field*, so it isn't some startling content that you were concerned with, but certain qualities of light.

SB: Yes, and in fact there you have the most ordinary representation of the experience of light. When two filmstrips are bi-packed, every solid object in either picture blocks the light completely from coming through both pictures, during the printing process (the same as when one holds two color slides back to back up to the light); and every manifestation of light in one of the pictures permits any shadowed or solid object represented in the other picture to come through without interference. This is the opposite of super-imposition, where shadowed areas in one picture are obliterated by the lighted areas in the other pictures. In superimposition, you print the two strips successively, one onto the other. In bi-packing, you print both at once. Now, what makes my use of bi-packing different from the "trick" use is that *Open Field* exhibits a control of light which is most equivalent to our ordinary experience of light—except that most people aren't explicitly aware of the ordinary. Let's say that one of my strips represents the scene before the eye, and that the other strip represents the viewer's imagination or memory images prompted by what's before his eyes. Then my equivalent of this experience, using the bi-pack technique, represents the most ordinary experience of light we have: from the outside in, so to speak, and from the inside out.

FW: Almost everyone has seen superimpositional sequences in films, and some people have seen whole films that are almost entirely superimpositional. One of the finest I've seen is Bruce Baillie's *Castro Street*. It's clear that his overlaying of images doesn't get to—and doesn't mean to get to—the combination of seeing-imagining you're speaking of. Rather, *Castro Street* is more like seeing with several pairs of eyes at once. That's quite different from *Open Field*.

SB: Superimposition couldn't represent this combination as well because the light would obliterate either the representation of the image seen or that of the image remembered. Through the bi-pack process, light, whether considered as bouncing in from the outside or, physiologically speaking, as sparked in the head by optic nerve-endings—flashing memories—would serve rather to illuminate images. Most people, of course, aren't consciously aware of this ordinary interchange (what they see/what they remember or imagine) in their daily viewing; but that is the way it works.

FW: Merleau-Ponty once observed that, since dogs may bark while they're asleep, we may suppose that they do sometimes have images. But man, he noted, doesn't just have some images painted on his brain: he can live in the imaginary. And I take that to imply that even before I live in the imaginary (as tears may come to my eyes during a sad reverie), my perceiving and my remembering or fantasizing are wholly interwoven in ordinary experience, like the warp and the woof of a tapestry which together produce the recognizable figures. Your *Open Field* seems to me to use the technique of bi-packing to weave with light.

SB: And it's continuous, that is, the entire film is bi-pack, from beginning to end. In that sense, too, the bi-packing isn't just an addition. I'm probably the first to use the technique straight, that is, all the way through.

FW: From beginning to end: this seems to lead to the notion of a "text of light" that we wanted to talk about. And the film by that name.

SB: Yes, *The Text of Light* was shot with a macro-lens, into an ashtray. But it's already a mistake to say that, because the lens is made of glass, the ashtray is made of glass, and all the other pieces of cut-glass that I put around and in the ashtray are glass. The sun hits the whole arrangement of glass, which bounces light within and around itself, making shapes which in turn just move along that special glass that the camera lens is. So I'm really photographing the sun. The ashtray is never visible as an ashtray, or any parts of it as glass.

FW: Any more than the lens of the camera is ever visible as glass.

SB: Right, I'm utilizing the lens glass to create shapes and patterns made directly of sunlight. One could say "indirectly" only to the extent that all this glass, including the lens, shapes it. So it's a film made as directly of light as possible. There's no object in it, unless the sun itself be the object, various sunbeams and what they shape.

FW: How did you come to the idea for this film?

SB: My camera had sunk down on its tripod, the macro-lens coming to rest beside the ashtray. I have the habit of looking into my lens before I move it because I'm very dependent on gifts. To me all of life is a gift, and certainly everything that I manage to make is a gift. I saw what looked like a forest, made of brilliant light-browns, a kind of blueish sky-like tinge, and greens touching up as if it were some kind of grass. That led to three months of sitting and photographing four thousand feet, a frame at a time, as I'd wait for the sun to move. The "forest" would grow, or transform into a landscape or something unnamable.

FW: That leads into some thoughts about color, which I think has been the most travestied subject in the entire history of philosophy and psychology. We have to combat to this day a conception of color as a "property of things," and thus a kind of dead content of perception, an opaque given. There have been uses for such a view, particularly in the development of the natural sciences, where it was useful to take color either as a simple given, or as a sign of so-called "primary qualities." These are abstractions that seventeenth-century physicists happened to be interested in conceptualizing. But color, as Merleau-Ponty has insisted, is in reality more an ingredient of the lived world that beckons us, that solicits a response. In that sense, a color is already an "idea," it has a concrete indwelling meaning, to which we in turn respond. There are psychological experiments showing that our whole way of being in the world is affected by color, not only the optical nervous system. Color can no longer be assigned the status of "secondary quality," some poor relative that the sciences allow us to keep like an eccentric aunt in the "third-floor back." Does this mean anything to you as a filmmaker?

SB: Yes, science seems only to have been interested in the causality of light or color, i.e., the sun shone upon the green grass, the brown cow ate the green grass, and we eat the brown cow, etc.

FW: I became vividly aware that color-seeing is an entire bodily response during a workshop with Charlotte Selver and Charles Brooks, in Mexico, on the terrace of a building where there was a lovely view of a bay. We spent the morning locating the eye muscles, and these in relation to our entire posture, until we could more or less voluntarily engage and disengage them. With our eyes closed, we slowly worked to the point where we allowed our eyes to find their natural resting-place. Then we began looking around. It was a different landscape than before, not just additional elements, but a whole different order of the visible.

SB: Yes, it would have to be. As I said some time ago in my book, *Metaphors on Vision*, most children first draw the sky yellow. There may be a quality of muscular control which specifies a range of color, so the sky looks blue to us. In a different mode, a child may just as normally see it as yellow.

FW: To render the sky at that time in Mexico, I might very well have reached for a yellow crayon. Not that I wasn't in some sense seeing blue, as I habitually do on a clear, sunny day, but that the *lived meaning* of that sky-color might have been better conveyed on paper by a yellow hue. And I don't mean that one color becomes a mere sign of another, like a word and its signification. The only theorists who have come close to understanding these things so far have been the Gestalt psychologists and phenomenologists.

SB: We're bathed in light, and we discreetly create lattices of interpretations, which become the conventional range of colors. Those who train us, whom I so much suspect these days, would I suppose have us all make exactly the same lattice, that seems to be their push. Maybe our only salvation is that we're incapable of it, each person continues to make a personal lattice. Which, if he but attended to and believed in, as an adult, would probably save his life, as they say. Most people most of the time see the world in black and white, and if you doubt that, just ask someone who's just walked around a room and come out of it to tell you what the various things in it were colored. Even though their body has danced and responded in different ways to the colors, they can't tell you.

FW: Yes, the problem in daily life, as Charlotte and Charles teach so beautifully, isn't so much to do something else, as to refrain from doing what we do to blind ourselves, and *allow* ourselves to see, to hear, to sense precisely whatever that allowing makes possible for us. The problem to which you address yourself as a filmmaker seems parallel, though different, too: to find cinematic equivalents for what it's given to you to see. And you must work somehow with the agreed-upon norms of light and color of film stocks, lenses, mechanical reproduction, radiant light, both natural and artificial, and now, in the last couple of decades, with the onset, so to speak, of luminescent light and color. In particular, there seems to be an issue, which is scarcely ever discussed in the arts—if at all—and which we've only had time to open up here—concerning radiance and luminescence, as we're calling them.

SB: Yes, I do believe there's a war between two hemispheres of the brain, and we've had to set up some dichotomies. Neither one of us has made TV or luminescence the bad guy, but I'm afraid these do represent a benefit only to humanity as mass—at the expense of person, as always.

FW: As I look back on this unrehearsed discussion, it seems to me that your work as filmmaker, and my own in phenomenology, converge in our common culture.

The point of convergence, I believe, is, as Merleau-Ponty put it in his *Phenomenology of Perception*, on the question of whether as human beings we can somehow foil that "ruse" of vision, by which our perceptions tend to simply lose themselves in an oblivion of objects.

All That Is Light: Brakhage at 60

Suranjan Ganguly / 1992–1993

From *Sight and Sound* 3, no. 10 (October 1993): 20–23. Reprinted by permission.

Suranjan Ganguly: You've been involved with film for over forty years as a maker, thinker, writer, and academic. Has your sense of film as film changed?
Stan Brakhage: In one sense it hasn't changed: from the beginning I had a feeling for film as vision. I didn't think it was related to literature or theatre at all, nor had it anything to do with Renaissance perspective. I was struggling all the time against the flypaper of other arts harnessing film to their own usages, which means essentially as a recording device or within the long historical trap of "picture"—by which I mean a collection of nameable shapes within a frame. I don't even think still photography, with key exceptions, has made any significant attempt to free itself from that. So I had certain instinctual feelings about film even before I made one.

SG: What do you mean by "vision," and how is it related to film?
SB: For me vision is what you see, to the least extent related to picture. It is just seeing—it is a very simple word—and to be a visionary is to be a seer. The problem is that most people can't see. Children can—they have a much wider range of visual awareness—because their eyes haven't been tutored to death by man-made laws of perspective or compositional logic. Every semester I start out by telling my students that they have to see in order to experience film and that seeing is not just looking at pictures. This simple idea seems to be the hardest to get through to people.

SG: But is it really so simple? In your films, to see without picturing is a composite of many visual processes, only one of which is open-eye vision, or what we call normal everyday vision.
SB: Open-eye vision is what we are directly conscious of but there's much more going on that we ignore. Seeing includes open-eye, peripheral, and hypnagogic

vision, along with moving visual thinking, dream vision, and memory feedback—in short, whatever affects the eyes, the brain, and the nervous system. I believe that all these have a right to be called seeing since they enable us to inherit the full spectrum of our optic and nervous systems.

SG: Can you define them?
SB: Hypnagogic vision is what you see with your eyes closed—at first a field of grainy, shifting, multicolored sands that gradually assume various shapes. It's optic feedback: the nervous system projects what you have previously experienced—your visual memories—into the optic nerve endings. It's also called closed-eye vision. Moving visual thinking, on the other hand, occurs deeper in the synapsing of the brain. It's a streaming of shapes that are not nameable—a vast visual "song" of the cells expressing their internal life. Peripheral vision is what you don't pay close attention to during the day and which surfaces at night in your dreams. And memory feedback consists of the editings of your remembrance. It's like a highly edited movie made from the real.

SG: How is film predisposed to embody these?
SB: Over the years I have come to believe that every machine people invent is nothing more than an extension of their innards. The base rhythm of film—24 frames per second—is sort of centered in its pulse to our brain waves. If you start a film at 8 frames per second and with a variable speed motor slowly raise it to thirty-two, you put the audience in the first stage of hypnosis. So the natural pulse of film is a corollary to the brain's reception of everyday ordinary vision. Then film grain approximates the first stage of hypnagogic vision, which occurs at a pulse within the range of film's possibilities of projection. Also, during editing, film comes close to the way you remember. And finally, if you cut fast enough, you can reflect within 24 frames per second the saccadic movements of the eyes, which people aren't ordinarily aware of but which are an intrinsic part of seeing.

SG: So virtually all your experiments were aimed at developing this relationship between film and seeing?
SB: My cutting has always tried to be true to the eyes, to the nervous system and to memory, and to capture these processes, which happen very rapidly. At one point I felt my montage—inspired by Griffith and Eisenstein—had to evolve to do justice to memory recall, so I began to use the single frame to suggest what the mind can do during a flashback. Then I began to use superimpositions because these occur constantly in the saccadic movements of the eyes and in memory feedback and input. I've done as many as seven superimpositions at one time—in *Christ Mass Sex Dance*—and I wish I could do more because there are more in

vision itself. Then I shot out of focus to capture peripheral vision, which is always unfocused, or used flares to give a sense of the body when it has an overload in feedback and literally flares—something you can see with your eyes open. In *Loving* a couple make love in the sun, and their optic system flares—it's really the nervous system's ecstasy—in oranges and yellows and whites. I had noticed that when film flares out at the end of a color roll you get those same colors, and I put them in because they are intrinsic to human vision as well.

SG: But of all these possible seeings, the hypnagogic has been the most important to you.
SB: Yes. I sometimes like just to sit and watch my closed eyes sparking, or the streamings of my mind. They're the best movies in town! But the flow is so rapid that to document it would call for a camera that would run 1,000 frames per second. All I can do on film is to grasp a little piece of it and then make a corollary. So my films don't reflect what I see when I close my eyes—only a symbol of that. The extent to which I accept that is the extent to which I can be true to what film can do.

SG: Since closed-eye vision is largely unfilmable, you had to find other means of representing it, and painting directly on to film became one way to do this.
SB: At the birth of my first child I was acutely conscious of my hypnagogic vision whenever I blinked my eyes. But it didn't appear in the film I made of that birth—*Window Water Baby Moving*—so for the birth of my second child, which occurs in Part 2 of *Dog Star Man*, and of my third in *Thigh Line Lyre Triangular* I painted on film to include what I had seen. I became very excited when I realized that my closed-eye vision resembled the work of the Abstract Expressionist painters I admired so much—all very Pollock-like and Rothko-like.

SG: Did you sense that they were also doing the same thing—recording their optic feedback?
SB: When I was living in New York in the fifties and sixties I became an avid gallery-goer. I discovered Turner, who is probably still the most pervasive influence on me because of his representations of light. I was also strongly drawn to the Abstract Expressionists—Pollock, Rothko, Kline—because of their interior vision. None of these so-called abstract painters—going back to Kandinsky and earlier—had made any reference to painting consciously out of their closed-eye vision, but I became certain that, unconsciously, many of them had. To me, they were all engaged in making icons of inner picturization, literally mapping modes of nonverbal, nonsymbolic, nonnumerical thought. So I got interested in consciously and unconsciously attempting to represent this.

SG: But it wasn't enough to paint. To find as close a corollary to hypnagogic vision as possible, you had to physically manipulate the surface of the film strip.

SB: I tried a number of different things, including iron filings under magnets! I would bake film before and after photographing to bring out certain chemical changes in the grain so that it would correspond to certain stages of hypnagogic vision. I once even herded brine shrimp into a pack to capture the quality of their movements. And I worked with household chemicals and dyes, and placed colored powders under vibrators and magnets. The making of *The Text of Light*, which involved shooting through a glass ashtray, was another way of capturing certain forms of both closed-eye and open-eye envisionment of light.

SG: And you would scratch on film and write on it.

SB: Words appear on film throughout my work. By scratching them I try to be true to the way words vibrate and jiggle when they appear in closed-eye vision—which doesn't happen very often. Also, by scratching them I can at least make them more intrinsic to what film is—they became carriers of light. Photographed words relate more to memory recall or just to the open-eyed present.

SG: Hand-painted sections appear in your work as early as *Prelude*, the first part of *Dog Star Man*, but in the last few years you've been making films like *The Dante Quartet* and *Delicacies of Molten Horror Synapse* that are wholly hand-painted. You even claim this is all you want to do now.

SB: I now believe that film is much more predisposed to what you can do with paint and scratches than with anything else. My hand-painted films are my favorites—I look at them again and again and they always feel like film, not as if they're referring to something else.

SG: What do you mostly work with?

SB: Acrylics—mostly translucent acrylics—and India inks and a variety of dyes that are variously mixed with or not with acrylics. I have also made whole films with Magic Markers. I use brushes at times, but basically it's paint on fingers, a different color on each finger. Usually I prepare the film first with chemicals, so that the paint can dry and form patterns, then during the drying I use chemicals again to create organic shapes and forms. Finally I go over it a frame at a time to stitch these patterns into a unified whole. If you watch me do it, it looks as though I'm playing the piano—it's very quick, very deft—but people forget that I have to paint twenty-four frames to get a second's worth of film. I have hand-painted films like *Eye Myth*, which is nine seconds long as well as *Interpolations* which runs for twelve minutes—the longest hand-painted film I have ever made.

SG: You've painted on all kinds of film stock, including 65mm Imax film. You also paint directly on footage you've found or shot yourself. What part of vision does that approximate?

SB: Let me say first that painting on Imax was very exciting—it was as if an easel painter had been given a wall, it was such a large space to work with. The model for painting on photographed film was closed-eye vision mixing with open-eye vision. Not very many people can see that, and it took me a long time before I could do both—see what I was looking at and also watch the nervous system's immediate shape-and-color reaction to it.

SG: Are the recent hand-painted films a new involvement with the hypnagogic, or the beginning of a completely new phase in your work?

SB: No, that's over. I don't want to make corollaries of my closed-eye vision any more—not consciously—because it limits me in what I can be conscious of. I feel my consciousness is no longer a very good arbiter, that it could even be a limitation on my making, which is another way of saying I'm now more nearly at one with the painting I do on film.

SG: So what is the new hand-painted work going to be?

SB: What's new is that I don't have anything else as reference other than what the film itself is showing me. Every time film reflects something that's nameable, it limits what it can do. If I can make films that refer to things that can't be lived through, then I feel that I'm giving film a chance to be in the fullest possible sense, and that makes me feel good. Now I really just want to fool around with paint on film, hoping to do so in such an open way that whatever is deep inside me, past all prejudice and even all learning, can come out along my arms to my fingertips, and with the help of these smudges and dyes sing a song like birds on a normal day.

SG: From 1979 to 1990 you worked on an extraordinary series of films—*The Roman Numeral Series*, *The Arabic Numeral Series*, the *Egyptian Series*, and the *Babylon Series*—where there's already a sense of leaving behind the hypnagogic for the very electrical patterns of thought before it even becomes thought.

SB: I've been going in and out of the Egyptian *Book of the Dead* for the last fifteen years, and I've studied Hammurabi's code very closely. When I made those films I was trying to do two things: to get a sense of the moving visual thinking of those cultures, and to see how out of it rose the glyphs—hieroglyphs—that shape their language. I tried to represent pictorially what occurs during this "seeing," and how within this flow of electrical coloration there are also bits of memory feedback that intermix with the hypnagogic and help shape the glyphs.

SG: So essentially you were trying to tap into a prenatal, preverbal, and pre-picture consciousness—the very womb of the image?

SB: Yes. We know that hieroglyphs are symbolic representations of the external world, but where do they come from? My sense is that they appear first as shapes in closed-eye vision. At the beginning of each film in the *Babylon Series*, I've scratched a particular Babylonian glyph, and then I go for the source of the thinking that produced it.

SG: So the films arose from a study of these written characters combined with explorations of your own moving visual thinking as a model?

SB: The first clear sense I had of these glyphs was when I was on a plane which was about to make a belly landing since its landing gear had malfunctioned. We were told to adopt the fetal position. It was then that I had a series of intense glyphs that was so powerful that even in that state I grabbed a pencil and piece of paper and drew them. Later I scratched them on to film and interspersed them with appropriate color flares that had also occurred at that time in my hypnagogic vision. The film was *"he was born, he suffered, he died."* As a result, I discovered how the mind can spark glyphs that seemed not pictures of events from my life but compound symbols of those events.

SG: The films are also meditations on light, which is not new to your work, except that this light is different, situated deep within the preconscious.

SB: What is film, after all, but rhythmed light? I've always agreed with that line in Pound's cantos: "All that is, is light." That's us and everything we're seeing, the dance of the light from the inside mixing with that coming from the outside in.

SG: How did you create the light patterns in these films?

SB: I didn't do any hand-painting or scratching, but photographed with various glasses, prisms, crystal balls, bits and pieces of tin foil, and whatever else was handy. I manipulated these with my hands in front of the lens. If I was lucky, I would get an equivalent of the light streaming and would combine fragments of ordinary photographed material with this light to create a compound—little meaningful glyphs of a sort. I also used filters. In fact, often with at least two filters in my hands I would color the streaks of light in various ways. And, of course, the prisms provided me with refraction colors, which I found intrinsic to moving visual thinking.

SG: One can enjoy these films on another level, as analogues to music. You've even called them "visual music."

SB: Of all the arts, music is closest to film, and I've had a long infatuation with music and film. I was very inspired by Charles Ives, who has several different sound sources going on simultaneously—a brass band on one side of the stage, a choir on the other and an orchestra in the middle—each playing their own music and it all interweaving. So I tried in combining sounds and visuals to push to the furthest possibility of a corollary between music and film, which is similar to Ives's combinations of different musical pieces, each retaining its own aesthetic integrity.

SG: At the same time, you've always held that sound in film is an aesthetic error. In fact, most of your films have been silent.

SB: Film is obviously visual, and, from an aesthetic standpoint, I see no need for a film to be accompanied by sound any more than I would expect a painting to be. At first I did make sound films, but I felt sound limited seeing, so I gave it up. My films were complex enough and difficult enough to see without any distraction of the ear thinking. But if I felt a film needed sound, I always included it. In the last few years I've even cut film to music—take *Passage Through: A Ritual* which I edited to a piece by Philip Corner—but that seems to be coming to an end. I believe now that you can only go so far with music, and then film is not music. It first became apparent to me fifteen years ago when I tried to cut exactly to the measures and shifts of a Bach fugue and the result was a mess. Since film clearly isn't music, I am now trying to find out what it is that film can do that's purely film. I really wish to open myself to that difference. I want to make films that are not even corollaries of music, that wouldn't even make you think of music.

SG: So a film that...

SB: ...will not be about anything at all. I wish I could be more precise, but it's hard to describe this in words. It was in a chapel—the Rothko Chapel in Houston—that I had a sense of nothing. What I felt looking at those paintings was completely distinct from a religious experience, something purely organic and sensual but that drew me out to the very limits of my inner being. That's where I think it all begins in the sense of the ineffable—and I want that to come through me into my work. I want that appreciation of nothing being everything.

SG: And anything that is referential deflects and limits that to some extent?

SB: Yes. A work which is too referential to things outside the aesthetic ecology, too dependent on something extrinsic, is not art. All this slavish mirroring of the human condition feels like a bird singing in front of mirrors. The less a work of art reflects the world, the more it is being in the world and having its natural life like anything else. Film must be free from all imitations, of which the most dangerous is the imitation of life.

SG: So when you speak of an "aesthetic ecology," you're speaking of the art work as a self-enclosed object?

SB: A work of art must be something with a world of its own in which everything that exists is interrelated so that it forms a whole, as do Rothko's paintings. And it must convey a sense of itself—for example, a film must show at all times some sense of it being an on-off projection of stills that flicker in the opening and closing of the shutter. The great films always do this—even narrative films have ways in which they do it. When I first scratched titles on film—in *Desistfilm*—I became conscious at once that they directed the eyes to what film is. Paint on film does that too with its irregularities and its rhythms.

SG: But isn't that too restrictive a definition? One of the complaints made about your work is that it fails to address the socio-political realities of the culture within which it exists.

SB: I think my films address that constantly. I don't think there has ever been a film that I wished to make that wasn't political in the broadest sense of the term, that wasn't about what I could feel or sense for better or worse from the conditionings of my times and from my rebellions against those conditionings. Take *Scenes from Under Childhood* which I made out of disgust at the Shirley Temple representation of childhood which was utterly false and served only to aid and abet the abuse of children. Or take the childbirth films. It was appalling to me that childbirth was a taboo subject, excluded from human vision, and that women were often barbarously treated in child-bearing and ignored as mothers within this culture. So there were political motivations that led me to make the five childbirth films. At the same time, I would add that if in these films I had tried in some conscious way to present a political alternative, I would have falsified the art process. As an artist, I have to be very careful not to allow social and political impulses to dominate because then I would falsify the balances that are intrinsic and necessary to make an aesthetic ecology.

SG: The childbirth films are part of a long cycle you made about your first family. Although there is no implicit political subtext, these films resonate with the sense of a life lived in a specific place and time and according to a specific vision. In a way they are probably the most "political" of all your films.

SB: I thought that if I photographed my daily life and photographed it as inspired by home movies or the amateur film rather than from what I had learned from film theory and the work of filmmakers such as Méliès, Griffith, Dreyer, and Eisenstein, and if I could also take inspiration from errors which I read as significant Freudian slips in home movie-making, then I could avoid drama. But I didn't realize the extent to which people in their daily lives reflect the movies and what they read.

We were plugged into the same literary/theatrical syndrome and our household to some extent was a template of what I wanted to avoid.

SG: How did you include Freudian slips in your films?
SB: I would study the raw footage so closely that it went beyond the average dream analysis in therapy. And I would find things in it that seemed very embarrassing, that I wanted to throw out, but, by the time I was through, they would become the center of the film. Also, while shooting, I would sometimes consciously try to catch what seemed like a true slip—and then in the editing put it in a context where it would reveal itself fully.

SG: In almost all these films there is a celebration of the trivia of daily life, a sense that the commonplace is itself sacred.
SB: For me, that's where we really live, that's what we really have. To stop the overwhelming influence of drama in film, I began to concentrate on the glories of an undramatic present, which is literally the tabletop. That is what peripheral vision is most involved with—the so-called mundane, which people use as a word of contempt when they really mean "earth." What they don't see is the potential for glory, for envisionment that's inherent in even doing the dishes, in the soap suds with their multiple rainbows, or in the dull edge of a plate that has to be scrubbed. If they could only see, only get involved with the wonders right under their noses—more specifically, if they could only see the movie playing on either side of their noses. All they have to do is close their eyes and look.

SG: Was there that hope behind the making of these films? Did you believe, like many of your contemporaries in the sixties, that film could help change the world?
SB: Yes, we really believed we were going to change the world. One of my favorite jokes was that I was working on the four-hundred-year plan. Well, I'm not any more. I have no world-saving ideas left in me. I would rather see my work as an attempt to clear aesthetic areas, to free film from previous arts and ideologies, to leave it clear to be of use to men and women to create formal integrities of various kinds which might help evolve human sensibility.

SG: Where is the avant-garde film movement that you helped to forge?
SB: There was no movement then and there is no movement now. What we shared was the uniqueness of each of us and that each of us was true to that uniqueness in his or her making, despite all attempts by society to pigeonhole us as a movement. But I must say that they succeeded, for the "movement" became an aberration of the sixties—a drug-induced, sexually motivated movie-making tangent to pornography—and that's how it is seen today even in the academic community. Instead,

we were a bunch of people who were dedicated to film and involved with the whole previous history of the arts in our concern to make an art. And this involvement we shared to some extent as "moderns." So you have a love of film, a love of art, a dedication to the arts. And one of the most vibrant ways to be dedicated to the arts is to be highly suspicious of every historical or inherited aspect of it.

SG: What about the current scene? Do you see anything in independent filmmaking today that you would consider innovative?

SB: There is much more uniqueness in filmmaking today than in the much-touted mid-sixties. But the irony is that it is now truly "underground"; in the sixties they said it was underground but it wasn't, now nobody says anything and it really is. It isn't affecting anybody; even the advertising agencies aren't renting their films to steal from them. And that's perhaps a good sign—that each of these filmmakers is doing something so unique that there is no real way to pick up a trick. To that extent, the art of film is truly moving into a realm of its own, happily free from commercial usages.

SG: Looking back over forty years of filmmaking, what matters most now?

SB: That I believe in song. That's what I wanted to do and I did it quite selfishly, out of my own need to come through to a voice that is comparable with song and related to all animal life on earth. I believe in the beauty of the singing of the whale; I am moved deeply at the whole range of song that the wolf makes when the moon appears, or neighborhood dogs make—that they make their song, and this is the wonder of life on earth, and I in great humility wish to join this.

Stan Brakhage:
The 60th Birthday Interview

Suranjan Ganguly / 1992–1993

From *Film Culture*, no. 78 (Summer 1994): 18–38. Reprinted by permission.

Suranjan Ganguly: Why have you stopped filming your family?
Stan Brakhage: Only one-third of my work while living with Jane was frankly autobiographical. That was fine because if I didn't make those films then we couldn't have held the marriage together, but in terms of what I've always been searching for, it was a passage through to other things. I don't film my family anymore partly because I think autobiography as a form is not good for film. It's very much on the record side of things—far too referential. Besides, I was never very interested in portraiture: very few of my films deal with people other than my immediate family or close friends. The big exceptions are *The Pittsburgh Documents* I made in 1971—*Deus Ex*, *Eyes*, and *The Act of Seeing with One's Own Eyes*—those were my social dramas of that period but, in general, I've always tried to get at the qualities of *being human*. My portraits are often about people's blurred motions, or things that are around them. For example, in *Dominion* (1974), you mostly see a man's nervous movements reflected on his desktop.

SG: Isn't it also true that Marilyn doesn't like to be photographed or filmed?
SB: Yes. One of the reasons why Marilyn doesn't like to have her picture taken is because, like me, she senses some falsification in that process. Now, I could have gone on photographing myself and the children—done a series of self-portraits—she has never forbidden me, but it's just that my sense of the aesthetic has changed, and that's largely due to my conversations with her. Also, after the second marriage I felt a strong desire to *have* my life rather than photograph it. So now I feel the autobiographical mode is essentially finished in every other sense except that naturally whatever I make will have something of myself in it, but I don't want to be conscious of that—I'd rather just let it happen.

SG: One of the reasons for filming your family and your daily life was to counter the influence of the other arts—especially drama—on film. Do you think you succeeded?

SB: I underestimated the historical flypaper I was stuck in. I didn't realize until much later how people in their daily living imitate the narrative-dramatic materials that infiltrate their lives through the radio, TV, newspapers, and, certainly, the movies. We went to the movies at least once a week and to plays, and I read a great deal to the children and they naturally acted out these things in their games. . . . It was ironic that I, who was an anomaly because I was working independently outside the studio system, created for myself a situation that was akin to that of a studio. To that extent, my work was tied to the whole history of cinema when I thought that wasn't the case. The films weren't free to grow aesthetically but dragged down by their subject matter. Despite all the evolutions of my film grammar and my inclusion of hypnagogic and dream vision, they were still tied to the more traditional dramatic-narrative framework. Moreover, while shooting, I would ask Jane and the children to keep quiet or be still, very basic things, but that pushed everything back toward drama. And then, although they were used to being photographed, they knew, like most people, when their picture was being taken, and that became a factor in what they did before the camera.

SG: But such moments were also important to your self-reflexive aesthetic.

SB: Yes, I did everything I could to recognize such moments and include them. Very often people look directly at the camera and sometimes even flash a smile, or I would include references to the fact that it was a film—flares, scratched titles, etc. *Dog Star Man* ends in a flare of sprocket holes. . . . I believe most artists whose work has any lasting value to a culture put out warning signs like these to say this is not a window into reality but an art work. This is why painters sign their names on the front of their paintings, or poets refer to the poem that's being written and to other poets. As Malraux said in *The Voices of Silence*, works of art speak to each other. And so there's a constant speaking to other filmmakers and filmmaking within my body of work.

SG: Was it hard to see those films after their subject—the marriage—collapsed? Did they have the same relevance for you?

SB: At first, I couldn't even bear to see snapshots of my previous life—I'd burst into tears. I was so twisted with agony that I couldn't even hold onto certain household objects, like a bunch of spoons, because they reminded me of the destruction of that life. So I had some terrors about those films—that I wouldn't be able to look at them again. But I found I could, and what is more I could watch them with Marilyn—the films had achieved an aesthetic to that extent, and one that was vibrant enough to sustain me.

SG: How did the children react to being filmed?
SB: For some, certain films are very bothersome. For example, Crystal finds 15 Song Traits in which she is crying, very disturbing, and the fact that I filmed her at that point. I now believe that in photographing the children I was engaging them in a creative process, a trance process that was physically far more demanding than they knew. As a result, their childhoods were distorted in subtle and dangerous ways. I am very aware of this now. Also, when an artist mixes his working process with his daily life, then there is a psychological imposition on other people who are involved. The children were not photographed continually—months or even half a year would go by—but there were long periods when there was some photography every day. It was more pervasive and, in that sense, more invasive of activities within the home which I now feel should be an area of privacy. There was an enormous invasion also of Jane and my privacy as well. So while I certainly achieved a better relationship vis-à-vis the children in the act of making those films than what I had inherited, it didn't go as far as I had hoped—all of which goes to show why that twenty-nine-year-old marriage, much celebrated in print and a constant point of reference within my art-making, finally collapsed.

SG: In the Hollis Frampton interview Jane actually complains of being used. . . .
SB: Hollis and I were both surprised by that claim. I think she felt used by the process coming through and directed by me, so I took her word for it then and still do now and feel condemned that a part of me couldn't see as well into her condition as it could with regard to the children. I must have been a terrible imposition on her. At the same time, I want to counterbalance this by saying that she always seemed very excited at being involved in the creative process, so I would invite her to look at the first edits and try to include her point of view in what I was making.

SG: Still, it must have been an enormous challenge to be housewife and mother and also face the camera.
SB: I think Jane was very much more a private person than she was permitted to be, not only vis-à-vis within the family, but with respect to the rest of the world. But she also seemed to enjoy the fact that people would come over and give her a lot of attention. Barbara Hammer even made a whole film on her in which Jane said she was a housewife and proud of the fact, so who's to know? There was that side of her which believed very strongly in being mother to her children and keeping house in that idyllic place. And I think what happened finally was that Jane increasingly felt that I was getting all the attention. And, as the children began to

grow up and she began to feel less enthralled being a mother, this fact began to hurt and disturb her deeply. . . . After the Frampton interview, I tried to represent her in ways she would recognize as being herself, and the first film that succeeded in doing this was *Hymn to Her*. She also felt a close affinity with the last film I made with her—*Jane*. And then there were her appearances in films like *The Loom* that moved her and satisfied her because she didn't feel used in them.

SG: To be fair, did you ever feel used in the process of making those films?
SB: I felt very used—ill-used—being given this burden of responsibility to stage-manage an unusually difficult family living situation at nine thousand feet in the mountains, subject to eight months of winter for a man who grew up a city boy. I was being used especially because I was inept in handling all that. It was hard to live there. I think I would have come to things that I have now come to very much sooner with a chance to better fulfill the intricacies of them. But there I had to split my personality. . . . It's just so hard to live, and I think the films show that. But still, it's all a gift—a gift of life and a gift of light, which are really one and the same. So, despite it not being my kind of place, I had ecstatic moments up there. I was forced to open myself to the wonders that are available in the most difficult surroundings.

SG: Wasn't it common in those days to refer to Jane as your Muse?
SB: Many people thought she was the Muse and I found that to be utterly repugnant. For me the Muse is a persuasion. It often feels like a force in Nature that moves through certain people, but it should never be appropriated by human beings. At one point in history the Muses were called goddesses, now it would be more appropriate to call them manifestations of the unconscious, or, perhaps along the line of Jung's "collective unconscious," to call them genetic manifestations that people shouldn't presume upon. Jane never called herself the Muse except as a joke, but she felt that what came through my work was really her doing although it was I who was mostly photographing and editing.

SG: So, whose films are they? In *Metaphors on Vision* you claim the term "by Brakhage" embraces the whole family, not just you.
SB: Yes, and that was well meant. The films were collaborative works, but, finally, they belong to the Muse—not to me or to Jane or to the children. All of us were used in some evolution. When I associate the Muse with the unconscious, I'm referring to the unknown. Those films came through me from the unknown. After we were divorced, Jane told two of her friends that it was really she who made the films and that I was very good at following her orders. By that she meant she had been the real inspiration for the films she valued most, and I felt she was

complimenting me for being extraordinarily sensitive to her inspiration. But the final result was extrinsic to any of us in as much as none of us could have conceived of them that way. And they came through with my style which is visible regardless of the subject matter or the techniques. I was the maker, for better or worse, and yet I wouldn't have been able to consciously make anything of any significance whatsoever. The only time I like to look at one of my films over and over again is when it is a product of this trance process.

SG: And this trance process would extend to the editing of the film as well?
SB: Yes, I would edit the material hoping to achieve an aesthetic ecology. That was always my intent without ever presuming to know whether I had succeeded or not, and I lent myself to that process in the most traditional ways—what you would normally expect from poets, painters, or composers—that their work is essentially under trance and largely alone in these final aspects of the making, even if they are working on a mural with people to help them. The impulse that distinguishes one mural from another comes essentially through one human being. I was trying to do that with film which was regarded as a communal art when I was growing up.

SG: But before you would enter into a trance, you would consciously think about the film you were going to make?
SB: I studied home movies as diligently as I studied the aesthetics of Sergei Eisenstein, beginning with *Songs* all the way to *Scenes from Under Childhood*. I turned to them for inspiration. But my films were different in that they were rooted in daily living rather than in the events that home movies tend to celebrate. What is embarrassing about certain amateurs is that they try to get everybody to jump around and act as if they were making a Hollywood movie which they can't. They are not showing the particularities or the *peculiarities* of their most mundane—i.e., "earthly"—surroundings and events. They would much rather photograph a staged birthday party than a normal day with their child. . . . I believe if we don't really focus on where we live, then great dangers arise in human psychology, one of which is to live in a past that is utterly falsified by human thinking and project into a future that is utterly impossible. Or we get bored and need drama. So, trying to stop the overwhelming influence of drama in film, I began to concentrate on the wonders that are under and on either side of our noses—more specifically, the greatest movie in town if only we would look at it.

SG: But at the same time you were turning that experience into myth, into . . .
SB: True. By focusing on the particularities of our daily life I could provide for Jane and the children and myself an alternative to the strictures of traditional family living. So the impulse to make those movies—as practically everything

in my work—arose out of a desperate living urgency to transform my sense of the constrictive family life. It was a need that Jane and I shared very vibrantly together. *Dog Star Man* is a good example, a myth which deals with the breadwinner—myself—being photographed by the wife, Jane (for the most part), climbing a mountain to chop down a tree, to bring home some firewood. . . . That's the human story, spread out, all the way to the stars and down to the microscopy of the man's vascular system, with everything in between metaphoring various historical stages in this brief climb of a mountain. We needed that metaphorical distance.

SG: But wasn't there a danger of taking that myth too seriously, of losing sight of the commonplace?

SB: In one of her scrapbooks Jane describes herself as an ordinary goddess. She has now changed her name to Jane Wodening—which is the female version of the god Woden. All this shows a predisposition to the goddess aspect of daily living, so both of us remained entranced by the most traditional, and, for myself, most dangerous presumptions of human existence on earth. All the same, there was a kind of glory and beauty to it. For a certain crowd in society we—the family—were like movie stars. We stood for certain ideals of the 1960s. . . . As an orphan and as a multiply-abandoned child, I respected the values of family living, and wished to assert their goodness and subvert what I felt was wrong. I wanted to create and sustain an inspired image of family living, and, if those films inspire me today, it is because there is a fair and honest representation of that image in them. I believe in those values, and thus run counter to some of the more virulent polemics of our time which would have it that family living is done for.

SG: Whenever people talk about your vision of childhood in these films, they go into a sort of rapture and invoke Wordsworth and Blake.

SB: I think it's misleading to relate me to Wordsworth—I who had no childhood at all. . . . I was after the emotional truth and the spiritual truth. And there was a tiny Weegee aspect to me too—only the bare truth—and sometimes I went out of my way to get that truth by photographing what normally you wouldn't photograph if you were making an idealized family living film. There's a lot of crying in my films of the children, of Jane and of myself. You see children being cruel to each other in ways that an amateur would never photograph.

SG: And yet it all seems magical, the way you photograph the light and the house. . . .

SB: The films aren't idealized in a simple sense, but they are in the sense that's intrinsic to art. I'm trying to make a form representative of family living which is a little bit off of this earth. And as such those films sit there hanging in air.

Looking at them you would think that everything was beautiful to those people. . . . People who visited the cabin found it to be small, dark, and cold, but in the films the house looks bigger and full of light. And that's because those films were inspired by the children and their growing up and having a childhood that was utterly different from mine, and the fact that I could give that childhood to them. I was translating that over into film emotionally. So people were shocked that from this grubby little cabin came a palace of visions.

SG: There are moments in all these films that seem quite trivial and yet uncannily revealing.

SB: I had read Freud's *Psychopathology of Everyday Life* where he discusses the verbal slips we make every day, and that was the time when I was intensely involved with representing common everyday occurrences. So I tried to capture those unconscious slips—"errors"—that can divulge hidden truths and tried to weave them into my work.

SG: How did you go about doing this?

SB: Sometimes while shooting, I would consciously try to get at certain things that were revelatory, that were true slips. I would look for them and then, during editing, put them in a context where they would reveal something. They crop up all the time in *Scenes from Under Childhood*, and even more in the *Sincerity* series and in the *Songs*. In *15 Song Traits*, the footage of Crystal crying was shot when we were in Lexington, Kentucky. The first thing I shot on coming home—a week or a month later—was a caged canary. When the footage came back from the lab and I looked at it, I was astonished by the power of that cut. And it had less to do with the fact that here was a girl feeling like a caged canary than the toning between one shot and the other, and where and how the canary sits in relationship to her face, and so on. That was the beginning of that film, and I then began rummaging among past footage to find other things that I began to put together in editing.

SG: How did some of your contemporaries respond to the family films, for example, the birth films?

SB: Maya (Deren) was outraged at *Window Water Baby Moving* when I first showed it in New York because she thought I was intruding, exposing feminine mysteries that were inviolate, etc. I had not intended to do any such thing. In fact, I was in the room during the birth at Jane's insistence that I be present and be true to myself, and I could only be true to myself while working, i.e., filming the birth. But I still worry about what Maya said. I photographed childbirth so that I could be a part of the process which was forbidden to men. In fact, in those days men were *absolutely* excluded from any kind of participation. So I hoped the film would be a valuable source of inspiration in joining men and women together in the birth process. . . .

SG: Do you think too much has been made of these films to the exclusion of your other work?

SB: Yes . . . I'd like to mention here that people tend to overlook the two-thirds of my work which was not centered on family living and which through the 1960s and 1970s was prophetic, so to speak, of what I'm now mostly doing with film. The content of my current films is less mimetic and more "at one" with the unique possibilities intrinsic to film. I carried a camera with me and made films during lecture tours, in hotel rooms, in airplanes. . . . I also made *The Text of Light* after months of sitting and photographing ashtrays in the office space of a friend, and it is much more pertinent to what I'm doing now than anything I did then when I was autobiographically trying to inspire people with my films about the ideals of the family.

SG: Two of your recent films are *The Dante Quartet* and *Untitled (For Marilyn)*. What led you to make the Dante film?

SB: Thirty years of reading all the translations in English of Dante's *The Divine Comedy*—I even tried to learn Italian at one point—as well as brooding on the Christian concept of hell, purgatory, and heaven. The four parts are *Hell Itself*, *Hell Spit Flexion*, *Purgation*, and *existence is song*, and they appear in that order. It took me seven years to produce this nine-minute film, but what is appalling is that you can see it today only in a postage size version.

SG: Why is that so?

SB: I wanted the dimensions of the film to match those of an Imax screen which is about three to four stories tall and half a city block wide. A film that would be like an enormous mural painting. I painted the four parts on different stocks—*Hell Itself* and *existence is song* were done directly on IMAX film, *Purgation* on a worn-out 70mm print of *Irma la Douce* and *Hell Spit Flexion* on 35mm. But it proved too expensive to print them for Imax projection. I finally rephotographed the Imax and 75mm strips off a light box to achieve the 35mm and 16mm prints that are now in distribution. So I view it really as a sketch of the original film I wanted to make.

SG: The real challenge must have been to find the hypnagogic equivalents of Dante's three-fold vision.

SB: I made *Hell Itself* during the break-up with Jane and the collapse of my whole life, so I got to know quite well the streaming of the hypnagogic process that's hellish. Now, the body can not only feedback its sense of being in hell but also its sense of getting *out* of hell, and *Hell Spit Flexion* shows the way out—it's there as a crowbar to lift one out of hell toward the transformatory state—which is the third state—purgatory. And finally there's a fourth hypnagogic state that's fleeting and evanescent—a sort of heavenly feeling. I've called this last part *existence is song*, quoting Rilke, because I don't want to presume upon the after-life and call it "Heaven." So, what I tried to do in the quartet was to bring down to earth Dante's vision, inspired by what's on either side of one's nose and right before the eyes: a movie that reflects the nervous system's basic sense of being.

SG: How long usually are your hand-painted films?
SB: They can vary anywhere between nine seconds—*Eye Myth*—to twelve minutes which is *Interpolations*.

SG: To get a second's worth of film time, you have to paint twenty-four individual frames. For *Interpolations*, that amounts to a mind-boggling 17,280 frames! How much do you throw away?
SB: Some end up in the wastebasket, a few get clipped off into little strips that I frame or send to somebody—I've even sold a few. . . . Yes, it's a lot of work, but there are people who believe it's all very simple, or it's work that's not important because it has no roots in psychodrama or neurosis. . . . My biggest worry is: Am I degenerating? The danger with painting on film is that it could turn into decoration and when it does, I throw it away.

SG: You've cited a number of influences on your hand-painting, among them Viking Eggeling, Walter Ruttmann, Len Lye, Oskar Fischinger, Harry Smith, and Marie Menken. What about contemporary filmmakers like Gunvor Nelson and Carolee Schneemann who have both painted on film?
SB: I've known Gunvor since the 1960s and always respected her work, but now it has evolved into an expression of thought process, and while she doesn't paint on film, she does paint over imagery, working with a frame at a time, and has created a combination of photographed imagery and painting, beginning with *Frame Line* and leading to my favorite so far—*Field Study #2*—which has affinities with my work being about remembrance which includes hypnagogic vision or moving visual thinking to counterbalance the dangers of nostalgia or sentimentality. I also have a great regard for Carolee who, dissatisfied with the male viewpoint of my *Loving*, which was about her and James Tenney, made *Fuses* which more than any other hand-painted film is a truly visceral presentation of texture. She was also distressed by my use of paint in *Thigh Line Lyre Triangular*—she's a great oil painter—and I taking this to heart have evolved an aesthetic of paint-on-film

which eschews "the painterly." It's like Orpheus in the Cocteau film when asked, what is a poet, replies, "Someone who writes but is not a writer."

SG: Why are Eggeling and Menken so important to you? After all, they didn't work directly with the film strip.
SB: Well, take Menken. It's true she didn't directly touch the film in that way, but, as a collage filmmaker, she would handle her footage as if they were shapes and patterns she had painted and weave them in according to their lateral motions. That, to me, is "hands-on" work. . . . I think the more you're physically in touch with the material, the more you become aware that you're smudging the passage of light, altering it by hand, and altering each frame, and every smudge reveals more of the light as you lessen it. And film, after all, is rhythmed light. So what matters finally is if you can *give in* to the light. That's the integrity of working directly with hands-on film, which is also hands-on light. I find that very inspiring. I'd like to mention Harry Smith here—Harry, who wanted to be a black magician in some sense and smudge the light in order to blot it out, came to a stage which can best be described as Jacob and the angel wrestling with the light. And, at some point, it became clear to him that, despite everything he tried, the light was going to win. And Harry had the integrity to back off and put himself at the service of humanity by recording with audiotapes and open himself to the phenomenological world and be a pure conduit of what could come through him and what he could put on tape. And he probably would have done the same thing with film if he could afford it. And I really respect that.

SG: If *The Dante Quartet* contains something of your personal hell, *Untitled (For Marilyn)*, which is dedicated to Marilyn, seems full of that evanescent quality you just described as heavenly.
SB: That's currently my favorite film, and how that happened was . . . I've always wanted to go to church with my children but churches don't like young children these days, so I've felt excluded from a full family participation. When I was in Helsinki about two years ago, I went to a Greek Orthodox church, but its doors were locked, so I photographed through the window, and later began to paint on the film. The more I worked on it, the more I began to feel my church is right *here*, where I am with my family—the four of us gathered together in the name of something holy. And I believe in that.

SG: Since this too is a quartet, what are the four parts?
SB: The first and last parts have writing mixed with paint. The first one is public or social, a sort of outcry vis-à-vis the church and myself, and dominated by the straight line structures of the church, while the last part is a private invocation of

myself and Marilyn, Anton, and Vaughn, and then thanks to God. The two parts in between move from the one to the other. I think the hand-painted sections are the ultimate of all the *hypnagogic* painting I've ever done, and I think this will be my last hand-painted hypnagogic film. There's an intensity of feeling here that I've never achieved before.

SG: What do the scratched words represent?
SB: It's a way of saying thank you. By the end of the fourth part I'm so overwhelmed that I want to give thanks for the peace that has come with my discovery of this film church. At one point I felt so emotional that I wrote—"You"—but that didn't look right, and I felt I needed a small "y" since it was Marilyn whom I was addressing. Then that's followed by hand-painted passages of what I felt hypnagogically at the thought of her, and then I scratched Anton and Vaughn's names, and, in the end, there didn't seem anything left to do but write "Praise be to God."

SG: I now want to shift to the Faust films which were made just after the marriage ended and you were living in Boulder. It was your first collaborative project as well as your first sound film in many years. What made you revert to the dramatic-narrative mode which you had previously shunned?
SB: I think I was seeking ground, going back to my beginnings, to psychodrama, sound, and collaboration, which are all aspects of my early filmmaking. In that respect the Faust films certainly resemble the early psychodramatic works, especially *Blue Moses*.

SG: Was there any particular reason for choosing the Faust story?
SB: Faust, for me, is the major legend of Western man. Some thirty-five years ago I applied for a grant to do *Joe Faust*—a contemporary version—but I didn't get the money. The film I made in 1987 was about a young Faust who wishes to be old without having to grow old. . . .

SG: Why the reversal?
SB: It made sense. I didn't want to go back in time nor relive my life, and the young people I knew then had no desire for eternal youth; in fact, they didn't expect to live very long. And no one typified this more than the man who played Faust—Joel Haertling, a composer and filmmaker, who lived in Boulder and had his own power-electronics group, Architect's Office. He was the contemporary Faust I had been looking for.

SG: Who else worked on the film?
SB: When I moved to Boulder, Joel introduced me to some very gifted young

people, and we formed a group, "The Sunday Associates" and started an Arts Series with shows every Sunday at the Boulder Art Theater. They were my chief collaborators on *Faust*. By the time I made *Part 2*, word had got around that the mountain man and the family man was finished—prey to a bunch of Boulder hippies.

SG: To what extent was this a collaboration? Was there a script you created together?
SB: I would come back from a session and write a few lines which usually ended up on the narrative track. Mostly, I relied on the material people were giving me, and occasionally would ask them to do something twice. I was trying my best to draw on my own ideas of Faust and, at the same time, on whatever anyone could offer. I was going through a Godard phase—gathering people together to create the script and create the film ... but, despite all this collaboration, it still is a Brakhage film.

SG: But by the time you get to the last part—*Faust 4*—there is a falling off, a need to abandon this form.
SB: By *Part 4* I had to work my way out because I knew by then that I had to free myself from psychodrama, and from the dramatics of Faust itself, and inherit the landscape again. *Part 4* is an obliteration by single frame of the memories of the past in the swell of the earth and in the desert. Also, by this time, I had met and fallen in love with Marilyn, and the film resulted from a road trip we took during which I photographed the landscapes of the West and the Midwest. So, in *Part 4*, there is no story really but a going to the desert to rid myself of these "pictures" and encompass the whole spectrum of sky and earth and what lies beneath the two.

SG: Another film resulted from that trip—the *Four Visions in Meditation*. Is that related to *Faust 4*?
SB: It's a four-part film with each part about seventeen to twenty minutes long and it springs directly from *Faust 4*—in fact, the four parts are the fullest possible imaginable extensions of *Part 4*—what the mind can do as it turns back on itself.

SG: You've said they were inspired by Gertrude Stein's *Stanzas in Meditation*.
SB: The basic inspiration is from the poem in which Stein tries to free words from reference and allows them to exist, each with a life of its own, within the jostling of all the words across the length of the poem. Thus "A" begins to take on a life of its own as the letter "A" or the sound "A" within the poem. You can wring a story from the life of "A" or "THE" or whatever word she introduces and repeats. But Stein didn't merely treat words as sounds. They have very live traits as they evolve, and I tried to create a corollary of that by photographing recognizable landscape.

SG: The search for a new aesthetic is already apparent in *Marilyn's Window* which you made the year before and which is the first of a cycle of films inspired by Marilyn.

SB: I think *Marilyn's Window* marks the beginning of everything that my *photographic* work has now evolved into. It was made when I visited her in Toronto and asked her to marry me. It was also just after my eye operation which had led to a lens implant in my right eye and given me a new sharpened vision.... Marilyn had a room in her brother's apartment, and the view through the window was quite plain: three brick walls, a roof, things like that, but it seemed to me the whole world poured in through them. There's no way I can quite put that into words. I began to shoot with a fifty-feet cartridge load camera, and later in the editing the sea suddenly rushed in. And I added other images, some hand-painted.

SG: You like to call it your most perfect film....

SB: Yes, it's the most perfect film given to me—in its rhythms, its shapes, but I didn't know it then nor did I aspire toward any such thing. There's no way you can plot or script such a film. And yet life provides these illuminations often in very mundane circumstances, like the view from the window of a room of the woman with whom I was falling deeper and deeper in love, and it's important to open oneself to these moments. Also, it was while making this film that I had a profound sense of how each object, each living thing is utterly unique, and the shapes they make on film are also unique, and so are the compositional relationships between the shapes. That recognition gave me a whole new sense of aesthetics.

SG: And two years later you made *A Child's Garden and the Serious Sea* which, like *Marilyn's Window*, is about seeing the everyday world with new eyes, about discovering it for the first time again.

SB: This is the longest film I've done which is not divided into parts or sections. It's symphonic in nature, but I made it at a time when I was also struggling to keep the consciousness of musical forms out of my work. While visiting Marilyn's parents on Vancouver Island, Victoria, I was deeply moved by her home and garden which hadn't changed much since she was a child. And there was the presence of the sea. I could even smell it from the garden. I had brought my camera hoping to film tide pools, instead I began to shoot the flowers in the garden, and the film grew out of those shots of the garden, the ocean, and a miniature golf course nearby. Anton was then about a year old, and there is a brief shot of him crawling along the grass in the distance.

SG: Is the film a child's perspective of the world?

SB: Not a child's perspective but a metaphor of a child's emerging consciousness.

In that respect the film goes all the way back to *Anticipation of the Night*, to a major theme in my work: the primal sight of children and their first encounter with the adult world. But, unlike *Night*, where the loss of that vision is mourned, in *Child's Garden* there is an acceptance. The images of the adult world impinge on those of the garden and the sea, but I treat them as a kind of aberration which doesn't overwhelm the primal gift of the whole phenomenological world.

SG: How was the film received?

SB: Both *Marilyn's Window* and *Child's Garden* have been misunderstood as an attempt to recreate Marilyn's childhood, of trying to see the garden through her eyes as she was growing up when I had no such intention. I have no illusions that people can see through somebody else's eyes except via aesthetics. We do not share each other's visions but a vision when it comes through an artist. To that extent, the integrity or the ecology of a work of art can override the intrinsic differences between each of us.

SG: Both films are silent, but, around this time, you had also begun to experiment with sound. And, like so much of the work after the divorce, this too has its roots in *Faust*.

SB: I think what pulled me back into a lot of sound-making was the same impulse, the need to go back to the roots of my filmmaking which lay in psychodrama. Sound is crucial for psychodrama principally because there's a lack of, what I would call, vision. What is psychodrama after all but the drama that's in the mind, and the extent to which you approach drama, even in the oblique way that I did in *Faust*, involves engaging with picture and continuity as well as a whole hierarchy of symbols. In the absence of vision, sound becomes a necessity to stitch the loose threads together and make it all bearable.

SG: So you haven't essentially changed your position about sound being an aesthetic error in film?

SB: No. Film is obviously visual, but Hollywood holds the opposite view, and the proof is that with most movies you can listen to the soundtrack and know what they are about without ever looking at them. For a long time only 2 per cent of my films were sound films because I felt sound interfered with seeing. Moreover, given the complex nature of my films, it was much harder to concentrate if the film had sound. But, at the same time, if I felt a film needed sound, I always included it.

SG: Did you study music?

SB: I was taught piano when I was three years old and living in Winfield, Kansas, and, when I was four and a half, I was singing solos because I had a high clear voice and could stay on pitch. And then I studied singing in Bisbee, Arizona, with a group of nuns who had taken an interest in my voice.

SG: How did that happen?
SB: There was a man in Bisbee, Arizona, who ran the local movie theater and he would go around photographing local events for a sort of Bisbee "March of Time" which he showed every week. He heard me singing in my backyard, photographed me and arranged a recording session. So I saw myself singing on screen and so did some nuns who felt I should have voice lessons. Later, at eight or nine, I chose to join the St. John's Cathedral Choir at Denver and sang as a boy soprano soloist until my voice began to crack. I also studied the violin briefly and was in choirs all through school, but I was primarily a boy soprano soloist who sang at weddings and funerals and on the national radio and had quite a life as a musical prodigy.

SG: Did you ever compose music?
SB: No. I was never good with numbers, and composers have to be mathematicians in a sense. The only song I ever composed is a round (sings):
>The bear is fur
>The fur is bear
>The bear is walking everywhere
>Here, there, near, far
>Bear furrrr . . .

SG: Quite early in your filmmaking, you began to experiment with electronic music. . . .
SB: I experimented with collage, or what was called "musique concrète," but I never kidded myself that I was a Goldstein or a Cage or a Varèse. After all, I'm not a painter or a composer but a filmmaker, so when I collaged those sounds, I was creating a corollary of what I was doing in film, and I've never done it except for film. The earliest collage experiments are in *Daybreak and Whiteye* where I made compound soundtracks with very primitive tape recorders.

SG: What about *Fire of Waters*?
SB: Yes, that's another early example and perhaps the best since it's really a silent film and the three short sound pieces stand out in a vast sea of silence.

SG: When did you first encounter electronic music?
SB: I was a year out of high school and back from a nervous breakdown at Dartmouth College when I went to a record store, saw a strange label, put on the record and first heard the music of Edgard Varèse. And it transformed my entire life like

the instant I first laid eyes on a reproduction by Jackson Pollock. Later I sought Varèse out in New York, and he let me sit in on his music lessons at home for free since I couldn't afford to pay for them. At the same time I was incredibly lucky to have met John Cage and to be invited to some of his sessions and music soirees.

SG: What did you learn from Varèse and Cage?
SB: Primarily what I got from them was the inspiration to make silent film. I was especially attracted to the instrumental aspects of their recorded live sound (for example, the hiss of tires on a wet street) and the fact that the sound could refer to the source of the recording (a passing car). This is a corollary of film because, when you turn on the camera, you automatically pick up reference. Even if you shoot totally out of focus, there is a certain quality of say a car's movement which even if reduced to a blob of hexagonal lens-reflecting light is usually recognizable as that of an automobile.

What Cage taught me was to recognize the "unscheduled disturbances in the atmosphere" as airplane pilots say when they hit an air pocket—disturbances that are routine in what we hear around us. And it's terribly important that these ambient sounds be recognized. I edited the A roll of *Dog Star Man* by chance operations inspired by Cage, and then I created superimpositions with the B roll and imposed metaphorical contexts (by conscious choice) in relation to the original chance operations. So I have consistently allowed these unscheduled disturbances to enter my work and exist in relation to the referential images. Cage continues to inspire me in that respect, and a good deal of my painting is based on chance operations.

On the other hand, Varèse was anxious to create sounds within a certain space so carefully that the flute noise which travels faster by a microsecond than the oboe noise would mix at a certain point in the room. When I first went to see Varèse, he had maps of the Grand Canyon on his walls and was dreaming of a vast symphony of the universe where these slight delays of one sound texture or one pitch over another would converge in certain places and in certain ways.... I was fascinated by that and also with how Varèse would allow a recorded sound into his work to serve as a musical instrument. Take the jackhammer with its electronic echoes in *Poème électronique* or the waterdrop sounds that resound within the interpolations in *Deserts*, and consider how these references to the source of the sound are embodied within what is finally a pure sound aesthetic. That has taught me to resist the referent, to take on referential photography and contain it so that the references would not destroy the aesthetic of the film as *a film* experience.

SG: When you made *Interpolations* last year, were you consciously thinking of Varèse?

SB: They were originally inspired by the interpolations I just mentioned which were interwoven with the orchestral music of *Deserts* and which Frank Zappa later singled out and put on a recording. I had first heard them as single pieces, long before Deserts was completed, so when I made *Boulder Blues and Pearls and . . . last year*—a peripheral vision film about Boulder—I thought of Varèse and of using five of my hand-painted strips as complete pieces of interpolations within the film's photographed content. I wanted them to exist as a counterbalance to the referential—the photographs of Boulder. I finally ended up with five films that go together so well in 35mm that I have not reduced them to 16mm. What went into *Boulder* were some hand-painted strips in 16mm, so my *Interpolations* ended up not being really related to Varèse's *Deserts* or to anything I had originally in mind. They exist independently and constitute my longest hand-painted work.

SG: Can you describe how you work with a piece of music?

SB: Most people assume that I put on background music and then jam with vision or something! In fact, I never play music when I'm working on a film. I make visual corollaries of music and once even tried to cut a film exactly to a Bach fugue and the result was a disaster. On the other hand, there is a relationship between Messiaen's organ music and *Scenes from Under Childhood*, and you can take *Mothlight* and see how it is related to a Bach fugue in the sense that the shapes of the wings and the recreated flight of the moth among the flowers have recurring colors which are melodic, and that the shapes themselves with their recurring actions are true to the overall sense of a Bach fugal integrity. . . . In this sense, these are all pieces of visual music, and so are many of my hand-painted films. But now I very much prefer to set pictures to music, and it's usually the music that inspires me in the first place and the film comes out of that.

SG: Who have you worked with mostly?

SB: James Tenney was the first one to compose music for my films. For *Interim*—the very first film I made—he created a piano soundtrack, inspired by Samuel Barber's *Sonata for Piano*. And we recently worked together again on *Christ Mass Sex Dance* which was made in very strange circumstances. I photographed the rehearsals of the Annual Boulder Christmas *Nutcracker Suite*, hoping to make a children's film, but I ended up with imagery that had nothing to do with the *Nutcracker*. And, the instant I got back the film from the lab, I thought of Tenney's *Blue Suede* which is a collage of Elvis Presley's "Blue Suede Shoes" with the words broken up into a kind of sexual grunting, and it seemed perfectly suited to it, so I cut the film to the music.

SG: What was the nature of your collaboration with Architect's Office?
SB: Joel's group embodied for me a certain revitalization of ideals that had gone dead since the 1960s. Their music was built around communal ideas, so that musicians could retain their individual signatures while working together. And there was always room for chance operations. There were some extraordinary talents like Rick Corrigan who did the music for *Faust Parts 1* and *4* and with whom I've collaborated on several films since. And there was Joel. I set *Kindering* to one of his pieces which combined his son's voice with tapes he had picked up at a yard sale, and it was all very beautifully integrated. He evoked for me a quality of childhood that I hadn't really felt for a long time, so I photographed my grandchildren with his music in mind and then edited the pictures directly to the music. I also set *I Dreaming*, my self-in-crisis portrait, to his collage or "recomposition" of fragments of songs by Stephen Foster.

SG: He also did some very innovative compilation tracks for your films about visual thinking and seeing.
SB: Yes. I greatly admired Joel's collage abilities—he did an amazing track for my hand-painted film *Fireloop*, in which I use fire as a metaphor for the light-and-sound process that accompanies moving visual thinking. He also did a compilation piece featuring music by groups like Die Tödliche Doris, Zoviet France, Nurse with Wound, and the Hafler Trio for *Loud Visual Noises*, my hand-painted film about optic feedback in response to sound. And he played Faust, collaborated on the music, and did the entire track for *Faust 2*.

SG: I want to talk about one last sound film, *Passage Through: A Ritual*. Why did you decide to juxtapose long stretches of black leader with a gamelan soundtrack?
SB: The piece is by Philip Corner—*Through the Mysterious Barricades (After Couperin)*. After I heard the tape, I begin rummaging through two to three thousand feet of film which I had shot during the break-up of the marriage and put away. I was trying to pull out only what I could have shot that day and throw the rest out, and I ended up with about fifty feet. . . . The film consists of mostly black leader with very brief shots of photographed objects that are usually unrecognizable. And I cut them to the music. So there are these long dark spaces of music with occasional flashes of imagery. It was one of the hardest films to edit since the challenge was to find the exact place where a particular image belonged. If I stretched some of those places ten seconds longer, it would become absurd.

SG: What were you really after?
SB: I think it's a film about the dark night of the soul with moments of illumination

that are intrinsic to my present, where I am now. In that sense, the film is very cathartic.

SG: I noticed how despite the black leader, it's never completely dark.
SB: There's a shimmering of light all through and there are little sprocket holes in the black leader that are like stars of light.... The optic nerve-endings of the viewers interact all the time with this ephemera of light. The film proves that even with black leader you can't ever defeat the light.

SG: We're coming to the end our interview, so let me ask: What now?
SB: My main problem at sixty and for the last five years has been to get old *Dog Star Man* off my back, so that I can just start fresh and go on with what has been given to me to do. The whole grounds of my making have shifted and, furthermore, I think they're shifting even more radically. I'm content with that. I've gone from "Brakhage" to "SB" which could be any old son-of-a-bitch to not signing the films at all. I think more and more I'd like to inhabit with great humility the position of anonymous.... I'm not really that man who made those films in the past in any other sense than the aesthetic: the styles of rhythming that are intrinsic to my being. Only now I hope I've cleared a great deal of the usages out of it, and it can just come through me. It has taken me a whole lifetime of hard work to get to the point of just making a film. The irony is, that as I get there, I don't know what to say about it. I now treasure those works about which people don't write anything or even remember having seen because those are films that exist in a realm which defies the verbal. They are films that are given over wholly to the unconscious.

SG: Films like?
SB: Like *Nodes* and *Matins*. They are the kinds of films I would like to spend the rest of my life making—films that are, in the ordinary sense of the word, about nothing.... And I'm getting there. I was just dabbling with paint when I made this new unnamed film, and I didn't even think that I was making a film. And that's very hard to achieve. Since I lost a nerve in my right hand, my index and thumb fingers have become weak, so I painted this new film with my left hand and I think it's the best piece I've ever done with this hand. I'm encouraged by that—after all, the left hand is usually neglected; it began to come into its own when I began painting with my fingers, finding them more useful than brushes. Since I didn't use the left hand for my past work, it could be a more direct conduit for the feelings that are now in me—this was certainly the case with this film.... Now and again something like this will slip through me that's got a mysterious, intangible quality to it like some of Cornell's films do, especially the Lorca series (*A Legend for Fountains*) inspired by *Poet in New York*. They have a certain is-ness

that no map of the mind can decipher. They simply exist out there in the world, each film with a life of its own.

SG: I'm intrigued by that word you just used—"nothing."
SB: I don't know. . . . It's very hard to be clear. Nothing exists—take John Cage's silence or the silence I once heard in a Kansas cornfield. . . . I heard the dominant fifth in my ears and the beating of my heart. If something out there can be inspiring without manipulating a person, without that being with reference to anything else in the world, be a thing in itself, then that seems to me an epitome of human making and experience.

SG: Are you going to give up titles altogether in the new work?
SB: I'm thinking of grouping some of these films in a series called *Naughts* and others in a series called *Chartres*. But even that seems an intrusion, so at some point I hope I'll have the good sense to give up titles altogether. And the films will be "things" nobody can categorize verbally. I think of Michelangelo's "unfinished" sculptures in this respect which are so much more exciting to me than his *David* or *Moses*.

SG: Why "naughts?"
SB: I don't really know what "naughts" means. When I call these films *Naughts*, I'm very conscious of the pun with "knots" which suggests a crossing of wires and the fact that I haven't quite got to where I hope I will someday.

SG: And why the reference to Chartres?
SB: Those are works that came out absolutely unexpectedly as a result of being at Chartres Cathedral in 1992. . . . I think the rest of my life will be profoundly affected by the several hours I spent there. When I was at the Beaubourg Center, they even asked me whether I would be interested in coming back to photograph Chartres, and I said, yes, probably in a couple of years. It could happen, and, if it did, then I would take a camera into Chartres and see what I could do. But what is wonderful is that I'm *already* at work on Chartres Cathedral without any grants or even consciously thinking that this is what I'm doing. Now I hope there will be more of these, or there will be more *Naughts*, or there will be something else that I won't be able to fit under either of those categories, and that finally all categories will collapse and I won't know what to do.

Stan Brakhage

Scott MacDonald / 1996–2002

From *A Critical Cinema 4: Interviews with Independent Filmmakers*. Berkeley: University of California Press, 2005. Reprinted by permission.

11/30/96

Scott MacDonald: One of the things that struck me about *Interim* when I looked at it recently, is that it's so much better than I remembered it. I remembered it as pretty rough, but this time it seemed good enough to make me doubt that it's your first film. Is it your first film, or just the first film you decided to distribute?
Stan Brakhage: No, it is my first film. I also happened to see it recently and was embarrassed—as I was when it was made—about the chunks of dirt in the gate and other utterly unacceptable technical wrongs. But I was also moved by it; what it is in its innate being rings absolutely true for such a despairing, youthful love syndrome. It holds up. Of course, a great deal of credit has to go to Stan Phillips, who was the cinematographer. Several people contributed to making what, at that time, seemed an absolutely true, disparaging statement about the possibility of loving someone. Subsequently, thank God, we haven't found the possibilities of love as limited as they are in *Interim*. But in some rather cosmic sense, you could certainly say that love is very limited, a brief make-life fling on earth.

SM: Knowing that you became the kind of filmmaker you are, it's easy now to read *Interim* as a visitation of the spirit. Your protagonist is on the main highway, where you/he is almost hit by a car. He comes down out of the mainstream space into the underground, a world underneath what modern life has created, and there he has the visitation.
SB: Let me just say that my whole life's work has been a search among these themes that you have just expounded very well.

Perhaps the most vibrant, older-age exploration of the theme of love in *Interim* is *Untitled (For Marilyn)*—the parenthesis is there just so that while the film itself that no map of the mind can decipher. They simply exist out there in the world, each film with a life of its own.

SG: I'm intrigued by that word you just used—"nothing."
SB: I don't know. . . . It's very hard to be clear. Nothing exists—take John Cage's silence or the silence I once heard in a Kansas cornfield. . . . I heard the dominant fifth in my ears and the beating of my heart. If something out there can be inspiring without manipulating a person, without that being with reference to anything else in the world, be a thing in itself, then that seems to me an epitome of human making and experience.

SG: Are you going to give up titles altogether in the new work?
SB: I'm thinking of grouping some of these films in a series called *Naughts* and others in a series called *Chartres*. But even that seems an intrusion, so at some point I hope I'll have the good sense to give up titles altogether. And the films will be "things" nobody can categorize verbally. I think of Michelangelo's "unfinished" sculptures in this respect which are so much more exciting to me than his *David* or *Moses*.

SG: Why "naughts?"
SB: I don't really know what "naughts" means. When I call these films *Naughts*, I'm very conscious of the pun with "knots" which suggests a crossing of wires and the fact that I haven't quite got to where I hope I will someday.

SG: And why the reference to Chartres?
SB: Those are works that came out absolutely unexpectedly as a result of being at Chartres Cathedral in 1992. . . . I think the rest of my life will be profoundly affected by the several hours I spent there. When I was at the Beaubourg Center, they even asked me whether I would be interested in coming back to photograph Chartres, and I said, yes, probably in a couple of years. It could happen, and, if it did, then I would take a camera into Chartres and see what I could do. But what is wonderful is that I'm *already* at work on Chartres Cathedral without any grants or even consciously thinking that this is what I'm doing. Now I hope there will be more of these, or there will be more *Naughts*, or there will be something else that I won't be able to fit under either of those categories, and that finally all categories will collapse and I won't know what to do.

Stan Brakhage

Scott MacDonald / 1996–2002

From *A Critical Cinema 4: Interviews with Independent Filmmakers*. Berkeley: University of California Press, 2005. Reprinted by permission.

11/30/96

Scott MacDonald: One of the things that struck me about *Interim* when I looked at it recently, is that it's so much better than I remembered it. I remembered it as pretty rough, but this time it seemed good enough to make me doubt that it's your first film. Is it your first film, or just the first film you decided to distribute?

Stan Brakhage: No, it is my first film. I also happened to see it recently and was embarrassed—as I was when it was made—about the chunks of dirt in the gate and other utterly unacceptable technical wrongs. But I was also moved by it; what it is in its innate being rings absolutely true for such a despairing, youthful love syndrome. It holds up. Of course, a great deal of credit has to go to Stan Phillips, who was the cinematographer. Several people contributed to making what, at that time, seemed an absolutely true, disparaging statement about the possibility of loving someone. Subsequently, thank God, we haven't found the possibilities of love as limited as they are in *Interim*. But in some rather cosmic sense, you could certainly say that love is very limited, a brief make-life fling on earth.

SM: Knowing that you became the kind of filmmaker you are, it's easy now to read *Interim* as a visitation of the spirit. Your protagonist is on the main highway, where you/he is almost hit by a car. He comes down out of the mainstream space into the underground, a world underneath what modern life has created, and there he has the visitation.

SB: Let me just say that my whole life's work has been a search among these themes that you have just expounded very well.

Perhaps the most vibrant, older-age exploration of the theme of love in *Interim* is *Untitled (For Marilyn)*—the parenthesis is there just so that while the film itself has no title, it reverberates with the dedication to Marilyn. I've come to a sense in which love is not only *not* despairing but is not even brief.

That other theme of the surface and the *undersurface*, where things *really* happen, represented in *Interim* by the protagonist going down under the viaducts, is very much reflected in *Commingled Containers*, the first photographic film that I've made in a long time. I made it just before I went in for my bladder cancer surgery. *Commingled Containers* was shot in Boulder Creek here in town. The surface in this instance is the stream; the undersurface is a series of beautiful, cellularly contained, semi-repetitious but never repeating patterns of light, in great quietude. Now, this may seem too facile a comparison going down under the viaducts in a dramatic sense with going beneath the surface of that creek to film the light and life of that body of water—but I believe that in both cases I was doing basically the same thing, and in fact the sense of desperation that drew me into Boulder Creek to shoot *Commingled Containers* was very similar to the desperation of the man in *Interim* being drawn to that plunge under the viaducts.

SM: How did you come to make *Interim*?
SB: Well, I had had a very rich life of movie-viewing, unusually broad for those days. My mother would give me money to go to double features, which were quite ordinary in those days. I'd come out of one movie and have something to eat—a hot dog or whatever—and then go into the next, and sometimes a third. She would pick me up after the movies. Movies changed rapidly enough in those days that I rarely saw a movie more than once, unless I wanted to. We're talking about my life as an eight- or nine-year-old, or even a bit younger. I was constantly at the movies; and they were, in fact, my alternate parents.

SM: Do you remember particular films?
SB: Oh yes. *The Mummy* so moved me, created in me such identification with the monster, that I wrapped myself in sticky adhesive tape and went out on the street to frighten people. I hadn't realized how painful it would be to unwrap myself! And earlier than that, I remember being terrified of Disney's *Snow White and the Seven Dwarfs* which is, I believe, the first movie that I saw. This was during the war years, and I remember the newsreels—there was a theater completely given over to newsreels—where I saw all the war news which, many years later, came to be the focus of *23rd Psalm Branch*. At this newsreel theater, I also saw such things as a boa constrictor eating a lion, or whatever; a pig being stripped to the bone by piranhas in thirty seconds; and there were all these strange travel features. So that was also part of my movie-going.

And then later in high school I had my experience with Jean Cocteau's *Orpheus* and knew that film could be an art—which was very surprising to me. By this time, I was very involved in the arts, in poetry primarily, but also in drama and music.

So first Cocteau's *Orpheus* and then a couple weeks later his *Beauty and the Beast* gave me experiences that were close enough to my involvement with poetry that I was certain that film could be an art. Then I began searching for it elsewhere, in Rossellini and de Sica, who were primary influences on *Interim*, and in Orson Welles, and so on.

Then later, during my brief stay at Dartmouth—the one uncompleted semester before my nervous breakdown—I saw certain silent classic films and other foreign films.

SM: This is 1951?
SB: Yes. I would have been class of 1955 had I come back to Dartmouth. Back in Denver, I remember sitting under those viaducts in *Interim* with my high school friends, in a car, all of us in various degrees of despair—myself from the loss of what I had thought a college education would be and hadn't been. As I remember, a friend in great despair, who had been in the marines (this was during the war in Korea), said, "It's too bad that artists can't work with film because it's too expensive." And I just saw red. I remember it vividly. I said, "We'll *make* a film," And, sure enough, we did find cameras—amateur cameras in people's attics—and started in.

SM: *Interim* did show you that film was a medium you could work in.
SB: Yes. For a long time, I thought of myself as a poet making films like Jean Cocteau; but when it became clear that film was what I really *could* do, my life became devoted principally to film.

SM: You became a relentless experimenter. Looking back, I'm surprised that I thought of *all* your early films as *Brakhage* films, without really conceptualizing what that meant. Now, what strikes me is the clear evolution toward that period in the late fifties and early sixties that produced, among other films, *Anticipation of the Night*, *Sirius Remembered*, *Window Water Baby Moving*, and what has come to be understood as your particular approach. Did you have a sense back then that you were moving toward something? Did you think about the overall process of your development?
SB: I had had a sense since I was nine years old that I was some kind of an artist. I had thought I was a poet, and I had continued to think so into my early twenties when I was living with Robert Duncan in the middle of the San Francisco Beat poetry movement. I met Michael McClure and Kenneth Patchen and Jack Spicer and Robin Blaser, Kenneth Rexroth and Louis Zukofsky and began having a sense of what a poet really was. All this powerfully confirmed my poetic aspirations.

But, more and more, I felt there was this *visual* possibility. As I began reading about artists, it began to seem quite natural that, because my eyes were weak and because I had never been content to accept this weakness, and had continued to struggle against it (at seventeen I had even thrown my glasses away), the road of most possible creativity for me would be along the line of the eyes.

SM: How bad were your eyes?
SB: Pretty bad, actually. I had a bad astigmatism. I was walleyed: that is, my right eye was always adrift and didn't focus well. I had to really struggle to come to focus. I couldn't take focusing for granted. And much of what you and others have described as my experimentation is just a part of my scrambling to come to an understanding of how you achieve sight. Something that other people just have naturally, I had to *earn*. One time, an optician, on looking into my eyes, said, "Well, by your eyes, physically, you shouldn't even be able to *see* that chart on the wall, let alone read it. But, on the other hand, I have never seen a human eye with more rapid saccadic movements. What you must be doing is rapidly scanning and putting this picture together in your head."

Anyway, to get back to the question, I wasn't *trying* to invent new ways of being a filmmaker; that was just a by-product of my struggle to come to a sense of sight. And it seemed reasonable to me that film ought to be based on human seeing, and not just the physical eyes but the mind's eye: that is, what happens when the eye receives images from the outside and how they interrelate with remembered images on the inside of the mind. How do we arrive at our seeing and then imagine with our sight?—we put dove's wings onto a cat and "see" a griffin.

SM: By the time of *Anticipation of the Night*, you're allowing yourself to represent the way you really do see, with all the supposed limitations, and to accept the reality of that as a means of making visual art.
SB: Many years later, when I met the poet Charles Olson, he made quite clear the importance of accepting what's been God-given to you to work with, of accepting your limitations as the special gifts. My eyes were the weakest part of me really; either I was going to be destroyed by them or they were going to become the path through which my creativity could flower.

My sense, very early on, was to figure out what my talents were, what was God-given to me to do. Whatever you mean by God. I don't mean to sound religious, but there are certain things that *are* given, that are intrinsic within us; and that was very much Olson's message to me in that great encounter I had with him, and which is celebrated in the letter to Jane at the end of *Metaphors on Vision* about my being very clear about what my natural sight is and accepting it and going with that.

SM: When did you start to see underground films by Americans?
SB: Shortly after making *Interim*, I went to San Francisco. I attempted to study at the California Art Institute, and then just ran off with a camera with another student—because they weren't teaching us anything. We took it for a week and jammed one roll after another into it, and learned how to run it. That was during the same general period when I was meeting the poets.

Then I went back to Denver. With some of my friends, we formed a little film society and brought in Von Stroheim's *Greed*, Kenneth Anger's *Fireworks*, which was important, Maya Deren's *Meshes of the Afternoon*, and several other classic movies.

SM: Were you aware of Cinema 16, and Art in Cinema, and the film society movement in general?
SB: Vaguely. But it seemed quite remote. When I went back to San Francisco the second time, I continued to make films, and discovered Art in Cinema, Frank Stauffacher's great series at the San Francisco Museum of Art. And he brought in Isadore Isou's *Venom and Eternity* [aka *Treatise on Drivel and Eternity*], which caused a riot. It was a deeply meaningful film for me.

I also got to see Chris MacLane's *The End*. James Broughton. Sidney Peterson. At that point, I was living in the storage room where Broughton kept all his films, and I had access to Broughton's originals and outtakes and was studying those and the work he did with Peterson, also. I bounced back and forth between the West Coast and Denver for a number of years, and at one point I met Peterson in LA, when I was working at the Coronet Theater for Raymond Rohauer, who was showing all kinds of banned and forbidden films from his vast collection. I swept up the theater and was a night guard in exchange for admission and access.

Gradually, God knows how, I made a series of films, shooting a roll at a time with whatever money I could beg or borrow. I didn't resort to stealing. I'd get odd jobs at times, doing some photography and this or that, and earn enough money to be able to make *The Way to Shadow Garden* or *Flesh of Morning*.

I had recognized that while *Blood of a Poet* suggested the possibility of cinema art, in the sense that meant the most to me, as did Cocteau's *Orpheus*, I saw also that both those films were filled, as was Buñuel and Dali's *Un Chien Andalou*, with Hollywoodisms. There was something very disturbing to me about this and about the overriding fact that narrative drama dominated everything. The dice were loaded clear back to the Greeks. Well, not just the Greeks, of course, because it's West *and* East, and it doesn't really matter whether you're dealing with a Kurosawa or a John Ford movie or with a Greek play. East and West, the world over, there's something intrinsically confining about narrative dramatics—and yet, of course, I also love them. I go to the movies all the time; and I care very deeply for drama.

Anyway, I had a sense that this loaded dice of drama could eventually destroy us all. I mean, if you think of all the forms of all the different arts, the one that changes the least is narrative drama. Because theater is also an edifice, and what is an *edifice* but something solid that doesn't change? Drama is always set up to come to the end—and the end can be happy or unhappy, or tragic, if you like, whatever—but there will be an end. Everything *is* designed like an equation, to come to the end.

Now, if you think about it, that is not true in the history of painting or music or poetry. These forms are ever more open and open-ended, especially as we come into full-blown Romanticism. Somehow, the theater hasn't evolved in those directions, except perhaps through the not-very-often-staged work of Gertrude Stein, for example.

So I began to be more and more leery of narrative drama in my own work, and my evolution has been to try to find a way out of the dilemma of the dramatic in film. The whole concept of photoplay began to be embarrassing to me, and by the time of *Anticipation of the Night*, I had developed a form that had shaken at least some of the shackles off. . . .

The qualities of a work that will make it last often aren't visible to the makers. They're just stuck with the work that has come through them, usually in some degree of trance or some kind of desperate state. And even though they may feel obligated—as I certainly have often felt—to go out and speak for the work right away, to help give it a life on earth, the work is often very difficult for them, too. They are its first audience and find it as difficult as other audiences do. That's something I think a lot of people don't understand. You have to take the work on faith, both as an audience and as a maker.

Whatever faults there are in *Anticipation of the Night*—and there are many—it was produced through a process of *such* absolute sincerity. I mean, it was desperate making, and it was a gift to me and not one that I accepted easily, because it did start riots and lost me friends and brought every kind of abuse down on my head. But what am I to do? I have to trust my process. All I *can* trust is that this work continues to insist on being made, even when I'm passing through bladder cancer surgery, chemotherapy, and every other goddamn thing—three operations in two months—and I'm still going to my office to make film splices! I know that I'm not mad. I may be a fool, but I'm not mad. There *is* an integrity to this process, and I will continue to struggle to try to raise the money to get the films printed—horrible as that struggle is going to be at this time—and to push the work out there where there are only about four places in the United States where it will probably ever be shown. It was the same with *Anticipation of the Night*: when I made *Anticipation*, there was *only* Cinema 16, and Amos Vogel wouldn't show it! In Europe it created a riot, and *that* was awful. I didn't enjoy any bit of it.

SM: When I show *Anticipation of the Night* now, this same overall history happens, but it happens in a microcosm. My students will revolt, and in discussion or in their formal journals, they'll try to think of new ways to tell me why this can't possibly be okay, why they are *not* going *this* far *this* time. But two weeks later a substantial number of them have come through that reaction and are feeling invigorated by the film. Over a generation there has been some movement, I think. The same thing does happen, but the pain is over quickly, and for at least some, the pleasure begins.

SB: I'm delighted to hear that, not just for the usual reason—my own pride in having let that work come into being through me—but because the thought process embodied in *Anticipation of the Night* is far more important than the plot that ends with the hanging. This thought process is a way into new envisionment for people. I believe and hope that it can have its life on earth for the betterment of humans or at least for the reenergizing of humans—whether it's *betterment* or not, who can say?

We always need new vision. As Ezra Pound said, "The arts are the antennae of the race and cultures go blind without them." I feel that *Anticipation of the Night*, in its humble way (and along with so many other films by me and others), has had something to do with a new way of perceiving, which also means a new way of thinking about what you have seen. And I'm delighted if people can begin to get over the disturbance of the newness of it as rapidly as you say.

SM: I have to confess that, as many times as I've seen *Anticipation of the Night*, I cannot get my eyes off the textures and the colors and the rhythms of the film; I can't *see* the story. I know from reading Sitney's analysis that there is a story, about suicide, but I cannot see it.

SB: Maybe you're just wiser than most in your ways of viewing, because the truth is, the story is very insignificant and, in fact, is flawed because, in the end, I *didn't* commit suicide—though, of course, I *had* thought about it. I'm glad I didn't commit suicide, but, all the same, the film had come to a point where when my decision changed, it could not re-realize itself in a new mode. Otherwise, the film is music, visual music.

SM: It's almost as though there was a battle between the new Brakhage and the old Brakhage. *Anticipation* completes the movement into a second way of doing things. And even though I can see that there is symbolic import to this or that detail, I'm immediately drawn back into the texture, the musical flow. Something in me fights seeing the film in that earlier way, as a psychodramatic story.

SB: It's also true that music can be spoken of in terms of story. Some music lends itself more to that possibility; we call it "programmatic music." You tell a story, and the music is about that. In Debussy's *La Mer/The Sea*, there are the storms and the peaceful periods. That's a kind of story. And there's even a story dimension in Beethoven. There are themes and, if you can think of the themes as characters, they have interrelationships with each other and then come finally to a resolution. I don't see anything wrong with thinking of film in much the same way. The difference, of course, is that in music the sounds only rarely evoke with exactitude anything audible in the everyday, ordinary world, whereas with film, unless you are painting on film or really working hard to achieve something completely nonobjective, you *are* involved in pictures of things that are nameable.

Last Sunday, at one of our gatherings with friends, Phil Solomon made an interesting critique of narrative drama. He said, "When you see the first shot, very often you have a sense of infinite possibilities; by the time the filmmaker has given you his/her second shot, your possibilities have been reduced to half. And so it goes. A fifth of the way through the movie, you're on a treadmill that leads in an inevitable direction. And that is the limitation of narrative drama." I think that's quite true. He was comparing narrative drama with other modes of making, especially with the more poetic cinema where you can live in the continuous present and can always have an infinite number of possibilities.

SM: That's certainly clear in *Anticipation of the Night*, as compared with your early psychodramas, which have to go somewhere. *Anticipation of the Night* can go where it wants.

SB: I wish I had known that when I was editing! I was so hung up that *this* was the end. Partly, the idea of my suicide gave me the bravery to do all kinds of things with film that at the time were considered absolutely monstrous. Who could even imagine such editing? You almost had to be tilted on the edge of death in order to . . . but then actually I *didn't* have to die, except in the sense that you could say that we will *all* die in the end. So I guess there's nothing terribly wrong that there's a noose at the end of the film.

SM: And since we do die in the end, the challenge is to see what we can see while we can still see it.
SB: I guess I'm at peace with *Anticipation*. But I certainly prefer your way of looking at it.

SM: *Sirius Remembered*, which was made right after *Anticipation*, is still one of my favorites of all your films. And it certainly goes in a very specific direction and has a very specific end, but somehow the development of layer after layer allows for a different kind of visual freedom to take place so that the film doesn't feel limited by its "story."

SB: It also creates empathy for my grieving over the death of a pet; I'm not brooding over my *self*.

SM: Is *Window Water Baby Moving* the most rented of your films?
SB: No. Probably *Mothlight*. *Window Water Baby Moving* is still hard for some people to take.

SM: That's a film I cannot teach without. I show it in nearly every course, partly because it's remarkable how little students know about the body and especially about the female body-in-process. During the sixties, it was hard to imagine that anything could be more conservative than the fifties but, on a certain level of colonizing the body, we may be worse off now than we were in the fifties.
SB: I think so. There was a period when people began to be able to look at *Window Water Baby Moving* and feel it and see it as a film. But then that turned around to a large extent. I don't think this period is quite as bad as the fifties, but to some extent, people are removed from their bodies and, maybe it is getting worse now with the computer, which doesn't sweat, has no saliva, is not sticky, is so unproblematic. There's a science fictionish tendency to stop thinking about the body altogether.

SM: To show, as you do in *Window Water Baby Moving*, that the body is actually a process and that during the process of birth, things flow—many of my students are amazed, shocked; they swear off being parents! Anyway, forty years later it's still one of the most powerful films I can show.
SB: They used to faint. We used to warn people. At almost every show of any size, someone would faint. They didn't crash down, but someone would end up lying on the floor. There was such fear. Whenever I presented the film, I talked to people about it, trying to make it easier for them, advising them to leave the room if they felt they couldn't take it. I don't recall any specific show, but New York City was always a worrisome place for the film. New York had a very uptight, highly developed censorship court, so whenever you showed in New York, you were running a risk, at least until 1963, 1964.

SM: One of the things that makes the film so powerful is that it's silent. Your shift into silent film has to do with a concentration on seeing, but was there a specific point in your life where you just said, "Okay, I'm not going to do sound anymore"?
SB: Gradually it became more and more apparent to me that my abilities as a composer of sound were not keeping up with my abilities as a visionary; sound was tearing the films apart. I was desperately trying to keep up with my burgeoning envisionment, and as the films kept developing visually, I just had to forget

sound. What sound can you put with *Loving*? *Anticipation of the Night* takes courage from that and just says, "Okay, we're just a silent film." Then *Wedlock House: An Intercourse*, and *Window Water Baby Moving* go on from there: sound is hardly conceivable.

But then the question would rise again: *Shouldn't* I have sound? Fortunately, it didn't come up again until almost 1962, with *Blue Moses*, where the sound came first, and the picture is almost an illustration of the sound.

I never wanted to make a polemic against sound, you know. After all, I had done all this studying with Varèse and Cage, and I had great composer friends like Jim Tenney. But I was never capable of achieving adequate sound, except under unusual circumstances where the vision was either deficient or intentionally low yield, the way the visuals in *Blue Moses* are. I was perfectly aware of my own faults, as I had also become aware of my poetic limitations earlier, and had discontinued my pretensions to be a poet. Just because you *want* to write a poem doesn't mean you're going to be able to. It's like *wanting* to be in love. You may want to be, but you either are or you're not.

These days I would want to be almost anything *but* a filmmaker. Who wouldn't? I'm not even sure what a filmmaker is anymore. But I am what I am. It's always a question, do you accept what you are? Are you honest about that? And for me, anyway, the art gets a tremendous strength if one is honest about what one *cannot* do, and I simply couldn't do sound well.

3/23/97

SM: At what point during that first pregnancy did you and Jane know you were making a film? Was it something you set out to do, the minute you found out Jane was pregnant?

SB: It was more complicated than that. First of all, there was a strong desire on Jane's part that I be present during the childbirth, and I wasn't really wanting that burden. I thought I might faint. I rather think I would have had I not been making a film, and something in me knew that. Though that was not exactly how I came to make the film either.

In a way, it was suggested by the doctor: once he learned I was a filmmaker—he assumed a commercial filmmaker—he said, "Well, I always wanted a film of the childbirth process to show to women and their husbands." That's how I was able to come into the delivery room. The hospital, after agreeing at first, reneged on their offer, but the doctor was interested enough in having the film made that he agreed to come to our home. Then we had to hire a nurse and rent some very expensive emergency equipment. It got very complicated, but the possibility of my being in attendance when the child was born was dependent on my filming it.

So naturally enough, aside from whatever the doctor thought I was doing, what type of commercial film he thought I was making, I began wanting images previous to the birth.

SM: When we look at *Window Water Baby Moving*, the domestic seems an idealized, comfortable, generally happy space for you. Is what we're seeing an idealization of what it was? Was there continual strife about the making of the film?

SB: Well, as I said, I really didn't know if I could go through the birth without fainting. I'm not the kind to weather childbirth; but, in fact, two things were very important to Jane: one, that I *be* there and, two, that it be at home; and both of these were very hard to arrange at this time.

I wanted to take some images of Jane in the bathtub showing the pregnancy before the actual birth, and she got very, very shy—understandably. She had never been approached this way before in her life, and very few people have. And in her shyness she said, "Oh, I can't do this." So I said, "Okay, okay," and I tore the film out of the camera and spread it all over the floor and made a big dramatic scene and said, "All right, let's forget it!" And then a half an hour later she bravely relented. She had pulled her courage together and said, "Okay, we'll do this." That's pretty much the way my relationship with her was all along. Then she engaged in the work and even took the camera at the end and photographed *me*.

I would always show the edited sequences to her, not only of that film but of any film I made. I wanted some sense of the feminine to be in my work. I had *enough* to know I wanted more, so I was always open to Jane.

SM: About the material before the birth that we see in the finished film: you went back after Jane relented and filmed again?

SB: Yes. In fact, at that point she was quite open. It became an important bonding for us, too, in the sense that (except in a way in *Wedlock House*, where she was acting), she had never been involved to that degree in one of my films. In some way the idea overwhelmed her at first, and then she realized it was necessary for me, and from that point on, she was open to any photography that I would do.

Her holding the camera at the end of *Window Water Baby Moving* was at her insistence, not mine. I think it's pretty obvious I was too far out of my head to be able to do any directing—she said, "Give me the camera!"

SM: After the birth, how long did it take to put the final film together?

SB: Once I did begin editing, it went rather quickly. I was, as the title suggests, very loosened up and taught in new ways by Gertrude Stein's writing: I've been reading Gertrude Stein since I was about nineteen. She was coming into my aesthetics pretty strongly at that point.

SM: *Window Water Baby Moving* not only gives birth to a new baby but pretty quickly to a whole new sense of who you are as a filmmaker. There's the obvious part—the whole theory of child vision—but also, soon after that film, you begin working on what becomes your first epic, *Dog Star Man*. *Dog Star Man* includes many of the kinds of work you had done up to that point, but it goes much further than just *including* it, it becomes a much larger, more expansive kind of vision. I'm curious about how that project took shape.

SB: A number of things happened. First of all, *Sirius Remembered*, as its title suggests, is rather important here: *Sirius* is the "Dog Star." *Sirius Remembered* was made on the occasion of the death of our family dog. The ground was too frozen to bury Sirius, so we went out into the New Jersey woods with him and just laid him on the ground, so that he could have a natural setting and a going-back-into-the-earth, just like all the wild animals that die in the woods. Then, of course, for a time, I kept visiting his frozen corpse and finally was filming the corpse. So right after the childbirth film we have a consideration of death. Part of the tactic of that film reflected a wish to *revive* that dog (I feel tears coming to my eyes even now as I speak about that moment).

We had not had Sirius very long, but his death immediately followed my punishing him: I spanked him for having licked the new baby, and the next day he managed to get himself run over chasing a car. There was an enormous sense of guilt. I hadn't trusted him enough. I hadn't had *sense* enough to know that it might be all right for him to lick the baby. It might not have been; I might have been absolutely right to do what I did—I don't know. Sometimes a pet *can* be very dangerous to a new baby. In any event, there was not enough sensitivity, and then, coincidentally or because of that, he was dead. So those themes—of birth, of death—reverberated.

Certainly, *Sirius* is a very visceral, physical film that set off in my mind senses of the Dog Star, and therefore Orion, and a whole set of abstractions. But then it was my job to bring these abstractions back to earth, so I have a dog, a star, and a man. And I have a cat, an earth, and a woman. What happens to such an equation? Certain parallel themes started reverberating from what was probably just guilt over the death of this dog. How do you *envision* all that? *Dog Star Man* was almost like an equation, you see, a hieroglyphic, taking shape in the mind.

Sirius was shot in Princeton, New Jersey. It was *edited* in Colorado, while I was starting to shoot *Dog Star Man*.

SM: Is the superimposition in *Sirius* your first use of that technique?
SB: Yes.

SM: It's a beautiful and suggestive film in its use of layers.
SB: *Sirius* was a much more important film than *Window Water Baby Moving* in

terms of my development as a filmmaker. *Window Water Baby Moving* was an anomaly in many ways, in terms of my later filmmaking. I don't mean that as anything *against* it, but it wasn't seminal like *Sirius Remembered* was.

Or, to give another example, you could say that *Nightcats* was seminal in the development of *Anticipation of the Night*. But *Loving*, which came right before *Anticipation of the Night*, I would *not* regard as a seminal work, but more the use of a mastery of certain things put in the service of some necessary revelation. A seminal work, to me, is something that cuts ahead: you don't know where it's going or what it is. *Sirius Remembered* was made in a trance, so I also didn't know really what it was.

We drove cross-country with a lot of footage that was later to be in *Scenes from Under Childhood*, *Sincerity*, *Duplicity*.... I had piles of film, though often I couldn't afford to process it. And I began photographing our life more regularly. So while all these various reverberations off a thread of guilt are twanging in the brain, there's *also* a sense of rooting down, of photographing the *most* mundane things of everyday life, and a developing sense that there must be some relationship between the two.

Arthur Eddington's *The Nature of the Physical World* was an important book for me at this time. A number of science books began being important to me, and I subscribed to *Scientific American* for several years. Gertrude Stein was continuing to be more and more important, and also Pound and Joyce. The epic structures of the longer films began taking shape.

At any rate, here we were back in Colorado, living in my wife's parents' house in the mountains, and at some point I asked them, "What can I do to help out?" Jane's mother and father were teachers, and Jane had the baby, which was *her* life's work; and for a while I couldn't get a job of any kind. Her parents suggested I collect firewood. That became my job, and I did collect enough firewood so that they were still burning it five or six years later. Then I began sensing that the central character of a film could be a woodsman—the woodsman is certainly a central character in many fairy tales—and I began photographing myself. Then I *did* get a job, which was to make two films based on Colorado legends—one about the Utes [*The Ballad of the Colorado Ute*] and another about a couple of miners who fought over some gold [*The Colorado Legend*]—so suddenly I had the use of expensive camera equipment and film at below cost. Because I was doing these commercial films, I had a way to be working on *Dog Star Man*. And I was reading a lot of mythology: Graves's *The Greek Myths*, and so on.

SM: I always think of Sisyphus when I see you climbing up that hill—
SB: Yes, he was certainly a primary figure in my mind, but I wanted to embody legends from around the world. I was reading the Norse legends of Gilgamesh, and

so on. My sense of it, in my bitterness, and there was coming to be a lot of bitterness in me by this time (despite the baby and my second baby coming and all that could have made life more joyful), was that the tree—the mythic structure, the metaphor for human culture—was dead, and all that it would be useful for was to chop up and burn for firewood. In a way, the story of *Dog Star Man* is a simplistic, embittered statement, something that someone might toss off at a bar, getting drunk. Remember, I was living in my wife's *parents'* house as a creature that they did *not* understand at all. I was *completely* suppressed in every part of my life except the filmmaking. And looking around me—we were coming out of the fifties, one of the most awful, intolerant times in the twentieth century—whatever felt brave or heroic *to me*, either culturally or aesthetically, seemed to be completely strange to the world around me.

SM: It's easy to read this Sisyphus-like climb up the mountain as an attempt to drag film up onto the mountain and make it an art equal to other arts.
SB: Well, that was certainly *always* in my mind, but the way I would have put it is that film was an art—from Méliès on, we had had obvious signs—and by now that ought to have been clear enough, though there *were* problems about how to make it *last*.

SM: *Dog Star Man* has a very unusual structure that is evident even in the catalogue description of the film: *Prelude* is twenty-five minutes, *Part I* is thirty minutes, while *Part II*, *Part III*, and *Part IV* are quite brief (seven minutes, eleven minutes, and five minutes, respectively). I'm curious about how that structure developed.
SB: Well, I had a belief in the compound. When you do lay out all the possible combinations of the superimpositions in those last three parts, of the A, B, and A, B, C, and A, B, C, and D rolls that are used in *Parts II, III,* and *IV* you *do* get a proportion that is more classical. In other words, I start with the *Prelude*, which was put together just by a variety of chance operations—I was operating under some of Cage's ideas about chance to try to create a dreamscape of the mind, to get a spill of the unconscious. I had a sense of the unconscious, not so much in the Freudian or psychoanalytic sense but as a chaotic world of chance operations.

Now, we all know that it's very Freudian to understand that things that you pass by quickly during the day, things you don't even notice, can create your dreams for that night, and as they do so, they can, and quite ordinarily do, reach back and touch your most ancient memories. But my sense was *also* that that *dream* you are having is affecting the whole *next* day. So *Prelude* is the dream; then comes *Part I*, which is the actual attempt to climb this mountain. Of course, the mountain by this time has been so photographed and edited that, for one thing, its trees recapitulate, rather subtly, too subtly for most people, the history of human architecture and suggest Greek pillars at one point and Gothic stained glass windows at another. But all the way through, as this man climbs, there is an attempt to mimic the mud hut, the log cabin, the cathedral, eventually even the skyscraper. It is very important to me, by the way, that the Dog Star Man never climbs to the *top*, only somewhere up there, and this is after falling down, and the Armageddon of the forest fire (which *was* a real forest fire, by the way. I had to go and fight it, and when I finished fighting it with all my neighbors, *then* I photographed).

As you come to the later sections, things get more complicated. *Part I* has a lot of poetic complexity going on in it, and multiple meanings, but it's *dominated* by a narrative, so it goes along telling its tale, and everything is in the service of the tale of that climb up toward the plateau. *Part IV* suggests much more complex meanings. If one doesn't think *Part IV* is long enough, one could run it again and again and again.

Let me put it this way: as you add more layers, more rolls of superimposition, and if everything is stitched together in *meaning*, then *complexity* ought to be equal to *length*. Maybe you could say it's the difference between prose and poetry. Even an epic poem is always struggling to be brief, on the one hand, and to be Truth, which we know is full of complexity, on the other hand. What is great about a poem is that there are multiple layers of meaning so interlocked with each other that you could say *that* is the most exact and complete meaning that we can manage with language. In poetry a word will mean *exactly* something, something that could be thirty-five or fifty different things simultaneously, but then *that* will have exhausted that particular but complex meaning. And that one word is all tangled with all the other words that it is in alignment with, and all *their* alternative meanings.

This has always been my sense of working with superimposition, beginning with *Sirius Remembered*. In every superimposition you have an exact, finite number of possible meanings, far more than any single layer could produce. And so, each of the combinations of pictures in superimposition ought to be equal to a much longer, single, unlayered strand of image. The later sections of *Dog Star Man* may seem shorter, but once you begin to explore the many layers and the connections between them, what may seem to be short becomes far more substantial.

Fred Camper has always much preferred *The Art of Vision* to *Dog Star Man* because it *does* use a more classically proportioned presentation of the *Dog Star Man* material. All of the material is laid out at length; and when you show all the possible combinations of the four layers of superimposition possible with those four rolls, *Part IV* is about an hour and a quarter.

Another interesting question is, what is *The Art of Vision* vis-à-vis *Dog Star Man*? Is it a work that's become finally more outer than inner?

SM: Could you talk about the sources of the other kinds of imagery in the film, especially the scientific imagery: the blood flowing and the images of the sun?

SB: The next project that helped me make a living, while working on *Dog Star Man*, was a film for the physicist George Gamow, who was teaching at the University of Colorado. I had gotten to be, and still am, close friends with his son, Igor Gamow. He and I together photographed through a bat's wing to get the blood cells moving through the veins and arteries.

SM: So you actually did that filming yourself? I've always assumed it was educational found footage.

SB: No, that was my footage. I also went to the slaughterhouse and got some sheep hearts, which are the closest to the human, and Igor wore them like a glove and operated the valves—that's how I got *that* material.

The only thing that I *didn't* photograph in *Dog Star Man* are the high-altitude observatory images of solar flares. It was important to me that, among the other myths that were operative in this work, the life and death of a star as scientists picture it—*their* myth—be included. I have always viewed science as another set of myths, which are constantly changing. In order to use those images, I had to justify that they were being used correctly according to scientific views. It was quite a day when I went up to the high-altitude observatory and showed *Dog Star Man* with all these scientists gathered around, expecting another science film. I defended it on a symbolic and mythic level.

SM: What was their reaction?

SB: They were charmed and excited, and immediately gave me permission to use their footage. I got to know quite a number of scientists through George; that was always going on quite consciously in relationship to all the reading I was doing. I did not want the literary to dominate *Dog Star Man*, so in every way possible I am clashing symbols so that they reverberate. I wouldn't say it's an antisymbolic work because it *is* using symbols, but it's using them to "make it new," as Ezra Pound would put it.

There is also a lot of astronomy in the film. Someone (an amateur who had done a lot of stop-motion photography of clouds and stars) gave me a couple of Rube Goldberg–like boxes that allowed you to set your camera to make time-lapse material. That's my time-lapsed photography of the stars in the film. The moon was photographed through a child's telescope just jammed up into the lens, and opening up and photographing, with a lot of luck.

And then, the main thing, to me, was to get the film down to earth, to daily living, so that's why you have all the images of the man and the woman and the baby at the hearth. That's what the wood is going to be chopped up *for*: to burn in that fireplace and warm that baby.

6/3/97

SM: I'm interested in talking about *Scenes from Under Childhood*. One general question that comes up when I'm talking about those films with students is, how did this idea about child vision develop? And to what extent was it a function of seeing your own children born and watching what they were experiencing as they grew?

SB: It was very largely that. I was very involved with the children and, at one point, was horrified to realize that I was guilty of what I came to call the "Shirley Temple syndrome": in other words, of finding them very cute and thinking of their lives as bucolic and happier than mine—in other words, not meeting them on the level of their own lives. And at that point I decided to start photographing them, because *that* enabled me to see more deeply into what they *were*. I had this sense in the back of my mind that a film might come out of it, but that was not the initial impulse. I wanted to *see* their world.

Now, I also understood that you can never really see inside another person's world; so at the same time that I'm looking at *them*, I'm remembering, as best I can, my own childhood. *Scenes from Under Childhood* arises out of a superimposition of those two things. My children were providing tender material, which I gathered; and as it came into the camera though the lens and later, during the editing process, my memories of my own childhood were sparked by their activities and in one way and another found their way into the films.

SM: The catalogue description of *Section 1* mentions fetal beginnings. I'm not clear how fully the four sections are meant to represent a chronology. Were you thinking that *Section 1* covers the transition from before birth to just after birth?
SB: Well, not exactly. *Section 1* envisions fetal beginnings in the same way you might say something invokes something. And it seems a little odd, but you could say it is *me* remembering *them* remembering something of their fetal beginnings; or, better still, myself *imagining* them remembering fetal beginnings *and* also remembering some sense of such a thing in myself. My feeling is—though I have no way to prove it—that children close to their births are actually remembering something of their life in the womb and the birth itself, whereas adults can only imagine it—though some adults do claim they have a sense of these experiences.

SM: Are you also conjecturing that, especially in the final months of prenatal development, babies see in the same way that we have closed-eye vision?
SB: Yes. What we call "closed-eye vision" is for me the template in the mind upon which all further formative envisionment is to occur. So there is an outside limit to human seeing, which is implicit already in the womb.

My sense of that is fortified by scientific experiments that have shown that there is rapid eye movement in fetus eyes, very similar to the REM movement of dreaming in adults and in children, too, for that matter. The fetus can be said to dream, and it seems reasonable that very young children could be remembering something of their dreams in the womb. When children are very young, they remember things from a year or two earlier rather remarkably, and then there comes, gradually, a period where they don't remember much about the first several years. A four-year-old will remember a great deal of his or her one-, two-, or three-year-old life. Later, that is reduced to a very few scenes. I think it's because there is such a catastrophic shift in the psyche at that point.

SM: As a result of learning words, language.
SB: And the various other restrictions on the free flow of memory.

SM: When I've taught *Scenes from Under Childhood*, I've usually suggested that the opening passages of *Section 1*, where we're just seeing colors—very bright reds and then increasing varieties of color—have to do with the eyes adjusting to the overwhelming reality of light. After the womb, the sun would be incredible, shocking. The color red that dominates those early moments of the film has always struck me as the same color I see when I look at the sun with my eyes closed.
SB: Yes. You've got exactly what I felt I was doing.

SM: Did you finish *Section 1* before you did *Section 2* and so forth? It looks to me as if 2 and 3 were done almost in tandem.
SB: Well, the same fund of material, which by this time had gotten to be five or six thousand feet of film, was being drawn on. In those days, unless something had a quality of envisionment that had been exhausted in some earlier work, I would save it rather than throw it away. So, yes, essentially, the sections are chronological; they're trying to show the progressive growing up of the children.

SM: Recently, when I was looking at *Sections 2* and *3*—and this had not struck me before—the color range seemed to change. *Section 2* tends toward reds, and *Section 3* tends toward blues and greens. There also seemed to be other echoes between those two sections that aren't relevant in Sections 1 or 4.
SB: What you said about *Section 1*—that it traces a recognition of the subtleties of colors coming out of this reddish field, which is like closed-eye vision of the sun (plus what I call the remembrance of womb life)—distinguishes that section. If you remember, the baby in that section is in an almost fetal position created by the distorting glass through which she is photographed. And so, all of *Section 1* is kind of a separating out of colors, a variety of colors, within this reddish field.

Similarly, you could say that each successive section has certain biases of color, until you get to the fourth part, which has a wide spread of color, most obvious in the towel scene, where the various colored towels are going into blanks of color. There's an increasing accent on color recognition.

Also, in that fourth section I come to a suggestion of the larger world, with the city scenes at the end, the baseball, the model airplane.

SM: Is some of the city material in *Section 4* actual home-movie material from your youth?
SB: No, but that's a wonderful compliment! I did shoot it as an adult, but, of course, the main drive of this film is to give that sense of time travel, as if I were drawing from the inside of my brain the styles and qualities of life of my growing-up period. I'm delighted that you felt as if that imagery might have been photographed when I was young.

SM: Even the cars participate; they don't look like late-sixties cars.
SB: That would not have been a conscious thing, but unconsciously I'm sure I was trying to exclude anything that might look too flashily up-to-date. The model airplane certainly was something that began to be a fashion when I was very young. Also, the scene where the two boys hold the little model cars they are playing with against their penises is a suggestion of transition to adult empowerment, both physically and mechanically. So there are all those suggestions that permit *Section 4* to provide a closure appropriate to *Scenes from Under Childhood*.

SM: The film ends with photographs of buildings. Are *those* childhood photographs?
SB: Those are from my childhood, yes.

SM: Your films are the family movies maybe we wish we had.
SB: Or do we? You may think you wish you had them, but the interesting thing is that my grown children are not very involved in looking at those films.

SM: Were they ever?
SB: Not really. They'd look at them when they came out, and that seemed okay. It was a normal part of their growing up, a daily activity. But they haven't shown much interest in their own photographed lives as children. Occasionally, they will ask to see the births, but otherwise they are not really interested—because, in a way, it isn't really *their* childhood. *They* are not remembering their childhood the way *I* was imagining them. The films confront them with *my* feelings about *my* own development, which they are only the occasion for.

And by the way, that was quite conscious. When I first started photographing, I got down on the floor and was rolling around with them with the camera, but I realized quickly that that was too much the Shirley Temple syndrome. So you'll notice that, pretty consistently throughout all of the footage in *Scenes from Under Childhood*, the viewpoint is slightly above and looking down at the children, to keep that sense that this is *adult* envisionment, and that it is affected by and affects the quality of the *maker's* childhood coming through and coloring, shaping, twisting the forms—through apple jugs or whatever—into the production of an aesthetic.

SM: You may find that as your kids get older, they'll get more interested. My son also doesn't go into the drawers where the images of his childhood are, but I think at a certain point he may become interested in reaccessing that material.

SB: Perhaps you're right. We'll see. I continue to be interested in it, even in my own photographic representation in it, and I marvel as I look at the images and remember.

When I began to take *Scenes from Under Childhood* on college lecture tours, I noticed that college-age people have *never* cared for this work. After talking to a number of people, I deduced that maybe it's because they're still too close to that period of their lives and *don't* want to remember. They're trying to climb up *out* of childhood. *Scenes from Under Childhood*—unlike almost all envisionments of childhood, which are sugarcoated and nostalgic, and presented within a general aura that things were better then than they are now and that the soul was cleaner or purer in childhood—stands *absolutely* against that, and it gets some of its inspiration for doing that from Schumann, and, of course, from Freud, and from many other sources.

My own sense of it is that *to the children* childhood is very hard, gruesome, an often utterly impossible world, just as adulthood is for adults. Children are in a state of almost constant terror, mixed with hysterical happiness, which can also be terrifying in an instant. And childhood is grubby, and they sit sometimes as if in a haze (*Section* 3 particularly is just this haze of repetitive slight shifts of tone and color) for long, dull periods, which people tend to connect with school but, in fact, are equally prevalent in home life. At home kids just sit around: "Mommy, there's nothing to *do*." The fact is that very often there *is* nothing to do; everything *is* boring.

SM: I think that most people would assume that what *you* mean by the slower passages—I mean all the way through the film—has to do with the child's being more perceptive of the specific phenomena around him or her, not that it's boring or terrifying.

SB: But that's exactly, from my viewpoint, what you *do* with boredom. You sink into it; you begin to be aware of the slight subtleties that are left in the gray field. The only thing that can be done with the dull civilization we are now having is to be fascinated by the *endless* riches of variance within the dullest, grayest field.

1/30/02

SM: How did the Pittsburgh trilogy evolve?
SB: Sally Dixon, when she was head of film programming at the Carnegie Museum, brought me in as a lecturer. She and her friend Mike Chikiris (a photographer for one of the local newspapers) picked me up at the airport and were asking me about films I wanted to make. I told them I had just tried to arrange to be in a police car in Boulder for several days, to photograph the ordinary, everyday activities of the police. I felt that the police were very maligned and that they weren't appreciated for what they primarily did. I wanted to try and *see* for myself if maybe they *were* as monstrous as many of my hippie friends told me they were. But I suspected maybe not, probably not. Certainly I, who was always subject to bullies, wouldn't want to live in a world in which there were no police to go to for protection. So I was open, but at the same time, had a healthy paranoia about police—from use of police by mainstream society to put down protests and rebellions, from the beatings.

SM: At this point, the only film imagined was a police film?
SB: Yes. For some reason, I still remember also telling Sally and Mike that it was a big mistake for NASA not to send an artist to the moon, because all the pictures we were seeing were so dumb—like bad B-movie science fiction, Flash Gordon. I said you've got to remember that Columbus had Americus on his ship, after whom our country is named. Americus was the cartographer and also the one who made pictures so that people could have a sense of what had been discovered.

It turned out that Sally had connections, and she arranged for me to ride around in a police car, go into a hospital—on a later trip—and finally into the morgue. The hospital was very open and excited, so long as I had signed releases from everyone who was photographed. The only similar complexity with the morgue was that I could not photograph the face of a corpse in a way that it would allow it to be recognized. And I understood that, perfectly well, and found it not too difficult a prescription.

SM: When you were going into these institutions, it was still fairly unusual.
SB: Forbidden.

SM: Now it's hard to channel surf without seeing an operation or a police show.
SB: Though I haven't seen one of those that can match *these* films. My secret was that I wasn't after what was making society so nervous, I was after an art. And all three situations provided me with the occasion to make art, and art that related to my own experiences: my own fear of police, and my dependency on them; my hospital experiences. I'd be dead many times over were it not for doctors and hospitals. Even at that time, I'd been in danger of death six or seven times. Like the people who gave the process its beautiful name—"autopsis" literally means "the act of seeing with one's own eyes"—*I needed* to *see* these things, to see something of what it *was* to be just turned into furniture meat. After experiencing several days of photographing autopsies, I felt that suicide would be very difficult, if not impossible. There's something sadly ridiculous about the dead, and why would you turn this complexity of a wondrous human possibility into a hulk of decaying matter?

SM: The structure of the three films varies. Both *Eyes* and *Deus Ex* seem to echo a day/night/day round-the-clock schedule. I've always figured that *The Act of Seeing with One's Own Eyes* was a much more difficult film for you than the other two—
SB: Oh, much more difficult.

SM: And that, as a result, its trajectory seems more involved with your coming to grips with the experience of being in the morgue.
SB: But I think day/night/day *is* reflected in *The Act of Seeing*, just more subtly. If you recall, there are bright, almost overexposed images where the white sheets and flashes of the still camera that someone's using create a lot of bright color; *and* there are also these dark areas, where the shutter closes up, and it's almost like falling into the pit of someone's chest, or whatever. There are lapses into the dark, almost like fainting, and I was *close* to fainting very often during the making of that film. Part of the process of the film as an aesthetic structure is to allow the viewers to manage to accept what they're shown, so they can continue to watch.

SM: Near the end you seem to have a kind of epiphany and become almost a child yourself in the excitement of exploring what seem to me to be landscapes. The camera becomes a plane swooping through these strange formations.
SB: Oh, I'm glad for that. To me one thing that saves the film is this little tiny bit of reflected sky that's caught in a little puddle of liquid in the armpit of a corpse—a little blue ephemeral thing that can stand for all of Spirit, which otherwise would be missing.

Also, I think it's funny that at the end a little man in a little bow tie is seen reciting all this horror into a tape recorder. He turns it off, and the film is over. *The*

Act of Seeing is full of jokes like that—it's black humor to be sure, but humor. The fly crawling on a toe. Or the zipping up of the body bag soon after a knife comes down and "unzips" a whole torso. Those moments are there to lighten the load of watching.

SM: At what point did you think there would be a trilogy?

SB: I knew by the time I was doing the third film that they would go together, and originally I thought there would be more. At first, I was thinking things like, "Oh, I should do *firemen* now." And there were attempts made to try to secure me a chance to film basketball, football, and other kinds of major social events. These would have been okay to do but wouldn't have had to do *at all* with what my deep unconscious had already recognized as three films that go together and that do not need anything else.

The trilogy begins with the police, who do what it is that the rest of us forgo doing: they go and deal with the misery and the blood and the suicides and the murders and the trash. We've hired these people to do that job, rather than reach out to our neighbors. They're the *eyes* of the society. I had a sense that there's the private eye and there's the public eye. These are the public eyes. "*Polis* means eyes," from Charles Olson, was also important to me.

Then you have the hospital, a stand-in for God—as you know, in Greek drama, when the playwright doesn't know what else to do, he brings in the *deus ex machina*: actors were swung out over the Greek stage and lowered onto the stage, where they spoke for the gods. In a way, our modern equivalent of that is the hospital. Watching the doctors, you almost get a sense of the Church. I feel that these hands moving to rescue this poor broken heart are kind of an epiphany of religious/spiritual feeling.

SM: I like your metaphor in the Canyon Cinema catalogue of an Aztec ritual: the long shots of the operating-room work as a kind of elaborate ritual—

SB: Except that instead of tearing the heart out; they're trying to revive it. And then the third film is about the idea that nothing shall have died without our knowing why. The trilogy makes a circle at this point, because almost all murderers are caught by the autopsies. Usually, murderers make every attempt to disguise that a murder has even occurred. Many times, we wouldn't know there was murder at all without autopsy.

SM: Have you always thought of these films as documentaries? I see more and more documentary historians including you.

SB: I always have, and for a while I hoped to be allowed to present my films at the Flaherty Seminar, in fact, Ricky Leacock, no less, fought for me, but we never got anywhere. Now I'm gradually winning the argument. I always had a documentary streak in me, and in fact, my biggest argument with P. Adams [Sitney] was about this issue. I said, "I am *foremost* a documentarian, among all the other things you might call me, because I photograph not only what's out there, but the act of seeing it. I'm documenting the very process whereby something is perceived." He always argued with that. He needed to keep the outside and the inside separate, I guess. I love that you have the sense at the end of *The Act of Seeing* that it's landscape. There are wondrous landscapes inside this body, and it's a terrain that, yes, we need to *see*.

4/12/99

SM: At the moment when you made *The Text of Light*, what was happening for you?
SB: All during 1974 I was involved with light, even in *Dominion*, which is a portrait of the American businessman Gordon Rosenblum, who owned the ashtray with which I photographed *The Text of Light*. I had known him since high school. Now, in *my* mind his "dominion," what he was lord of, was really some light moving across his desk. That's putting it far too simplistically, but you get what I mean.

SM: When you began *The Text of Light*, did you know this was going to be a single large project?
SB: No. I'd had a hard time shooting *Dominion*. Gordon was very uptight, and I was trying to get an image of him behind his desk in his office with the macro lens. I don't even know why I put that on, except that I was trying anything and everything. I was pretty desperate because it felt like a rare opportunity to get a portrait of a man of economic power. The same impulse had earlier sent me to do "the Pittsburgh trilogy" and would later result in *The Governor*. So there I was, struggling. This macro lens kind of sags down onto his desk, and I remember it had a little bellows, and even the bellows kind of sagged down. And only because I had the habit of looking through a camera before I moved it (I often got gifts that way), I peeked into it and saw a whole forest of glassine trees. I looked up and said to Gordon, "My God, what I'm seeing is incredible. I don't know how this is happening!" I looked again, and this forest had changed slightly. And we finally figured out that it was light bouncing off the glass across his desk from underneath his glass ashtray. Then, as we watched, a little river seemed to appear and flow through it. I said, "Oh my God!" I didn't do any thinking at all, I just gave up on the one project and started on the other. (I went back later and made *Dominion*.) Anyway, I'm in there with this camera, taking individual frames. Finally, over a period of time I accumulated several pieces of glass, all kinds of glass, and arranged them near this very fine crystal ashtray. I could move through the whole spectrum by shifting

and adjusting pieces of glass. There were crystal glasses, and a cheap knickknack glass ball with some indentations on it, and the secretary would bring in this or that from her knickknack shelf, and we'd try it for a while. Some things were useful, most things weren't. I was always shooting into the ashtray, never into any of the other glass. These other kinds of glass were used to give me ways to affect the interior of this ashtray.

SM: Did you shoot the whole film in his office?
SB: All in his office. His office had windows all around the side so that you had the sun all day long as you moved from window to window. In the morning you got the early morning sun at one end of the building, and at sunset you would end up in the kitchen at the back with the sun setting. I moved the pieces of glass from window to window. A lot of the time I just used the ashtray, but I also had all these other objects to draw on.

SM: How often did you shoot?
SB: I would start shooting in the morning, usually. I had been in the habit of staying overnight at his office, which had a little guest room. I just began staying there rather regularly and would get up in the morning, start photographing, and then move from window to window and end up in the kitchen and have supper. It was a time of great ecstasy because the visions that were given to me through this process were just as you see.

The first shots I got back seemed way too smooth, and I never used them. What I began to do—we're talking daylight Kodachrome here—is to tap. The camera was screwed down with U joints, and I loosened those slightly, and by tapping slightly at the edge of the lens I could get it to move just a fraction to the left, then take a few frames, then a fraction more to the left and take a few more, and then tap it back the other way—so that the results had a handheld quality. A little way into the film I began thinking of it as a world, and just in order to hold my sensibilities together, I began thinking of myself as passing across a planet something like our own, but not entirely like ours, passing through its four seasons, and its mountainous and forested areas, and so on.

I wanted the film to be rough, not smooth and locked down. I owned a gadget with a timer that would have allowed me to just click off frames, but I couldn't bring myself to use it.

Later, a lot of people thought, "It's rough because he's using inferior equipment," but that wasn't it at all. The roughness was very hard work: I had to try and imagine how many shifts to the left and then back to the right would be feasible within a minute without the result looking just jerky. Very few, right? I had to spread each visual development out over several minutes of film running time, which was actually an hour and a half of shooting time or more.

SM: Were you always looking through the camera as you did this?
SB: Yes. And just to keep from going nuts—because in some cases I wanted more change than you could get if you were sitting there shooting frames constantly—I would often have a book, and be reading. I'd take a frame and would have a rough sense of how much more reading I could do, seven or eight sentences or maybe a paragraph, before exposing the next frame and creating a certain, subtle visual development. I read half a dozen books while I was making *The Text of Light*, but I was always looking when I took a frame.

SM: How close was what you were seeing through the camera to what you ended up having?
SB: Very close, for two reasons. First, I had real saturation because I was shooting one frame at a time, and second, I was using Kodachrome, and I had come to know Kodachrome like the back of my hand. Anyone could get an expensive ashtray or even any drinking glass with a thick bottom and try the same thing. If you look deep into the glass, holding it where the light can come through, it will begin to reveal the world of *The Text of Light*.

SM: How long were you shooting in Rosenblum's office?
SB: Most of a year. And then I took another year to edit.

SM: How much of what you shot ended up in the finished piece?
SB: You know, I don't really remember. My rough guess is about half. Again, there was gorgeous and glorious footage which I destroyed pretty quickly after I finished editing, because I thought that the temptation would be too great to go and make *Text of Light II*, *Text of Light Meets the Wolfman*, whatever.

SM: I was reading your little essay on Jim Davis last night and you draw an interesting comparison between Davis's light and yours: your light is always on some level embodied, whereas his light seems disembodied. Davis's light is *real*, but it's also almost entirely abstract, whereas the light in *The Text of Light* always seems connected with something material: it's light that's been transmogrified by bouncing off a physical reality.
SB: I think that's an interesting distinction. Of course, as you know, Jim inspired *The Text of Light*. I think I might never have made it without him, and that's why I dedicated it to him.

In the end I came to see Jim's films as a meditation on the imagination of light.

SM: One of the things you talk about in your essay on Davis is your being tied to the history of Western art. It's certainly true watching *The Text of Light*. I'm always thinking, "Oh that looks like Munch's sky above *The Scream*."

SB: Or Turner, who I think is a major inspiration on that film. As was true for *The Wold Shadow*, the film that got me back into painting, *The Text of Light* is almost a history of Western painting. The second-to-last shot, for example, is almost Clyfford Still. The last shot is more ambiguous and allows the film to end. But *The Text of Light* is partly a history of Western landscape painting and means to carry that tradition on, the way *Dog Star Man* is thrashing about within the history of architecture.

SM: As you edited *The Text of Light*, you had a considerable amount of material—

SB: That was one of the toughest films ever to edit.

SM: So how are you keeping this huge piece in your head? It's wonderful to watch, but to remember the specifics, moment by moment . . .

SB: This may be why the seasons come to be a way of structuring music and other forms, because if you've got four seasons, that gives you something to hold on to. Certain things in *The Text of Light* look like winter, certain things look like spring. Of course, spring and summer can also look very similar, but there's a kind of a gold and a heat that's characteristic of summer and so on. So that gives you a way to distinguish footage—not all of it, but a lot of it. *The Text of Light* starts in late fall and moves into early winter; another section starts in deep summer and moves into early fall. Each movement includes the end of one season and the beginning of another. There is also a movement down from a kind of rocky prominence into more icy waterways that are melting, and finally into swamps. These were ways to hold onto the material and keep from going totally crazy. Now I wouldn't have had to do it that way, but I think these structures are comforting to audiences; it's harder for them when you're into pure visual music.

SM: Did you score it at all?

SB: Oh, I always have a tendency to write quite elaborate notes on the boxes of film and to draw sketches, like you find in *Metaphors on Vision*, apropos of *Anticipation of the Night*. I haven't kept all that stuff because I feel I made that process clear in *Metaphors of Vision*. There's no point in putting people through the process over and over again, with every film. But I do need to find ways to help me hold things together. In a long work like *The Text of Light*, you're risking insanity.

    I also depend upon the film to tell where it's supposed to go. A lot of the making really is just that. Something needs something else, and I'm searching, searching, searching, and suddenly, *there's* something that seems to *be* what's needed there, so I try to put it there, and it doesn't have the right rhythm. So then I go back and search and search and search and find another thing that seems like it should be there, and this one also has the right rhythm—but not the right color; it doesn't work with the melody of color that the sequence has set up. I go on searching, searching, searching, and finally all of *these* things are satisfied, but it looks like a *tree* where we haven't introduced it. More searching. You can truly go mad. And then suddenly you might find fifteen things in a row that just go together perfectly. And here's the hard part: you're holding in mind also, for a year or at least for many months, certain formal imperatives that have to be accounted for before you end, in order for the work to be entirely cohesive. At the end of *The Text of Light* I reveal a globe—not the ashtray, just a globe that came along during the process. It's the symbol of this cohesiveness.

Another Way of Looking at the Universe

Ronald Johnson (with Jim Shedden) / 1997

From *Chicago Review* 47, no. 4 (Winter 2001) and 48, no. 1 (Spring 2002): 31–37. Reprinted by permission.

Stan Brakhage: There are some who would caution us about our use of language, who would say that there's no point in saying things like "primordial," that it's ridiculous to talk about a camera that's invented in the late nineteenth century and a projection mode and so on, and then to talk about how it's touching the primordial mind—they'd tell us it's absurd.
Ronald Johnson: Well, we've still got at the base of the spine that reptilian brain, so everybody's brain still goes back to the beginning of time. I don't see why we can't use "primordial."
SB: And I could make the case that film just by the very fact that it was invented within the last century, or just a century ago—is beginning at a beginning, is fit to begin where anything began. And its closest kinship is cave painting. It's at a cave painting stage at best in its development.

RJ: That's one of the reasons that Guy Davenport is so fascinated by the cave paintings. Suddenly we realized that art itself was a human thing, that went all the way back. It's always been there. Man has always been gifted to articulate his perception of the universe in a very graceful and perceptive way from the very beginning.
SB: Why do you suppose?

RJ: I don't believe necessarily in God; I believe in a transcendence or something. I believe that brains were made to communicate with the universe. Life was always tending towards the human brain, so that the universe could start talking to itself. And the cave paintings make that very clear, because they're very technically agile and can handle certain things very well. Of course they were looking at animals, and lived in an animistic universe. And art became a conversation with their world.

SB: I don't want to overstate this case, because I'm living and enjoying much and appreciating nature, and my films show how much I deeply care. I'm paying homage to and re-presenting nature as one aspect of my work, and creating anew in thanks for what's been given to me. But also there is that thing I have—my sense of those cave beginnings, or any kid making a collection and storing it somewhere in the attic, hiding it, showing it maybe to his or her closest friend: all that is the anomaly of being human and being at odds with the given phenomenological world. So that's my feeling of it.

Jim Shedden: Stan, you were talking last night about incomplete literary epics, and suggesting that incompletion was part of the form. How about film cycles or film epics—have you finished any of yours?
SB: Yeah. *Dog Star Man*, and its fulsome spread as *The Art of Vision*. *Scenes from Under Childhood* is unfinished. It cost so much, and the grant was taken away, so I had to back up and kind of put an ending on it, and abandon it, so it's unfinished.

JS: You once divided your work into "The Book of Film," "The Book of Family," and so on.
SB: People always made the mistake of labeling me as the mountain-hero-family man. And even across that period when Jane and I were together, when I made so many of those films, only a third of my work had anything to do with family. The rest of it—two thirds of it—was about many other subjects, about things that I was encountering on the road, or even up there. So at some point I had a sense of what could be called a book—in the sense that you can call a cathedral a book—what could be called "A Book of Family."

"The Book of Film" is where film presents that that only film could present, that's not leaning on picture or reproduction or anything, that by grace of thanks for all that's been given to me, for all the pictures that I've had across my life, that there come from me things that could only come from me that's given back in thanks like a little bouquet in the night, of the unnamable, the ineffable. And so in that sense, all of what other people would call my abstract films, which as you know I don't regard as abstract at all, are the most concrete pieces of my making, because they come most directly from my synapses and my thinking. The sense of style, just like people can tell the difference between my signature and anybody else's, is unique to me. And not for anything that I need to be proud of just that when I etch, as I'm now doing on film, my signature is integral with that making, not out of some school training or look-ma-no-hands, or how-smart-I-am, but because that's the me that was given to me to be.

RJ: That's one of the reasons that I put the palm print in *ARK*—
SB: Yes, that's so beautiful.

RJ: —so that they could read my palm anytime that that's still reproduced. It's also the entry of Orphée, Cocteau's *Orphée*, into the underworld. He puts his hand out into the mercury to go into the underworld. That palm print is me and nobody else.

SB: And also that's one of the earliest things that we have from our ancestors. I mean imagine taking a straw and blowing dye through it on the cave wall leaving your hand print just like that, like you have in the book, fingers splayed, just like that, on the wall, sprayed around by blown paint, with the dawn of the human. Last night, after everything was over, Nick Dorsky was the only one that saw that when the going really gets rough in *A Child's Garden and the Serious Sea*, that is, when we're sunk in all this adulthoodedness, and the child's imagination is trying to make it leap into some semblance of flower, something fit to weave with the sea, Nick saw that my hand starts becoming integral in the lens. You can see parts and bits and pieces and shadows of my hand blocking things out, stopping them, so my hand comes in to shape, to struggle with and grapple literally with the environs. And Nick saw it come to this point where, and I agree, where Eden *does* get restored. But it's not as it was before, it's now more remembered. It's there amidst a series of emblematic pictures, like the child and the man and the boat and the crow. It's not as it was. It's remembered, and it's among a series of things.

RJ: *Paradise Regained*. Nothing is never the same.

SB: Yeah, in essence. But isn't that what you're working with in *RADI OS*? You may have, and I'm so grateful you do, and I'm envious in a way, a happier sense of the universe than I—but Milton did not.

RJ: No. But he was telling a biblical myth, I wasn't. Blake rewriting *Paradise Lost* had another thing too; he didn't believe old Nobodaddy was God. Blake is definitely an influence with me: you see things and create things, and that is paradise.

SB: What about "No ideas but in things"?

RJ: Oh, I believe that.

SB: I can't, you see. I work with ephemera. I can take pictures of them but they remain forever representations. I did try very hard, and took the kinds of pictures that would be supportive or inspired by the concepts of Williams's "No ideas but in things," but in fact it's not that applicable to film, whose nature is to be fleeting and moving on. It's a weave of light that's forever dissolving.

RJ: I've written a piece called "Hurrah for Euphony" for a young poet, where I say, "Poetry is quick with specifics." "Quick" points to "the quick and the dead." When you get the specific things, that's where poetry is alive.

SB: That's where film starts becoming picture, or illustration, so that's a danger for film as I see it. But what film can do is lift these specifics so they can be made to reverberate. You can create inferences, since the eye is always roving. The eye is *very* open to a reverberating spread of what we would call metaphor, I guess, in language, open to a multiplicity of visual means, but not an endless multiplicity. There's a skein or a net of great exactitude. So you can't say one can come and see anything into it because that's just a mess. But within that exactitude this spread is available to a wide variety of individual approaches, each given time. Or a person can across a lifetime, as I hope, see the same film over and over again, and see now this aspect of it and now that, and finally have the whole complexity of it.

RJ: There are a lot of people out there—we're differentiated as artists—but there are people who don't ever really see things as they are. These people are "seeing camel in the clouds," as Guy Davenport puts it. I mean that's not the way the artist works. A cloud is a cloud is a cloud.
SB: Yes, but it can infer a camel, and still be a cloud, and if you can do that, then you've got the same as what I'm talking about with Kathryn Mackay's painting here—that it can be a flat, and absolutely have a fulsome sense of depth. But if it is also a flat, it doesn't run what is for me a risk, and I'm kind of surprised that you would want to drift into a painting, if you can have the assumption that you can drift into it. So I want there to be space in there, and light, but I want it to be quite clear that it's something for me to look into, not walk into.

RJ: That's because we're twentieth-century people.
SB: But we're *right* in being twentieth-century people!

RJ: Well . . .
SB: Think in terms of the land-grabbing and "real" estate that came out of the Renaissance, and its trick of space.

RJ: But that's further on down the line. Henry James couldn't look at twentieth-century art. He could see Turner perhaps—
SB: Pound couldn't even look at twentieth-century art!

RJ: —his painter was John Singer Sargent. But that's the way the world was viewed at the beginning of the century, before we got to Modernism. And that's what made Modernism. They said, "No, there's another way of looking at the universe. . . ."
SB: "Another way of looking at the universe." Well, I guess I'm a progressivist. You're probably right. But I'm moved to think that there is a move to a sanity of

recognition of the universe that comes with that openendedness that begins with Romanticism without that being dependent upon stitching things along the line of fact and logic. I see this openendedness as our only hope.

Except for poets, I think language is a damnation of human sensibility and in the blind mouths of politicians is destroying us all. And I think also that narrative drama, as a form that's unchanged since the Greek, is a trap that's loaded people with the dice that makes it very possible that the Third World War will be in Jerusalem and all the apocalyptic visions of drama will be fulfilled. People will move to try to fulfill those prophecies if we don't move to get out of the three-act play. We should either get it down to a two-act play or a six-act play, or do any damn thing to break up this narrowed concept which has become really narrowed through the sieve of motion pictures of what it means to be dramatic with each other, and what drama is.

JS: [inaudible question about the Bible]
SB: Well, the Bible is many different kinds of books—the one I have is the King James translation—and it's set in the forms of plays, poems, essays, stories, etc., so that one can have the recognition of the various forms that are in the Bible, and as such it's a collection that is filled with much goodness and much that's to me questionable, if not uninteresting. I can take it as all of it seems so far as I can tell aesthetically interesting. It's beautiful language—these King James translators are great translators.

RJ: And we grew up with it. You can't get away from it, even if you don't believe in it. We're steeped in the language and the images. Well, you know I took the Psalms and made a long poem out of them, which again turns into Orpheus and Eurydice. I learned from Zukofsky that you can make up a rule. So what I did with the Psalms was I took one letter out of it, so you had "Palms." And then my rule was that I had to have at least one word from every Psalm and that they had to be in sequence, which gave me a lot of leeway. And so I turned them into the songs of Orpheus.
SB: I don't know this!

RJ: It's right in there.
SB: It's in *ARK*?

RJ: It's in the Foundations.
SB: As you're speaking of it is not the way I read it. I must have skipped a cog there as I was reading it.

RJ: Well, *RADI OS* gives you the process of what I was working with, but Palms—if you take the "s" out of Psalms—then that tells you the process I was working with. I don't anywhere in the book say that it's made out of the Psalms. That's left there to infer. Because I found in doing that, although I was telling another thing than the Psalms tell, you can tell by the profundity of the language, I was able to get another thing by using someone else's words. It's like Lucas Foss's Handel, where he cuts it in pieces, which is what influenced me to do *RADI OS*. He said, "The spaces are mine."

SB: I can't help but like what John Cage said when taken to Handel's *Messiah* and seemed kind of irritated and bored as they were leaving and the people that took him said, "Don't you like to be deeply moved?" And he said, "Yes I do, but I don't like to be pushed." Which could apply to Milton too.

With Stan Brakhage

Philip Taaffe / 1997

From *Philip Taaffe: Composite Nature*. Ed. Raymond Foye. New York: Peter Blum Edition, 1998. Courtesy Peter Blum Edition, New York. Reprinted by permission.

Philip Taaffe: Your titles are wonderfully evocative, you're an extremely good writer.

Stan Brakhage: Thank you, but that's still not a poet, right? In fact it's almost the opposite. To be a good writer is to almost preclude being a poet. I love that statement in Cocteau's *Orpheus*, where he says, "What is a Poet?" And he answers, "One who writes, but is not a writer." I'm always struggling with that. I don't know whether I betrayed language or it betrayed me, let's say it was a mutual betrayal in my crucial late teens. But I've had the good luck to be in the company of truly great poets all along the line, like Robert Duncan, Kenneth Rexroth, Louis Zukofsky, Charles Olson. And people of my own age, Michael McClure, Robert Creeley, Ed Dorn.

PT: You've dealt with animals in your work quite a lot.

SB: Oh yes. The one that springs to mind in relation to your present work is *The Domain of the Moment*. The title is a phrase by William James, where he is attempting to describe that moment when one suddenly feels at the mercy of the universe, like a great emptiness. I won't try to paraphrase William James, but it's an incredible concept. As I read his statement about it, that which he feared so much, I came to have this sense from the animals around me that they lived in this condition most of the time. Only humans struggle to be out of it. So I made four portraits: one is a little chicken. One is of a guinea pig, one is a raccoon, who has a kind of interaction with a dog, and then the final one is a snake, eating a mouse. These are multiple superimposition works, very layered.

PT: We're right on track here. When did you make that?

SB: Late seventies, early eighties. I also made a film called *Bird*, which was inspired by a guy who taught here in Boulder, Robert Bakker, the man most in charge of the idea of the hot-blooded dinosaurs. A big bearded guy with his bib overalls, out in the field most of the time, but he'd come into town once in a while. This is dinosaur country. He wrote a book called *The Dinosaur Heresies*, which I highly recommend. It makes the case, absolutely to my satisfaction, that there's no reason to have two phylum for birds and dinosaurs—they should be one phylum. When we lived up in the mountains in Rollinsville, I had a guinea fowl, and this was the smartest creature in our barnyard, which had goats, chickens, cats, geese, and so on. It was by far the smartest creature among them, and it couldn't have had a brain larger than a pea. I had a complete vision of it as dinosaur.

PT: I suppose the mind is always looking at related families of forms in trying to put something in its proper place. There's a continuous process of classification going on all the time. We confirm our understanding of something through a steady accretion of similarities, until we come across a difference that makes it fall completely outside of our experience. I've noticed that birds are very reptilian. Not only the talons, but the scaly feet are extremely reptilian. I keep these Chinese roosters at the studio, and they have hairs and feathers growing out of these lizard-like claws. They have a distinctly reptilian feeling . . .
SB: You also have a painting with beetles. I see you've named them scarabs rather than beetles. . . .

PT: I called the painting *Scarabesque*—that was my impression of what Thelonious Monk would have titled that painting. I've always admired Monk's playfulness with titles: *Epistrophy*, *Misterioso*, *Brilliant Corners*. They seem to express the same oddness and angularity of his work.
SB: That sort of titling serves to place the work at one remove from language, in a way.

PT: There's an interesting book by Lawrence Weschler about the conceptual artist Robert Irwin, which takes its title from an epigram by Wilhelm Schlegel: "Seeing is forgetting the name of the thing one sees." In other words, to really see something, to observe it, is to forget what it's called. To have complete communication with the thing itself.
SB: Okay, but that's ten times, maybe a thousand times harder to do in a representation than it is in everyday life.

PT: Still, philosophically I think it applies. The idea of something arriving at a point of descriptive accuracy that is nowhere near what you expected it would be.
SB: Visually, what we share with language is iconography or hieroglyph. At any

moment, however big you make your beetles, they can become hieroglyphs for beetles.

PT: It would be good to get rid of the word and just deal with the image itself, which was Burroughs's idea.
SB: That's what I was trying to get at in the beginning of *Metaphors on Vision*: "Imagine an eye unruled by man-made laws of perspective, an eye unprejudiced by compositional logic. . . ." It's an attack on language, actually. The real trick it seems to me is to have it namable but not have that at all interfere with seeing it in the first place.

...

PT: I get a better understanding of a painting's structural requirements by dwelling on it for sometimes long periods of time. In superimposing further imagery, I may finish a work several times. In this manner there is an accumulation of elements and meanings.
SB: For me that accumulation of meanings creates a certain irony which I take it to be at the center of your making, of which one aspect is this involvement with the decorative.

PT: I think it's important that you mention irony in connection with the decorative because this issue needs to be placed in a larger cultural context. I do try to subvert the decorative in various ways, even though it is not always easy to recognize how this has occurred in a given work. I believe I'm much closer to a minimalist position in that I favor austerity. I generally use decorative motifs in a carefully restricted and iconic way. Also my choices are *very* much about personal association and memory. I try to invest the work with a psychic energy which makes me less immediately concerned with loveliness of pictorial composition than with finding the best means for holding the energy there.
SB: One way I held my sanity together across that fifteen-year period that I commuted every other week to teach at the Chicago Art Institute, was by visiting all of the Louis Sullivan buildings. That famous Sullivan quote is wonderfully applicable to your work. What we mean by design: the purpose of the flower for the plant, which he seems to be suggesting, is indeed decorative or attractive or sexy—it is also a natural and necessary exfoliation of the leaves and the stem and the whole root system. So what is the present-day argument? That the decorative has been used as a pejorative in relation to painting?

PT: Yes, it certainly has, with the exception of Matisse, perhaps. Actually, the origins of these anti-decorative arguments are to be found for the most part in modernist architectural theory. Mies van der Rohe's reaction to nineteenth-century architecture was to strip things down to their bare essentials, to a very focused structure. The use of proportion and planar space was considered embellishment enough—anything more had to be seen as antithetical to progress.

SB: Once stripped to "essentials" a new order of complexity just naturally occurs—creates a new mystery. I know in the arts, the whole of it is for me a mystery, and we're all in a holy pursuit of the most ancient form of being human. I invoke those caves. There's nothing older, and they are very mysterious, some of them as much as three miles underground and sealed airtight shut, which is the only reason we have them today, sometimes with only one set of fingerprints in the clay. Made on a subterranean cave wall by tallow light with berry juice—what is that? We're deep in a mystery here—a holy ancient calling that's the most intrinsically human thing you could possibly think of.

PT: This is another side of the story that we haven't discussed, an artist's motivation coming from a place that is completely private. The drawings are meditations, but they're also public. In the beginning it is always a completely private vision, but the ambition or the motivation is to give that to the world. I often find myself poised between two poles of thought. The one, as Matisse said, is to make a painting as a luxuriant armchair. And then, on the other hand, you have Georges Rouault saying, I don't care if anybody ever sees anything I do, I'm creating this purely as a form of prayer, a private visionary meditation, and that is all.

SB: I'm somewhere between the two, also. I'm envious of Rouault's being able to say that, and I may someday be given that possibility, as I get older, I can hope. But I'm somewhere in between, because I also feel the burden of an evolution of human consciousness that is moving through the works that I've cared most about, by my contemporaries and myself. I feel the burden of this new possibility of exteriorizing moving visual thinking, as it's never existed before. I also feel a burden of Abstract Expressionism in relation to this new possibility, which for me is the new great frontier of human consciousness. So these are the two burdens that keep me social to an extent. But when I'm working, forget it. I can't allow any of that in, and I will go to any lengths to exclude it.

PT: This brings up another question I wanted to ask, which has to do with this issue of transcendence, and how our *everyday* circumstances need to intersect with that point on a constant basis. We create because we feel these ancient sources of motivation. I think we both feel that strongly. We're doing what we do because there's something behind us that is propelling us to act out a certain ritual. It's a form of magical engagement, shaping something that goes against a lot of what we experience. So much of what we do stands in opposition to what we have to confront culturally.

SB: The arts will automatically undermine the given status quo. At the same time, artists tend to be the most conservative people on earth, contrary to the myths that are propagated about them. I've said again and again that I'm not to be credited so much for the art which comes to me in a trance state. I'm just running along panting after forces or persuasions or muse-buzzings, or god or angels or whatever you want to call it, just trying not to screw up, to get it somehow so that it has a life of its own. I'm being midwife to this creation. I don't understand it any better than anybody else. What I'm to be credited for is having stayed alive to be able to do that in an incredibly hostile time. When everything was out to destroy and defeat me, I kept on reading, and opening myself up, so I had as wide a life experience to pour through me, and as deep a comprehension of other artist's lives and makings coming through me, and I tried to be honest about what I was doing. Honesty with no sense of hubris, as if I knew what was right and what was not. I cannot praise something that I'm unable to see. I have to be able to comprehend in order to make art. That's got me in the worst trouble imaginable.

PT: And that is why you are one of the great sole practitioners of the art of cinema. Any adversity I have had to face in order to do what I do, I'm sure pales by comparison to the obstacles you have been forced to contend with. Nothing less than an act of sheer transformative will would have enabled you to preside over those magnificent magic lantern poems of yours.

SB: Well thank you. It is the magic of art, its transformation possibilities, which people most fear. Formal aesthetics contain magic powers, but most people don't know how to comprehend art aesthetically. Many artists also eschew aesthetics for direct magic power in their works. All my life I've witnessed the perils of the practice of magic by artists. Most people just don't have the wisdom and the strength to wield this power. Artists are all the time in this category, right? There are great dangers in the arts. Abstraction is very dangerous—as you know very well.

PT: I'm glad you said that. As far as I'm concerned it's got to be dangerous if it's going to me any good.

SB: Very dangerous. That's why you're being very careful. On the other hand, to make a representation of something risks being either stupid or facile or passé. And it is also dangerous. When you make a picture of something, in a way that's vodun, and it's not been good for humanity. White Magic is for me. My whole case against Black Magic is simple: you have to move a mountain, so you apply your energy, the same as if you were moving it a shovelful at a time, for however many generations it takes. You pass that energy on in a useful form to others who also share in it, until finally that energy has been accrued, and then if you have to you can move the mountain because it's already been paid for. Black Magic says move it now, pay later. The temptation of Black Magic is that people always have good reasons—beneficent, humane reasons for needing to do some big thing. Like go all the way to the back brain and start forward, But it has to be paid for a shovelful at a time. Or else, like the installment plan, you're in debt, with interest. If you're borrowing against the future you have to pay the interest, right? There's great power involved, and what kind of a saint can resist that kind of power—when you can put someone to death just by incantation. How many are saintly enough to exercise that power beneficently?

PT: We're surrounded by these dangers. We live in a time in which the whole possibility of human survival is really very much called into question, and the dangers are increasing. They're certainly not diminishing. It's curious you should mention incantation because it's an activity that bears a certain parallel to the art-making process. I made an experiment a couple of years after I got out of art school. I was living in the General Theological Seminary, an Episcopal seminary in Chelsea. One night I went to see Antonioni's *Red Desert*. When I came back to my room I started working. I had a cheap little tape recorder on the drawing table, and I wanted to do my version of *Red Desert*. I wanted to get inside this haunted industrial landscape, this weird sensuality, this sense of demise that I recognized in the movie. I was drawing with oil sticks, and as I started making these gestures I began speaking into the microphone. . . .
SB: You were giving these lines characters. . . .

PT: That was part of what I was trying to do. I suppose the experiment was to see how long the vocal narrative and the linear or gestural narrative could coexist, keep generating one another, before language fell away.
SB: And probably you talked less and less the more you got involved in the work. You see how comparable that is to Gertrude Stein's *Stanzas in Meditations*: every word must be a character, as if in a novel, so that "a" and "the" have lives as they move through the poem, until finally it's a cast of thousands that are murmuring their own stories. (I'm very dependent upon the wisdom and friendship of Stein scholar Ulla E. Dydo for much of my thought here.) The larger truth behind that is we are made up of particles that are absolutely unique, with no two alike. Certainly these cells have likenesses unto all of the cells that make up our body, but let's just stick with the brain for the moment. The brain has all these cells inside, and each of them is having its own individual life. They have parts you can name, each has a nucleus, and a connective tissue that looks a certain way, but no two are alike. They are then variously cooperating in whatever it is we are, or imagine ourselves to be in some conglomerate sense. But there is no actual or literal space in there.

And unless your painting is in some sense being true to what the individual lives of those cells are, you're not evolving in any way.

PT: One thing I want to reiterate about this process I was describing when I was speaking into the microphone and making these marks and trying to refer to my immediate memory of this film, is that it was some form of incantation. And I believe there is a connection between this previous exercise and my present incantatory use of silkscreen. The repetitive printing of these animals and fish takes place in trance-like episodes, where the drawing, or the shifting of the paper, is an exercise in getting someplace else, in bringing them into a more elemental condition, perhaps. The best of them seem like entrance ways to another reality. They suggest something which is compelling beyond themselves.

SB: When we go through the womb we have fins at one point, we have gills, we look very much like those curled rocks we find in fossils. We are of earth in that sense. Although I firmly believe that it does not matter if anybody else ever sees it, you cannot just think it, you have to put it into material. Once you put it into material it's in the world. We are here to work with material, we are not walking on water. Just sitting and thinking it is not enough. But if in the making you want to be true to the brain, if you want it fully in the painting as the mind, then all you can achieve is fishness: not fish, but fishness. I don't know how else to put it. Because otherwise you're making a symbol that's pointing to something outside. Brains do not have fish stuck in them, they have fishnesses, they have an energy in there, they have traces of something that can be invoked as fish.

PT: We're getting into difficult semantic territory here, but I think you're loosely referring to the Platonic thought-form, the image we implicitly know to exist, from which all particular examples are derived. The fish was certainly a dominant Paleo-Christian symbol.

SB: But instead of having a symbol that gets more and more hardened, like the valentine heart, you clash these things, or imprint them doubled. They double over on each other, they start reverberating. You may have the shadow of the same thing, or a near-symmetry, on opposite sides.

. . .

PT: Symmetry is death. Nature forbids symmetry.

SB: Yes, and you avoid it. I fear symmetry very much. I've used it in some films, but always delicately off balance. It is to me, if not necessarily evil, something tangent to that: dangerous.

PT: Do you think it's the danger, or the appeal of danger, encoded within symmetry, or does the use of it act as a kind of charm against something more dangerous?

A protective charm to deal with these dangerous issues in order to stop something from unraveling that would be truly catastrophic?
SB: Yes, truly catastrophic would be to lose the back brain. Or to pretend that there weren't things that seem to be happening again and again, or to pretend there weren't things seeming to be symmetrical. So the trick is very delicate. Things can seem symmetrical, like a snake, but it's quite clear right off the bat they are not. Language either becomes at one with the shape or it ceases to exist and then it's irrelevant. To try to pretend that we haven't named things, to try and pretend that we can go back and be primitive is to me the horrible danger. That's what so many people try to do as they go through their teens over and over again, try to pretend they're primitive. All of Germany decided it wanted to be primitive again and shuttled eight million people into the furnaces. You avoid the name dominating, and you avoid symmetry dominating. And those in a dry way are two of the most interesting things about your work. In the wet way, you're burrowing into the back brain, from which ground you now say to me you want to evolve the human form.

...

PT: What is this fear of fern forests, Stan, can we get to the bottom of this?
SB: [Laughs] They're too much the same on one side as the other, though they're not identical. But they give the impression that this might be so, and this makes me very nervous.

PT: They're also self-generating, self-pollinating, I believe. What about the pleasure principle as an impetus for making something? I will honestly tell you that my most fundamental decisions as to what gets incorporated into the work and how I go about doing things, are closely determined by what I anticipate the pleasure yield to be. Not to say that those decisions won't also be agonizing as they are played out.
SB: Yes, of course, and you need to have your own bag of tricks to stay alive. But let's face it, the other thing you're doing when you're making marks, and talking into the tape recorder, as you have done, anthropomorphizing those marks, and creating a story—you're trying to give yourself something to hang on to, something as solid as a detective story.

PT: Clues....
SB: Yes, while in fact you are drifting off into this terrifying realm. Because those marks end up essentially ...

PT: Haunting you....
SB: Because they are essentially unnamable. So you're protecting yourself, you're

holding on to something. I also invent little stories, or I whistle colors, I sing: red red red green, blue blue blue purple. Or else I talk to myself, hang onto little stories, little scenarios. But finally that isn't going to have much to do, if anything, with what eventually the work is when finished. I've just used these little tricks to survive the making. And then when the work is done, it has its own life, and it doesn't care what I did to get it there.

・・・

SB: We did touch on the necessity to go back to the grounds of one's own most sexual privacies, as a springboard into wherever you're going, artistically. Basically your work is meat, meat patterns, and here you are trying to be Ellsworth Kelly. You've gone to an opposite extreme. . . . But desperately you are trying to work through ritualistically all of the geometric, which essentially is not going to be a part of your making. It isn't, is it?

PT: Well, it was a way of getting things going, of constructing a foundation. In order to arrive somewhere else, it is necessary to pass through another domain; a new phase of possibility is entered through an existing place.

SB: It's also a way of getting to the front brain, because that's where those geometries come from. They don't exist in nature, either in your meat physiology or anywhere on earth, except for chance. There are no straight lines, there are no real triangles. There are shards of crystals that look like they're geometric, until you go at them with the microscope and then they all have wobbly surfaces. The geometric is a late human idea, and it exists more as an idea. I'm not speaking against it, you understand: it's an effluvia. . . .

PT: I see it this way: take this lemon peel here on this table, and the shadow it makes on the tablecloth. Focus in on this shape, distill the line, take this part of nature and accept it as a building block, something you can utilize to go somewhere else. One then takes that "abstraction" and puts it on a surface, and that provokes a certain set of associations. One examines what those associations are. On the basis of those associations you construct other material that you want to incorporate into this original idea. Now you have this new set of material, of which some can be applied and some cannot. There's a radical empiricism at work there somehow. It's also about an abstract idea that becomes a story emerging out of nothing—out of pure observation. Just a perception of a very limited part of physical space that can be examined. This is a microcosmic scale. I've always been interested in the molecular separation between an object and the space behind it. I'm very interested in how we perceive that physical reality. I'd like to be able to apply those observations to a very different kind of pictorial situation than what we've known before.

SB: But the more geometrically you represent this experience, the more you have to limit seeing in the first place. One always has to limit seeing: one can't have everything all at once. I'm with you in that in the long run I want everything, but we can't have everything all at once. The more the geometries interfere, they become like language. They limit the possibility to see that lemon peel to an extraordinary extent in the first place, however you're going to represent it. There's the dilemma.

Fly over any country and you know when you're flying over human habitation or not, because it's all checkered and circled and triangled. The landscape is geometricized. What's lacking is to bring in the back brain. And in order to do that, you've got to have symmetry without having it. You've got to show that it doesn't really exist, even though it looks like it does....

PT: Can you define what an image is?
SB: Image is difficult. Picture I've defined. An image, I don't know, I've never tried to push that distinction.

PT: An image is more transient.
SB: It doesn't seem to me the naming would have to be that crucial.

PT: It's ineffable, what constitutes the experience. Does mirage better define this notion?
SB: It could be a part of a picture that is unnamable. I hear "mage" reverberating in it.

PT: Magician, magus.
SB: Yes. When you say image I then more want to talk about Impressionism, rather than hard-edged depiction. I like the word visual, because it escapes all these things. Moving visual thinking, then, is the center of my concerns.

PT: You also use the word envisionment.
SB: I suppose that means after the continuities of time, and out of all of that vision, what reverberates as meaning—the composition of the whole of it, what's meant. Again, it's tough because language doesn't quite describe it, otherwise I'd probably be a poet and not a filmmaker.

PT: For me, the deepest part of the process of making a painting is when I get into an almost incantatory state. When I'm working in this way, I can sometimes recognize a previous archaic existence that I seem to have been a part of. I'm revisiting an archaic moment. Now I know this sounds completely outlandish and presumptuous....
SB: No, not to me, not to anyone who studies DNA....

PT: I tell you, sometimes when I'm working on a painting, I'll put an element into place, and I'll see that in relation to something else; and I will have an experience of passing through the familiar terrain of a forest encampment, or sitting by a fire, part of some remote tribal archaic life that I have been a part of, I feel that very strongly. It's a recognition of an earlier existence, in the act of having experienced just a particle of that existence in a work. That's what really exhilarates me.

SB: You can have that as reincarnation, as some people do, or you can have that as DNA encoding. I can tell you just one story that's put me at peace a lot in this matter. They had little cut-out silhouettes of hawks and sparrows, and then they had little chicks who never did see their mothers and never were trained, and these chicks with no training were wandering around, and they pass the shadow of the hawk over them, and they all go crazy and start running in all directions. Then they pass the shadow of the sparrow over them, and they go about whatever they were doing, pecking and scratching without worry. And they didn't get this info from mommy, they got it genetically. That's enough proof for me, and there are a lot of other examples. Charles Olson spent the last years of his life trying to understand the outside limits of being human. What we're really sharing at the outside of being human, in the womb as well as now, is a kind of a grid, if you could call it that, and here's where language gets awkward. There is a kind of grid which is lit up, even in the womb. We know fetuses dream. What do they dream of? Something's lit up in there, this dreaming grid which is being shaped, upon which all the imprimatur of their later life will rest—all the ways in which they can imagine or be. And I think that has to be informed by genetics, by DNA. That has to be where we are the most alike. It's unimaginable that it could be anything else. I think that's what I in my way, and you in yours, are trying to reach, and give representation to.

PT: Perhaps that's why I need to go back to Ireland and investigate my Celtic roots. I think I have some shamanistic past, but I'm not sure I'm ready to brag about it.

SB: There's a playful side to all of whatever the making is, but basically, it's dangerous, it's not socially acceptable, and there's no choice. It's imprisonment. There is this real fear and sometimes hatred of the artist and of visionary experience.

PT: It's clear to me that the art we appreciate, the art that we find most overwhelming and compelling, that we pay attention to, is the most dangerous stuff, in terms of the risks it takes. It's a raw challenge to how things have been done previously, and this puts us in a state of temporary disequilibrium. We know that this information must be dealt with, which is exactly what we demand, it's what we expect.

SB: The darkest continent of the world is the human mind. For me none of this is a question of decoration. It is seriously a question of art. That's a discipline you share with people that goes all the way back to the ancient caves. It's the earliest record of being human, and that gives you a stable grounding in some sense: to be an artist even though everyone uses the term for everything other than what it should be used for. And it's such an annoying shit factor in your social life—one is so often embarrassed to open one's mouth to say it. But the truth is, if you hold to that you have a touch with all humanity, and this is some protection against these dangers. It makes you very small in relationship to the whole endeavor, because it also includes those known and unknown artists who tried and failed—those who never made anything of any significance—by the millions.

PT: Or some of those great manuscript painters of the Middle Ages—we'll never know who they are, those contented or malcontented monastics.
SB: Or all those people who did beautiful, great things, that were just lost or thrown out with the trash. It puts one in this great arena which I literally need when I'm uncovering these layers of the mind. I need it going on all around me and that's why I work at Potter's cafe in downtown Boulder, in this atmosphere of businessmen talking, of fans watching the football game, of tourists.

PT: Why do you do this, instead of working at home?
SB: To keep from going crazy. I do not paint or etch on film in a solitary room, at home or in my office. I can edit there but I can't dig out the material. I need to be sunk in with my fellow human beings, so I'm not alone with it.

PT: Do you think artistic statement excludes equivocation and speculation, and a negative way of describing things? Describing something by naming all the things that it is not. Do you think that's a valid approach?
SB: That's certainly an exhaustive way to go about it. I don't know. It's valid if the heart of the person doing it is good, is dedicated to goodness. It's intriguing. Rilke at some point wanted to get rid of things in the world altogether, and the way to do it was to name them—that was an actual positive ideal. Then you would be left with the truth. The truth is always what you fully believe down to the bone at the given moment, and it can't ever be anything else than that. When you deal with fact, you're into the sliding world of science, which changes its facts faster than people change their laundry. Nowadays scientists have far more presumption. Now they think they know. That means they know less than when they didn't think they knew. As a child, do you remember having hypnogogic visual experiences?

PT: Yes, I really loved the optic feedback, when I rubbed my eyes. Looking at the sun and seeing the veins in your eyelids. Looking at colors with your eyes closed. This inner kaleidoscope.

SB: We very much share that. In periods when I'm mad enough to push toward myself as a realist filmmaker, I'm trying to paint as near an equivalence of hypnogogic vision as I possibly can. I fail miserably, but usually turn out something else that's so wonderful to me that I can fortunately just go on and evolve various ways of creating a visual musical equivalence. There too I feel particularly related to you, because I feel in the length or varieties on a theme in your work, you're really extending over time. You could almost be a filmmaker like Viking Eggeling or Hans Richter, both of whom started out making scrolls. They finally stumbled into film because they couldn't accommodate the scroll medium to the length that their work was demanding. Your painting from the Vienna Secession catalogue was like that.

PT: You mean *Megapolis*. That was about thirty-five feet long by twelve feet tall. I like working on a large scale. I can fit so much more inside.

SB: There is a sense in much of your work of real color and real form similar to what I've invested in making some of my works, like *Mothlight*, or *The Garden of Earthly Delights*, using a real, collaged, flattened object. Only you do it with paint.

PT: I like how you described *Mothlight* as having to do with the attractiveness of death: the fact that the moths were attracted to this warmth and light, and that killed them. It's a way of showing that feeling or reality on film in a very palpable way.

SB: That was certainly the personal reason for making it. I felt I was being killed by the process of creating by being drawn to the light. And the moths certainly were, right before my eyes. Then there was this question of what to do with their bodies, which started all that off. It was *very* important to me that I didn't kill any of them in the making of that film. There's a later work that's more related to painting, actually, pressing Alpine mountain flowers between thirty-five millimeter film, so you have the images in much larger scale: *The Garden of Earthly Delights*.

PT: I notice you use a phrase which I use quite frequently, which is aesthetic ecology, to describe a state of equilibrium in a work, where all the parts are functioning within the general system. Nothing wasted.

SB: Aesthetic ecology, yes. To me it means more than balance: it means nothing should just have dropped into the work from heaven. You could have something dropped in from heaven, but that would be an anomaly, and you should, then, have prepared for that anomaly. You can't slide on too much of that—that suddenly things will just occur. A place has to be made, things have to be generated. I'm talking about a continuity art, across time, the way it comes into existence, how it interacts with everything else. And my great teacher in this respect, is Gertrude

Stein. Her ultimate poem is *Stanzas in Meditation*, because there every word has a life of its own, as if it were a character in a Tolstoy novel. Whatever they tangentially describe or obliquely indicate, all these words also have a life of their own, in between the lines, which you might call their soul.

PT: I think the phrase "aesthetic ecology" can also apply to the fact that, in the awareness of making something, you have to energize every frame. Every cell has to have a life energy. There's a cumulative effect as a result of all of these energy sparks. It's a funny psychological problem, how to treat one's chosen material. I love calligraphic gesture and will very often scrape litho ink over glass deliberately to make an impression on paper from that. But there's a fine line between appreciating a certain gesture or mark, giving it its due weight, and not feeling too precious about it. And I think the material has to be treated in a very ecological way, so that one makes good use of these resources, accepting them for their potential and for their capacity to be integrated within a larger scheme of things. They have a practical use value—as well as having a particular beauty. There is the more inclusive, loving part of the story, and then there must be a ruthlessness, which has to do with knowing what belongs where.

SB: For me the really arduous and disturbing chore of furthering what's known as Abstract Expressionism, in contemporary terms, in terms of the human mind, lies in uncovering that whole streaming of moving visual thinking that is and always has been free of language. Because of the Abstract Expressionist painters we have all these different areas of the unnamable—areas of now-shared, human nonverbal thinking that we can inhabit, travel to. . . .

PT: To inhabit the pictorial—that's a very important idea. You have somehow managed to calm the better part of my anguish about not knowing what something is called, while I'm working on it. The pull of language is so great at times, that I might find myself conforming to the imaginary demands of a discourse which says that the identification of something has absolute primacy. Often in art those premature qualifications can be misleading and counterproductive. So from our conversation I feel more relaxed about that idea.

SB: Painting is where this new visual consciousness rose, and I think probably every evolution of it will occur in painting first. And I'll tell you why: people can only deal with so much. It is to me in one sense the same as the Impressionists, who went out into the landscape and in the rain and wind, and they sat there and painted from nature, and it made an enormous difference in human vision, right? Similarly, Jackson Pollock goes into his head, and finds some area that's never been expressed, and at great agony gets it out of himself. Many went nuts under this, literally went crazy and came to bad ends, not just the alcoholism and suicides, but literal insanity; trying to get this vision out of their heads. The beautiful, shamanistic clarities of these drunks, which is really mostly what they were: utterly sincere, desperate, crazy American drunks. What a thing for this to come out of. And then there are certain people who manage to go on being creative and achieve a certain kind of happiness, and it absolutely puzzles the hell out of me how they do that.

PT: I know what you mean. Most people are condemned to a life of at least partial torment. Perhaps the point is to bear it with dignity.
SB: And I yearn for it, of course, I want to be, well, happy is too superficial a word. But you know what I mean. I want to be joyful and present a splendor, a happy splendor to people, and to myself. One thing that you and I share that makes us forever not happy—you wanted to be a filmmaker and I wanted to be a poet, so we are in the first place failed—although we've had the sense to accept what was given to us to do.

Interview with Stan Brakhage

Pip Chodorov / 2003

From *Millennium Film Journal*, nos. 47, 48, 49 (Fall/Winter 2007–2008): 161–78. Reprinted by permission.

In February 2003, I had the opportunity to transcribe the audio recordings that Pip Chodorov had taped for his film *A Visit to Stan Brakhage*, a brief, fifteen-minute portrait film of the great American avant-garde filmmaker, commissioned for French television. The interview was to be Brakhage's last. At the time, I had known that Brakhage was ill, but listening to the tapes I began to doubt the extent of his illness. His voice was vital, even forceful at times. He laughed frequently. And with great patience—with a touch of weariness perhaps, for later I learned that the clarity of his speech had been compromised by the medications he was taking—Brakhage made the case for cinema he'd been making in over four hundred films for the past fifty-two years: the case for a personal cinema, visual poems of pure light, the reaches of vision itself.

In the interview's final question, Brakhage was asked if he could find a continuous theme throughout all his works. He paused deeply, the first and only time during the interview that his tremendous outpouring ceased. Gently, he avoided the question. It seemed that he had grown tired, or perhaps didn't wish to reveal himself. I was wrong. Moments later, Brakhage rebounded in a joyful song, and gave of himself in an altogether different and moving way. Singing, he exclaimed, "I can't give you anything but love, baby!" The following interview took place at Stan and Marilyn Brakhage's home in British Columbia on January 4, 2003. Stan Brakhage begins by reading aloud from his 1963 book, *Metaphors on Vision*.
—Genevieve Yue

Stan Brakhage: *Imagine an eye unruled by man-made laws of perspective.* Our whole structure of visual thinking is based on man-made laws of perspective and so on. But *imagine*, I say in my youth, *an eye unruled by man-made laws of perspective, an eye unprejudiced by compositional logic, an eye which does not respond to the name of* *everything but which must know each object encountered in life through an adventure of perception.* In other words, everything you see, you have to be having an immediate adventure with it. It's not canned in any sense. *How many colors are there here in a field of grass to the crawling baby unaware of "Green?" How many rainbows can light create for the untutored eye?* In other words, can we actually see the rainbow at all unless we're squeezing the eye in that particular way that causes that diffraction? *How aware of variations in heat waves can that eye be?* In other words, can you really see the quivering, the actual quivering little wavelets through which every little shaft of light is, you know, feathered onto your consciousness? *Imagine a world alive with incomprehensible objects*, imagine it just alive with things we don't know what they are, incomprehensible objects, and *shimmering with an endless variety of movements*, everything moving. There's not a moment of stillness anywhere, and *innumerable gradations of color*. I mean, you start naming the different shades of, let's say, these pants, blue-black? Are they gray-black? Are those socks then black-black? Are you taking advantage of this, of my whole spread-out being here? You have all these varieties. . . . Here's a blue. And you start naming: is this Prussian blue? Is this cobalt blue? Is this navy blue? And those are just blunt gradations, names that are given, and you can go on and on and on and you run out of words, finally. You'd end up with a dictionary full of words trying to delimit and otherwise describe a quality of blueness, very shortly, just along the line of these black pants and black shirt and black socks on this quilt which I will make no attempt whatsoever to try to describe. [*laughs*]

And all that shimmering and movements and gradations of color, *imagine a world before*—this is the point—*imagine a world before the "beginning was the word."* [*Max the cat enters.*] Hey, that was a good entrance, cat! [*laughs*] Look at the shimmering across that cat's body. It's just absolutely incomprehensible. At some point I became aware of that. Look at the brown blacks and the sheen of the blue black coming up, bouncing off. Look at how he enrobes himself, Max the cat, with the beauty of all that gradation—without giving it a thought. How do I know what he's thinking? Huh? You like that Maxie-moo? All that massive, shimmering, feathery, fragile, splintering, weaving, unweaving, revolving world in which we move, and live. I began to be aware of it in some overwhelming sense so I could no longer disregard it. I could no longer just take a shot. I could no longer do a take. I could no longer steal, in that simple sense in which I always had, like any filmmaker. I could no longer *shoot*. You can only do that if you're *using* film, if you're using what all the light is bouncing off of all around you and you're using it in order to tell a story or something like that—something that film is ill-equipped to do, actually. Film is so distractive in all the things that it presents as a possibility of recorded busy-ness that it's ridiculous in a way to chop it down to a love story.

I always liked best that Hollis Frampton said—great filmmaker, Hollis Frampton, who was a teacher, an aesthetician. He said the whole history of Hollywood movies—any movies, just the movies—was comparable to birdsong. He discovered after years of listening to the birds that there are only five things that birds say, and he discovered that there's only five things that movies do. They say "Good morning!" "I found a worm." "Love me." "Get out!" "Good night." And then there were variations of these. Some films, it was primarily "get out"—that's what most gangster movies seem to be—but also it was "love me" woven in there, and so on. At any rate, along these lines, you were telling every kind of movie that ever could possibly be conceived of or thought of, narrative or dramatic. Now you can see that film is ill-equipped to deal with that. Why? Because film is so many other things. You just open your eyes and you see what an overload you're dealing with, and in the midst of all that overload you're supposed to do such delicacy as "get out" and "love me"? No, forget it! They would be buried in a shimmering mass of . . . but of course, by the film stock itself, the bluntness of it, by the limitations of humans, they've shoved all these sensibilities through machinery. They have broken it all down to something that can indeed be made into a movie. But that was no longer interesting for me to be doing. I mean, my life was in too much of a crisis. I couldn't think of a reason to get up in the morning. Couldn't think of a single reason. I mean my childhood had been so wretched. Well, everyone's childhood is, but that didn't help me, to realize that not only me but everyone else was suffering the same indignation and horror. I was born in a natural condition of, you know, the heart of darkness—oh, the horror, the horror!

I early learned that I was not going to be able to do this kind of movie, because I was aware of all these things that I just read in this opening statement. The simpler way in which I found it out was I went to Hollywood, and I had an actual way to get a job there. I had what every young person dreams of, I mean a literal letter of entrée through some actors that I met in Central City, Colorado—Wendell Corey, Paul Douglas, and Jan Sterling and finally, via them, Charles Laughton. And the week I arrived in Hollywood to get that job, to carry a chair or whatever you do at first when you start in Hollywood, Charles Laughton got drunk with me and a couple of people and said, "Get out of Hollywood. Get out! It will kill you, it will destroy you!" It was a whole ugly night, between his lurching to the john, and the pissoir, and the vomit smell on his breath, and the horror and the anger over having accomplished, to me, one of the few great narrative films of Hollywood history, *Night of the Hunter*, and having had that taken away from him. Having had that film made and then it failing at the box office (as it happened, it fell out just that week I arrived in Hollywood). What was taken away from him was his chance to do *The Naked and the Dead*, one of the more interesting books of the Second World

War, you know, Norman Mailer's great book. So there I was, drunk in a booth at the Turnaround Theatre with Charles Laughton, being given every reason, as if I needed any, for giving up the whole course of narrative drama.

Pip Chodorov: Describe how you got to *Flesh of Morning* and why you made your *Desistfilm* in the first place. You were doing art before this, right?

SB: Me and art. Here. [*pulls out a drawing*] That's as good as I am, as art. We got pictures of Max here, you can see, not very good. They're good faith attempts. Here I am as a drafter, drawer of the large page. [*flipping pages*] Ho-ho! Looks like my answer to John Wayne riding across John Ford's Monument Valley. Or is this an attempt to make a background for Hollis Frampton's film, *Love Me*? [*flipping pages*] There, that's more "love me." In other words, I can draw ok, but I'm no artist. What I really wanted to do was to be a poet. That's what I've dreamed of since I was very young, since I was two or three—having no sense of what a poet was. Since I was nine, between the ages of nine and nineteen, I really wanted to be a poet. And in that period, toward the end of it, I wrote such things as, "Oh to find the lips of the sympathetic drinking water,/ Then to the softest unconcealings / Must one / Must one/ Must one . . ." Which is a lovely piece of verse—but no poet; won't find a poet there. [*flipping pages*] Now, there's another attempt at the cat. Look at that, what all that cat is. Here's my trying to see through my hypnagogic vision even, the blue sparks that I see embodied as a flashing manifestation of bits and particles of life of this black cat. I, at least, honor the one I'm holding—I'm keeping this one because at least it has something of the quality of Max's bodily mien. It's a nice little kitty cat picture maybe but a total failure.

So there I am as a drawer and as a poet. I believe that the muse who permits—who is that part of human consciousness that permits the creation of an art or not—allowed me to do something with film. I gave up any false poetics or singing or painting for that matter and was given film. Huh! And you can say, what! For me? Film—for me? Thanks a lot! Every time you turn around it costs a fortune, it'll destroy your whole life. Press the button but once and you've spent fifty dollars. But, anyway, that was the gift that was given to me, and so long as I remain true to that and the other arts (and I've always been very careful therefore to do so, to be so), I could be a filmmaker. But then that was going to lead me down paths as to what *film* could be. I think I've been clear, I've never been clearer about alternative paths I think. . . . However oblique I may sound at times, you know that I'm very grateful. "Grateful" isn't the word really. I'm very moved to be part of this and what you're doing. And without it, what's the point of anything that I did with the films—they aren't going to take on life sitting on a shelf, somewhere, you know, in some museum.

PC: No, it's important people can see them.

SB: I wish we could send them as films. . . . So that's where I'm essentially centered. I think people have to try to understand film as an art in this way. There is something that could be called the prose of cinema and that's all the movies that we see, all the five different stories that Hollis Frampton says movies can tell. That's the prose of cinema. I'm putting this in quotes: "It produces novels. It produces all our prosaic information including much of our documentation." It is really prose, just as it is in the books that we get at the library and read.

Then there's poetry, and poetry is something distinct. And the only problem with making a distinction of poetry is that people tend to think poetry is more important than, or greater than, or more significant than prose, or vice versa. That needn't be the case at all, and isn't as far as I'm concerned. I mean it is in the sense that I love poetry very deeply and I'm more involved with and care more about poetry, but otherwise there is a distinction between prose and poetry which is not based upon one being better than the other. One goes to the movies for a *certain* kind of experience just like one reads a novel for a certain kind of experience. And one would be hard put if you started trying to read a poem in the way in which you read a novel. I mean, it would be very discouraging in fact. Poetry would come to seem to be hard rather than, which it truly is, different. And I think those people who regard my films as hard are simply disregarding the fact that they're poems, that they're little cine-poems. They're to be looked at completely differently. You're not trying to find out who's going to ride off into the sunset with whom. Is this beautiful yellow shape going to ride off into the sunset with the purple phallic shape or what? No, it's absurd. A poem is a poem. And that leads me right into Gertrude Stein's "rose is a rose is a rose is a rose." She was the best definer of what poetry is in our time.

Let me give you two of her definitions that I think should do for us. She always said she distinguished herself and knew who she was because of her animals. "I am I because my little dog knows me" is one of Gertrude Stein's most blessed and beautiful statements. Now hear this one: "I learned the difference between prose and poetry listening to my little dog drinking water." There's a total difference in drinking that occurs with lapping it up, you know, getting your prose mouthfuls up. It's quite a curl of the tongue that the dog must do in order to quaff his cups. "I learned the difference between prose and poetry listening to my little dog drinking water." Ok, but there's a really deep and clear way in which you could come to understand my films as being some visual equivalent, something with pictures, which is more like poetry than like prose.

Gertrude Stein took one poem that actually turns out to be the most famous poem of the twentieth century. "Rose is a rose is a rose is a rose." It's famous because people laugh at it all the time, it's a big joke, and they're making fun of her and it and themselves, I suppose. But while they're doing that, they're forgetting—and I got a natural rhyme out of that, did you notice how it lent itself immediately to a rhyme scheme: "I suppose," "a rose"? It's a wonderful device for being clear. She, when pressed on the issue of what this meant, said "All I can tell you is that the rose has not bloomed so beautifully in English poetry for hundreds of years." Now poetry always did take certain terms and they become signatures. Rose means something in English poetry, it means something right off the bat as distinct from what it means in prose. In prose, you order at the florist shop—so many roses, a dozen roses or whatever. But in poetry, rose immediately has to evoke—voke, vocal?—has to evoke in the person the sense of birth, sex, death. And then it spins off in a kind of mysticism, the mysticism of the rose, the Rosicrucian, the holy rose, the rose windows of the great French cathedrals. But let's just take it as flat as you can, because that's how it was originally arrived at: she wrote it as a little poem that a little girl carves around a tree in a book called *The World Is Round*—a children's book that Gertrude Stein wrote. She meant it in the simplest sense—not having the most ecological sense of trees, one could be a bit horrified—but what she needed that tree for was because, probably without consciously realizing it, she needed to ring in the Tree of Life. Now that's the tree Yggdrasil, that comes out of the Norse, the Tree of Life, the tree whose hairs are stars, whose throat is the voice of the world, whose trunk is what the world is planted in. It's also the holy tree, the tree in Christian heritage, for example, on which Christ is crucified. That is where the tree is in our culture.

And then in relation to the rose. Let's set the tree aside for a moment and say "rose is a rose is a rose." Well how do we know birth, sex, and death in poetry? There's the sister that pulls in the wool, and then there's the one that makes the thread of it, and there's the one who cuts it. The first one is giving it birth; the second one is giving it its fulsome maturity, its life, its usefulness; and the third one is death—give it a snip and it's over. Sis. Three sisters and the three sisters of Fate are certainly famous enough—you can hardly read a page of Shakespeare without encountering them. They can come on vicious as in *Macbeth*, etc. "Rose is a rose is a rose." Now listen. If you're listening, you're hearing "sis, sis, sis". You're even hearing that that's moving towards snip. Sis sis sis. Rose sis a rose sis a rose sis. The three sisters are in there. A rose, arose, arose, a-r-o-s-e means like an arising . . . an ascension. It can be the ascension of Christ into heaven, it can be a hard-on coming to find its place. [*laughs*] A rose is arose, that can be arrows of Cupid shooting the arrows that pierce the hearts of lovers and make them fall in love. Rose is saros, sis arose, s-o-r-r-o-w-s is sadness of and, along with the arrow, both of those can also stand for death. Sorrows and death. The end. Rose-is, eros, e-r-o-s, the god of love out of the Greek. So within these few little words you have a whole gem of language that's interrelating, these words knocking back and forth among each other giving us a largesse that you can hold for a meditation piece for the rest of your life. And it certainly has served me well.

Now the tough thing to do when you come upon my films or any poetic cinema is to think of pictures in some similar way. If you're just making a picture to show the young man bringing the roses to the young lady, "ding, dong" the doorbell rings and there it is, a bunch of roses all sort of soft-petaled, mistily photographed, etc. If it isn't, in other words, a furtherance of the plot, of the love affair, of the story that the prose movie is telling, then it's open to all these other possibilities. In fact it almost inevitably starts becoming these other possibilities. They become probabilities, they become absolutes. And then one moves with every single picture—when you see a picture it doesn't just knock the story along, it takes all your own personal relationships to the flower, but not just the flower as a piece of language, but the shape of the flower, that it's so many-petaled, that its petals are all interwoven with each other in a certain way. That does open up into the rosace, into the rose windows of the great cathedrals; the mystique of the rose is already there in the shape. As a shape it exists and it moves as a shape along the line of our feeling and thinking and thus becomes a film as it's moving.

A film is something quite distinct and different from a piece of prose storytelling. Well that's what I do, and that's the difference. It takes a little getting used to, to open yourself to just letting the pictures flow over oneself and feel them in this way. And there's this: film is the very, very closest to music of any of the other arts because it relies upon time. It's a continuity art, it happens across a period of time. You have to read a poem, you have to experience a film across a passage of time. And across that passage of time you have to *feel* its textures, its color, its tones in other words. Now, to be sure, they are hearable tones as distinct from tones of color—blue, rust, so on. They are hearable: [*sings opening notes to Beethoven's Fifth Symphony*] "Buh buh buh buum." "Rust rust rust apple-green." "Rose rose rose—which can also be a color—pea-green." And one can go on editing a film so that it has melodies, so that its colors keep shifting and changing as one would expect them to when listening to a little piece of the Fifth Symphony of Beethoven. [*sings*] "Buh buh buh buum, buh buh buh buum." Then it all depends on how you place these tones and melodies, these tones of these flowers that are so pictured and what they come to mean as a compendium of music. Because it is really close to music, and it's dependent finally upon a mystique that none of the other arts have. I believe it was Carlyle who stated, quite correctly, that "all the arts aspire to music." And they do because music is the fulsomeness of what art can be: it can be experience. To wit, if one has the wits to make that of it, you're actually having a poem like you'd have a moment very close to your own personal being. You're not having it as something you're throwing out there, like a throw of the dice for chance. You're having a film that's close to your own heart's beat, like in music: 'Buh buh buh buum, buh buh buh buum." The feet begin to move, the heart beats as one listens to the symphonies of, or dance music of, a great composer. Similarly, in an auditorium where people are experiencing the poetry of film: we can't thump and stamp our feet (though sometimes that does happen), but basically there's a whole feeling in that auditorium of bodies moving. One becomes aware of one's body moving, of one's bodily being. And thus one is having the experience of some kind of loving, of a mystique, that is dedicated to the celebration of the rose, or whatever is being pictured, what is being photographed. It's the celebration of it in relation to everything else that's appropriate, that enlarges that celebration. You can say it is thanks that a human gives back for all the goodness that is given to our eyes as we move through life seeing, seeing. "Oh I see!" we say, which is really like saying "Thank you God for . . ." like in prayer. "I see." Which is considered the compendium of thought. "I see! At last I get it." And that doesn't mean I understand two plus two equals four. That means I feel it down in my bones. It's become one with me. I can dance it. I'd die for it. More, and harder: I'd live for it. I'd live for it. . . . And that's the best I can do on the distinction between prose and poetry in cinema.

PC: Could you say a little about how you've shifted your work towards more camera-less filmmaking and has your vision changed over the years, over fifty years of filmmaking?
SB: A little should be said about the way in which I see, because most would say that I see very strangely. Though I don't see in any way that's stranger than others can approximate or approach in their visions, if they want. But it is true that when I was very young I had what's called poor eyesight. I had a wandering eye, this eye always drifted wherever it needed to go. Which is called the thyroid eye of the poet and I had the thyroid problems that go with it. So that I had every reason to suspect I might be a poet, though I didn't know what a poet was, which was perhaps one of the major reasons I didn't become one at that time. I was dyslexic, clearly, what they call these days dyslexic. I had all kinds of asthmatic wheezing and coughing. I had practically everything wrong with me that you could have as a child. I was gasping and wheezing, I had a hernia so that if I wasn't wearing a truss, or if the truss slipped out of place, the hernia would jam down into my left scrotum and I would begin gasping for breath. I couldn't get my breath unless someone pushed the truss back into place. So I grew up wearing a harness through childhood just so I could breathe. I had thicker and thicker glasses, which was that terrible mistake people make when someone is having trouble seeing something. It seems to me that all kinds of people rush in and compound that problem by adding instruments through which they're supposed to poke and peer, and they're of

course doing the best they can, but it was a disaster for me until I outgrew it. There came a point where I set these glasses aside because I wanted a sex life. Clark Kent with glasses: that did not attract young ladies to young men when I was growing up, alas! So at some point, just so I could have a life in common with what was expected of a movie hero, I set the glasses aside and lost them finally. For several weeks I was as if blind. I could hardly cross the street; it was dangerous for me to cross the street. Then gradually, slowly I struggled through to my own form of seeing. Because I was sharp to every movement. I became aware of the slightest of movements and was clear about the shift of shape. Any shape-shifting that went on in my environs was quickly picked up by me, my mind coming at it, having to deal with it. I had an entire life that was searching for that, that I and I alone could have, where I discovered what again I share with all humans. And people can try this if they want. You take a hand and let your eyes go out of focus where you're not squeezing the eyes to get a focus on. And look at the lines on the hand as you move it, you know, the lines that we're supposed to read for the fortune of our futures. And let that hand drift somewhere until, while it's focused on infinity, on way out there, beyond the solar system, let it move until those lines of the hand come into sharp focus. For most people it's somewhere between nine and twelve inches. Without any squeezing at all, without any musculature of your optic nerve system, you achieve what's called natural focus. Whole societies painted for this area of seeing. The Mayans did. Charles Olson told me that that's why you read their pictures crawling on your back through caves where, as you look up with your tallow light, only somewhere between nine and twelve inches the pictures come into and out of focus for you. Societies were involved in that as natural focus. That was your focus which, oddly, you shared the most with other people. It's that irony that the word that you most share with other people is that which makes you most distinct: "I." "I." I share that with you! [*laughs*] And you and so on, with everyone.

PC: Did your ways of seeing change from decade to decade, and as you changed your film techniques?
SB: Yeah, because as I grew older I began to have the sense that I couldn't just paint my inner eye, my closest, most secretive eye, even if that was what I shared the most with other people. I was obligated to adopt, to some extent, the norms of my culture. So just as I started by making narrative dramatic films (certainly *Interim* is a love movie inspired by the Italian neorealists), similarly, as I got older, I went back to narrative forms with a renewed sense of what narrative could be. That film did not have to be slavishly tied to conveying a story. That it could also be playful, like *Blue Moses*, and search and range among all the possibilities of what a narrative figure, a character in a story, would be, might be. And then also, I felt a compulsion, as I moved towards films like photographing the birth of children, I

felt drawn to the shared societal sight. To what I share most as a culture with the rest of my fellow humans, you know? What do I share with them really, when it comes down to these crucial moments that are so deeply meaningful to us, like when a baby is being born? Oh my, such a moment. And at such moments one also moves to what all of one's contemporaries are. And let me say also that as I, getting older, began to face death, knowing I was in my forties—a man who's lived in the sun knows that his time is running out at some point—facing that sense of death, I also came to a more societal sight and made what's called the *Pittsburgh Documentaries*, the ones on the police, and on the hospital, on basketball. And *The Act of Seeing with One's Own Eyes*, which is literally what autopsis or autopsy means. So those shifted.

PC: We had just talked about the Pittsburgh trilogy....
SB: If it comes to where you need to share with people—we all need to share something close with each other in the face of death or birth, or sex—and in these modes of being one can be more drawn to the normal story, to the normal way in which people write, or paint, or sculpt, or sing songs, or make movies of these things. That's where you find my work pulled toward just telling a story or making a picture, where what's at play is my trying to reach out to the society in that simple desperation which I share with everybody, you know? [*calls*] "Hello out there!" [*laughs*] Somewhere we do have equivalent visions of the universe. But what's really exciting is how different we are from each other, too. So the ideal is to carry both along, and that's what I've tried to do in my work. And that's the function of poetry, really. That is what poetry just is and does. It is making the great dance in language, in the case of poetry, and in pictures, in the case of moving pictures, mine. The great dance where I can feel that I'm the closest to anyone else's way of seeing just because I'm showing the uniqueness of my seeing. That is something for *sure* that I share with everybody, that each and every one of us is completely unique. There'll never be any two creatures on earth at all like you [*laughs*] . . . or like me. Never ever again is it conceivable that there can be such a thing, because there is such a compendium of all things that have gone to make up what I am. Starting right on the cellular level, when they're starting to put together the bare bones of what it is I'm going to grow up with to be just as an animal creature. And then all and every little movement and shift and change in my life. That's why Gertrude Stein said when you say the word "red," everyone hears that completely differently. Some are thinking of reading, some are thinking of the color. And then if you say, "No, I mean the color red," you delineate that. And what a shift of reds we have before us, and what do they mean—in addition to the social things that have been attached onto it, one's communist affiliations and so on [*laughs*].

But within all this, art is what permits us to reach out across the chasm to each other. And to do so lovingly, like as a dance, with rhythm and with the joy of tone. To sing of oneself, and in joyful exuberance in relation to another. Loving. And, in one sense, that's why the most difficult thing for art to re-present—and I don't really think it's the business of art to re-present in that normal sense but to the extent to which it can be said to do that—the most difficult, perhaps, is sexual loving. I say sexual because I want to get right down and bring in the whole flesh body and everything that has do with it, not leave it as some ideal [*laughs*] only. I think that one of my struggles has been most critically there. To the *Lovesongs*. . . . Every time that I deal with lovemaking, it always seemed to me some kind of a failure. And Marilyn first made it clear to me why this was: because the acts of being involved in art as an aesthetic experience are so completely different from those of loving. Such an alternate, such an other, they almost don't seem to exist in the same world. But then the drive is ever more fervent to enjoin such differences, to create a film that truly is what it's about, and is sexual loving. I'm hoping that *Lovesong* achieved that finally, and certainly there have been little achievements, both with camera and with hand-painting along the way, attempts at least. But how do you get such feelings, the complexities of someone feeling loving [*picks up and starts to unwind a roll of film*]—and I'm using 35mm here, most of my work's been on 16 and a great deal of it on 8, *but* we'll be lavish today and pull out a hunk of 35mm—how in the world do you get such tenderness of feeling and being, of a person moving through the world? You can take a picture of some young man who's an actor portraying me or you with a bouquet of flowers, a picture of him walking up to a door that's opening with a lovely lass, a corny old forties picture. But is that a way to represent? It certainly would be so used. And yet it's blasphemy. In agreement with Marilyn's discouragement with representing love in film is Orson Welles. I think the only thing she shares with Orson Welles [*laughs*] is that he said it's blasphemy to attempt to show sexual lovemaking or prayer. Those two things can never be represented on the screen because it's just a blasphemy for that to happen. [*Marilyn, his wife, enters with a cup of tea.*] And here comes a cup of tea [*laughs*], thank you. Here, put it here, Marilyn, so we can make it into a movie.

Now this may be the blessing and the reason why I made a major shift in my work when in midlife crisis, fully expecting I was finished, Marilyn and I found each other, and she announced at some point that she did not like to be photographed. In fact, it was stronger than that—I forgot how you put it, but it was "I don't want to be photographed." And I was just shocked because so much of my life had been photographing the story of my life and suddenly that was being cut off at the knees, you know, cut off altogether. She did not want that, she, who I would be needing to be with for the rest of my life, and never any more autobiography coming out of me. It took, I don't know, thirty seconds or a long while, and suddenly I felt an immense sense of relief. As if I was relieved of an enormous burden and one that was almost hopeless to begin with anyway, to make the occasion of a film on the same grounds as that of loving. "Ode to a Coy Mistress": who knows the coy mistress, or if she was coy, or how she felt about a poem being written about her. All we know is it's a vast mystery and poetry doesn't finally seem to have existed only to send valentines to each other. In fact that would be a horrible denigration and usage of it. Well, anyway, so you have a movie where Marilyn brings me a loving cup, beautiful. I take it to be silver, but she said it's stainless steel, sent by Ken and Flo Jacobs as our housewarming present. You can see how it all falls into a story. This can be a little story about some loving, but what a delimiting of the loving feelings we're having, if we end there. That's just a little story: we did the shot, that's it, and what's next, you know? No. In order to have feelings that are appropriate to such a thing, I have to engage the most inner thoughts, the sparking and synapting of the cathexis of my brain waves ticking. [*Unrolls a section of hand-scratched, black 35mm film*] Here is one second carved onto this film that is an approximation of what I see when my eyes are closed and I'm remembering, putting together the members of something. I'm seeing at most the hints of shape, not an entirety of some photographed documentation, but hints that are left free in the line that they can reverberate with the sense of feeling that's appropriate to such senses of loving. This happens to be a little section that I'm working on called *Chinese Series* in which, after twenty years of studying the Chinese hieroglyphs and so on, I finally feel I'm emboldened to attempt to do a little Chinese film called *Chinese Series*. I thought this would be it, one second, and then I sent it to Mary Beth Reed who does the printing for me. I said "No, if you print it"—not knowing at what stage it will arrive—"you have to double-print it, do every frame twice because I don't want to be upstaging Hollis Frampton's one-second movie."

I thought that's it, then. But then I went on a little ways and one day I started going and I suddenly started doing, guess what? More! More! [*laughs, unrolling the film*] And I thought, what is this? But, of course, I knew what it was. It's exegesis. The Chinese had the wisdom that often they'd spend more time on the explanations of, or commentaries as they call them, of a painting or a poem that had been placed before them than they did on the original thing itself. So call that the original second, one-second, and call this what I have to say about it. Because these lines are all related to those first two seconds (if double-printed, two seconds), they're all commentaries on it. [*Unrolling more of his film, he comes to a short section that is all black.*] Now here's a little break. Is this it? Is that it? I can't believe it. No! [*laughs*] There's more that needs to be said. And it's made when I'm up to it, when I'm enabled. It is made with my fingernails, with my spit. I spit upon this and loosen the emulsion and that gives me just enough so I can get in there with the fingernails and usually, with my eyes closed, feeling what I'm shaping. Knowing very well that it's nicely delineated, the individual frames. Knowing very clearly the frame, I can get in there, and I can work from my meat out, to what this is. So, in one sense, you could say, "This is the spit of the poet!" The *spit* of the filmmaker, as I won't fancy myself a poet, nope. And it's made from the nails themselves, feeling, pressing, making an impress of whatever feelings there are to them in space and shape and so on. So maybe a little film is being born, maybe not, who knows, but I'm trying, I'm trying. [*laughs*] I'm trying from this sickbed to sing a song. So, what's tough about that? Well, I'm sitting here blathering and filling in the narrative—what's missing is the soundtrack! "Sound, sound!" You remember that pathetic cry when the movie comes on but they haven't turned on the sound: "Sound! Sound!" people call out across the darkened auditorium. [*laughs*]

Well, I've made a number of sound films too, and I honor those sound films. And I've been very, very careful. The great master of sound films, for me, is Peter Kubelka, and he's given me the caution to *not* do anything easily or capriciously. He honors that I went silent. You know if a man can't say it or has nothing to say, best silence for God's sake. Don't sit blathering which I fear I may be doing because I'm on a thousand hydromorphine milligrams a day here. Just monstrous how my body seems to gobble up narcotics, and it's important that it be known because I'm fighting through all that difficulty of narcotics to make an articulation. But if I couldn't, what would I do? I'd sit here and scream. Not probably get quite that bad, I'm being dramatic. I almost had to stop making movies and get out of drama. I've been very fortunate, I think. It may not seem right for me to say so, sitting here all crippled up with cancer. But the truth of the matter is I've been very, very fortunate and I'm grappling still and struggling with the cancer too. With "vision therapy" as it's called. Marilyn's sister is involved in teaching self-hypnosis, which has helped me. I did some of that previously in my life. In fact I think every film I've ever made was involved in self-hypnosis primarily. But then once you get into that first step you soon get into the grounds of vision therapy where one is literally grasping with the mind's eye, almost tactilely, almost with touch, the cancer itself, and struggling with it. But one has to know something about me: I would never grasp anything hideously, i.e., out of "that hideous strength," as C. S. Lewis put it. I would not hideously struggle to ruin my destiny. I take it as it comes, and not easily always. It's just that I don't fight and fight against whatever it is it's supposed to be. I just want to make things as good as I can for my loved ones and for film, yes, dear film that sustained me throughout so much of all my life.

PC: Phil Solomon had mentioned that you had a conversation with Ken Jacobs about how at one point you were all thinking of your filmmaking as new, something with which to change the world.

SB: Yeah, I remember that and I have those moments when I think we've failed somehow to implant poetry in cinema, or to bring out the qualities of cinema that are truly where film can be pulling. There's so much overwhelming attention given now to the movies and to every conceivable usage of film except that for which I most naturally feel it was born—to be a poem. So I feel very often that we've lost the social battle. The movies sail along; most universities don't even use film anymore. They don't know the difference between film and video. And so whatever cheap purveyor they can bring—by cheap I mean inexpensive purveyor of the image—that they can equip their classrooms with, suffices in their wants. And in fact it's moving; it moves very much as it does in relationship to prose and poetry and pictures and so on. For example, there is now a determination in many classroom teachings to do away with the original source material altogether. If you're doing a course on Don Quixote, for instance, you can say, "Well, we know enough now about the artist to know that they didn't know what they were doing. Cervantes didn't know what he was doing, didn't have the least comprehension, so why study and spend that much time on the original source?" And people in some classes are even forbidden to read the source! [*laughs*] They say, "No! One thing you do not do, you do not read *Don Quixote* but we read every fine text that's been written on *Don Quixote*, every critique of it and so on." Well I would say this is going to an extreme with what the Chinese seem to have done in a more balanced way with their commentaries. Their commentaries are lovely if you think of them as a furtherance of whatever it is that was given to them by the original poem or the original painting, and so they do their commentaries. But when it comes to forbid looking at the original source, one begins to suspect that there's a battery of people that cannot make a poem, that cannot make a painting, that have betrayed the muse in some deep sense, which means they have betrayed their own life forms in some way, and then tried to sneak themselves and all their ideas under the coattails of Cervantes without even the grace to honor the source material they're using. They're just an ultimate extreme of bastard academic that we've had biting at our coattails all along the way in the whole history of studying the arts. Why read Shakespeare when after all you could study Frank Harris on Shakespeare? Well, so I worry about that—what am I doing sitting here blathering when one could just be showing some film?

PC: Could you say something about the snail's trail in the moonlight and why is it you've made so many films?

SB: I said that I would rather think of what I was doing as making a snail's trail in the moonlight. The snail knows muscularly what he or she is doing and is at one with every shift and shape of body in leaving this line of exuded spit along the rose. There's an image for you that the poets like to pounce on, the snail smearing the rose or the leaf of the rose. But they're just talking with words when they do that. There's that other side that's just literal. In the moonlight one can, as I've seen snails do, leave a trail that can be lit by the moon, that's soft, gentle light in the dark. Not a gloom but rather a frieze of shapes and forms. Such as by Phil Solomon when he makes his *Seasons*, which is based on my paintings. He takes the paintings themselves and he takes them out for air, gives them air. I would rather think of myself as leaving a snail's trail in the moonlight than of someone sitting and consciously making an art.

PC: Can you think of something that unites all the different kinds of films you've made, from *Window Water Baby Moving* . . . from *Mothlight*, *Dog Star Man*, all the way to the *Chinese Series*, that is similar, that makes clear why they all come from you?

SB: Mmm. . . . No, it drifts away from me. Not because I'm drifty or lazy or whatever, though that I may be also, it just drifts away from me. . . . I think I'm done. I think I can't give you more than that. [*sings*] "I can't give you anything but love, baby! That's the only thing I've plenty of, baby! No-dah, dah. . . ." See, most people don't know more words than that to the song [*sings "la la"*] and I don't want to botch it up, it's such a lovely tune. So let's call it a day and a year. 2003, made it through to 2003, hard to imagine. Sun is coming out, if I was just a little stronger I could go to a movie. [*laughs*] I don't have the strength, yeah, I would love to. But, not today, maybe it will come back next week.

Additional Resources

Books

Barrett, Gerald R., and Wendy Brabner. *Stan Brakhage: A Guide to References and Resources*. Boston: G. K. Hall, 1983.
Brakhage, Stan. *Metaphors on Vision*. Ed. P. Adams Sitney. New York: Film Culture, 1963.
———. *A Moving Picture Giving and Taking Book*. West Newbury: Frontier Press, 1971.
———. *Film Biographies*. Berkeley: Turtle Island, 1977.
———. *Brakhage Scrapbook: Collected Writings*. Ed. Robert A. Haller. New Paltz: Documentext, 1982.
———. *I . . . Sleeping*. New York: Island Cinema Resources, 1988.
———. *Essential Brakhage: Selected Writings on Filmmakers*. Ed. Bruce R. McPherson. New York: Documentext, 2001.
———. *Film at Wit's End: Eight Avant-Garde Filmmakers*. Kingston: Documentext, 1989.
———. *Telling Time: Essays of a Visionary Filmmaker*. New York: Documentext, 2003.
Elder, R. Bruce. *A Body of Vision: Representations of the Body in Recent Film and Poetry*. Waterloo: Wilfrid Laurier University Press, 1998.
———. *The Films of Stan Brakhage in the American Tradition of Gertrude Stein and Charles Olson*. Waterloo: Wilfrid Laurier University Press, 1998.
James, David E, ed. *Stan Brakhage: Filmmaker*. Philadelphia: Temple University Press, 2005.
Keller, Marjorie. *The Untutored Eye: Childhood in the Films of Cocteau, Cornell and Brakhage*. Madison: Farleigh Dickinson University Press, 1986.
Nesthus, Marie. *Stan Brakhage*. Minneapolis: Walker Art Center, 1979.
Powell, Anna. *Delueze, Altered States and Film*. Edinburgh: Edinburgh University Press, 2007.
Sitney, P. Adams. *Visionary Film*. New York: Oxford University Press, 1974. Reprinted 1979 and 2002.

Vergé, Emilie. *Stan Brakhage: Catalogue Raisonné, Films (1952–2003)*. Paris: Paris Expérimental Editions, 2016.

Wodening, Jane. *Brakhage's Childhood*. New York: Granary Books, 2015.

Articles and Book Chapters

Arthur, Paul. "Qualities of Light. Stan Brakhage and the Continuing Pursuit of Vision." *Film Comment* 41, no. 5 (September/October 1995): 69–76.

Brabner, Wendy. "*The Act of Seeing with One's Own Eyes*: Stan Brakhage and Robert Creeley." *Library Chronicle of the University of Texas*, no. 17 (1981): 84–103.

Brakhage, Marilyn. "On Stan Brakhage and Visual Music." *Experimental Film: The Missing Frame*. Ed. Benjamin Meade. Kansas City: Avila University Press, 2010. 46–64.

Brakhage, Stan. "Telluride Gold: Brakhage Meets Tarkovsky." *Rolling Stock*, no. 6 (1983): 11–14.

Brakhage, Stan, and Malcolm Le Grice. "Stan Brakhage and Malcolm Le Grice Debate." *Cinema News* 78, no. 3 & 4 (1978): 3–4, 18–26.

Camhi, G. "Notes on Brakhage's *23rd Psalm Branch*." *Film Culture*, no. 67–69 (1979): 97–129.

Elder, R. Bruce. "'Moving Visual Thinking': Dante, Brakhage, and the Works of Energeia." *Dante and the Unorthodox: The Aesthetics of Transgression*. Ed. James Miller. Waterloo: Wilfrid Laurier University Press, 2005. 394–449.

Grauer, Victor A. "Brakhage and the Theory of Montage." *Millennium Film Journal*, no. 32/33 (Fall 1998): 105–29.

James, David E. "Stan Brakhage: The Filmmaker as Poet." *Allegories of Cinema: American Film in the Sixties*. Princeton: Princeton University Press, 1989. 29–57.

Nesthus, Marie. "The Influence of Olivier Messiaen on the Visual Art of Stan Brakhage in *Scenes From Under Childhood*." *Film Culture*, no. 63 & 64 (1977): 39–50.

Osterweil, Ara. "Stan Brakhage: Acts of Seeing." *Flesh Cinema: The Corporeal Turn in American Avant-Garde Film*. Manchester: Manchester University Press, 2014. 93–135.

Sitney, P. Adams. "Brakhage and Modernism." *Masterpieces of Modernist Cinema*. Ed. Ted Perry. Bloomington: Indiana University Press, 2006. 159–78.

———. "Brakhage and the Tales of the Tribe." *Eyes Upside Down*. New York: Oxford University Press, 2008. 243–58.

———. "Stan Brakhage's Poetics." *The Cinema of Poetry*. New York: Oxford University Press, 2014. 149–95.

Stam, Robert. "Seeing with Experimental Eyes: Stan Brakhage's *The Act of Seeing* with One's Eyes." *Documenting the Documentary: Close Readings of Documentary Film and Video*. Ed. Barry Keith Grant and Jeannette Sloniowski. Detroit: Wayne State University Press, 1998. 269–85.

Wees, William C. "'Giving Sight to the Medium': Stan Brakhage." *Light Moving in Time*. Berkeley: University of California Press, 1992. 77–105.

———. "Words and Images in Stan Brakhage's *23rd Psalm Branch*." *Cinema Journal* 27, no. 2 (Winter 1988): 40–49.

Interviews

Abbott, Rebecca. "The Avant-Garde in American Film: An Interview with Stan Brakhage." *Sacred Heart University Review* 9, no. 1 & 2 (Fall 1988): 1–13.

Andersch, Brecht, and Timoleon Wilkins. "Christopher Maclaine and the San Francisco Film Scene in the 1950s: An Interview with Stan Brakhage." *Radical Light*. Ed. Steve Anker, Kathy Geritz, and Steve Seid. Berkeley: University of California Press, 2010. 55–62.

Dillon, Karen, and Stan Brakhage. "Interview (mezzo)." *High Ground*, no. 4 (1998): 34–41.

Dunbar, Jennifer. "Stan Brakhage: Life Behind the Camera." *Boulder Monthly*, September 1979, 25–30.

Grossinger, Richard. "Interview with Stan Brakhge." *Io* 14, no. 3 (1973): 353–64.

Higgins, Gary, et al. "Grisled Roots: An Interview with Stan Brakhage." *Millennium Film Journal*, no. 26 (Fall 1992): 56–66.

Jenkins, Bruce. "Interview with Stan Brakhage." *Stan Brakhage*. Eds. Bert Sichel and Emilia Garcia-Romeu. Madrid: Museo Nacional Centro de Arte Reina Sofia. 83–89

Kawin, Bruce. "Interview with Stan Brakhage, Parts 1–6." *By Brakhage, An Anthology, volume 1*, 2-disc DVD set, The Criterion Collection, 2003.

MacDonald, Scott. "The Filmmaker as Visionary." *Film Quarterly* 56, no. 3 (Spring 2003): 2–11.

Mason, Marilynne. "Stan Brakhage's Last Interview." *Northern Lights* 1 (1983): 7–33.

Parent, Bob. "A Stan Brakhage Premier." *New Cinema Review* 1, no. 1 (September 1969): 10–14.

Perry, Ted. "Stan Brakhage Seminar." *Dialogue on Film* 2, no. 3 (January 1973): 2–11.

Pipolo, Tony. "Family Business." *Artforum* 52, no. 7 (2014): 254–59, 308.

Porte, Michael, et al. "Discussion." *Cinema Now: Stan Brakhage, John Cage, Jonas Mekas, Stan Vanderbeek*. Ed. Hector Currie. Cincinnati: University of Cincinnati. 23–28.

Still, Colin. "Brakhage on Brakhage, Parts 1–4." *By Brakhage, An Anthology, volume 1*, 2-disc DVD set, The Criterion Collection, 2003.

Journal Issues Devoted to Brakhage

Stan Brakhage: Correspondences. *Chicago Review* 47, no. 4 (Winter 2001) and 48, no. 1 (Spring 2002).
A Sense of Sight: A Special Issue Devoted to Stan Brakhage. *Canadian Journal of Film Studies* 14, no. 1 (Spring 2005).
Brakhage at the Millennium: The Words of Stan Brakhage. *Millennium Film Journal*, no. 47–49 (Fall/Winter 2007–2008).

Index

Abstract Expressionism, 133, 143
Abstract Expressionists, 68, 143
Anger, Kenneth, 20; *Fireworks*, 100; *Maldoror*, 21, 32
Antonioni, Michelangelo, *Red Desert*, 135
Architect's Office, 86, 93
Art in Cinema, 100

Bach, Johann Sebastian, 12, 72, 92
Baillie, Bruce, *Castro Street*, 61, 62
Bakker, Robert, *The Dinosaur Heresies*, 131
Baudelaire, Charles, 14
Beethoven, Ludwig von, 103; Fifth Symphony, 151
Bergman, Ingmar, 44
Blaser, Robin, 98
Book of Film, The, 125
Book of Job, 60
Book of the Dead, 70
Book of the Family, The, 125
Boultenhouse, Charles, 11
Brakhage, Anton, 86, 88
Brakhage, Crystal, 23, 82
Brakhage (Wodening), Jane, 4, 5, 6, 7, 8, 9, 10, 11, 12, 14, 16, 17, 18, 19, 20, 21, 23, 25, 26, 27, 29–50, 76, 77, 78–81, 82, 99, 105, 125
Brakhage, Marilyn, 76, 78, 86, 155, 156
Brakhage, Myrrena, 10
Brakhage, Neowyn, 23, 25

Brakhage, Stan: on act of seeing, 49, 50, 66–68, 70; on aesthetic ecology, 72–73, 80, 142, 143; on being a documentarian, 118–19; on chance operations, 22, 26, 91, 93, 109; on childbirth films, 10, 19, 24, 73, 82–83; on closed-eye vision, 22, 47, 55, 67, 68, 69, 70, 71, 112, 113; on distinction between prose and poetry, 149, 151–52; on envisionment, 69, 112, 113, 139; on film and music, 71–72, 92–93, 102–3, 151–52; on filming his family, 76–77, 78, 80–83, 114; on Freudian slips, 73, 74; on home movies, 25, 73, 80; on hypnagogic vision, 41, 50, 54, 66, 67, 68, 69, 70, 71, 83, 84, 86, 141, 142, 148; on ineffable, 72, 125, 139; on Jane's collaboration, 7, 10, 14, 17, 23, 25, 27, 106; on light, 45–47, 49, 51–65, 71, 85; on memory feedback, 70; on memory recall, 67; on moving visual thinking, 67, 70, 71, 84, 133, 139; on muse, 38, 79–80, 134, 158; on myth, 80, 81, 111; on nothing, 72, 94, 95; on open-eye vision, 66, 69, 70; on painting on film, 22, 24, 41, 47, 55, 68–70, 71, 73, 84–85, 86, 94; on peripheral vision, 60, 66, 67, 68, 74, 92; on problems with his eyesight, 29–31, 99, 152–53; on psychodrama, 22, 84, 86, 87, 89; on rejection of narrative drama, 28, 37, 59, 73, 74, 77, 80, 100–101; on rejection of sound, 72, 89, 104–5; on Renaissance perspective, 24, 29, 66; on scratching on film, 36, 69, 70, 71, 73, 86; on Shirley Temple syndrome, 73, 112, 114; on song as inspiration, 12, 74; on studying music, 89–91; on superimpositions, 61, 62, 67, 107, 110, 130; on symmetry, 136, 139; on trance process, 80, 134; on uniqueness, 34–35, 74, 154; on unnamable, 37, 63, 125, 137, 139, 143; on visual music, 71, 92, 142

Works:

Act of Seeing with One's Own Eyes, The. See *Pittsburgh Trilogy, The/The Pittsburgh Documents*

Anticipation of the Night, 3–5, 12, 25, 35, 36, 58, 89, 98, 99, 100–103, 105, 108, 122

Arabic Numeral Series, The, 70

Art of Vision, The, 110, 125

Babylon Series, 70, 71

Ballad of the Colorado Ute, The, 108

Bird, 130

Blue Moses, 86, 105, 153

Boulder Blues and Pearls and . . ., 92

Cat's Cradle, 7–9, 11, 37

Chartres Series, 95

Child's Garden and the Serious Sea, A, 88–89, 126

Chinese Series, 156, 159

Christ Mass Sex Dance, 67, 92

Colorado Legend, The, 108

Commingled Containers, 97

Dante Quartet, The, 69, 83–84, 85
    Hell Itself, 83
    Hell Spit Flexion, 83, 84
    Purgation, 83
    existence is song, 83

Daybreak and Whiteye, 90

Dead, The, 9, 11, 13, 17, 19–21

Desistfilm, 6, 36, 73, 148

Deus Ex. See *Pittsburgh Trilogy, The/The Pittsburgh Documents*

Dog Star Man, 11, 13, 14, 17–19, 21, 23, 26, 77, 81, 91, 94, 107–11, 122, 125, 159
    Dog Star Man: Prelude, 11, 13, 17, 21–24, 26, 69, 109
    Dog Star Man: Part 1, 5, 17, 26–27, 109
    Dog Star Man: Part 2, 68, 109
    Dog Star Man: Part 3, 109
    Dog Star Man: Part 4, 109

Domain of the Moment, 130

Dominion, 76, 119

Duplicity, 108

Egyptian Series, 70

existence is song. See *Dante Quartet, The*

Eye Myth, 69, 84

Eyes. See *Pittsburgh Trilogy, The/The Pittsburgh Documents*

FaustFilm, 86–87, 93
    Faust, Part 1, 93
    Faust, Part 2, 93
    Faust, Part 4, 87, 93

15 Song Traits, 78, 82

Films by Stan Brakhage: An Avant-Garde Home Movie, 24, 25–26

Fire of Waters, 90

Fireloop, 93

Flesh of Morning, 100, 148

Four Visions in Meditation, 87

Garden of Earthly Delights, The, 142

"he was born, he suffered, he died," 71

Hell Itself. See *Dante Quartet, The*

Hell Spit Flexion. See *Dante Quartet, The*

Horseman, the Woman and the Moth, The, 54
Hymn to Her, 79
I Dreaming, 93
Interim, 6, 44, 92, 96, 97, 98, 153
Interpolations, 69, 84, 91, 92
Jane, 79
Kindering, 93
Loom, The, 79
Loud Visual Noises, 93
Lovesong, 155
Lovesongs, 155
Loving, 8, 68, 84, 105, 108
Marilyn's Window, 88, 89
Matins, 94
Mothlight, 92, 104, 142, 159
Naughts, 95
Night Cats, 108
Nodes, 94
Passage Through: A Ritual, 72, 93–94
Pittsburgh Trilogy, The/The Pittsburgh Documents, 116–19, 154
    Eyes, 43, 76, 117
    Deus Ex, 52, 55, 58, 76
    The Act of Seeing with One's Own Eyes, 76, 117, 118, 119, 154
Prelude. See *Dog Star Man: Prelude*
Process, The, 59
Purgation. See *Dante Quartet, The*
Riddle of Lumen, The, 29
Roman Numeral Series, The, 70
Scenes from Under Childhood, 36, 43, 73, 80, 82, 92, 108, 112–16, 125
Sexual Meditation: Open Field, 61–62
Shores of Phos: A Fable, The, 59–60
Sincerity, 82, 108
Sirius Remembered, 11–16, 37, 98, 103, 107–8, 110
Songs, 80, 82
Text of Light, The, 59, 62–63, 69, 83, 119–23

Thigh Lyre Line Triangular, 24–25, 68, 84
23rd Psalm Branch, 97
Untitled (For Marilyn), 83, 85–86, 96
Way to Shadow Garden, The, 100
Wedlock House: An Intercourse, 5–7, 43, 105, 106
Window Water Baby Moving, 7–8, 9–11, 24, 68, 82–83, 98, 104, 105–7, 108, 159
Wold Shadow, The, 122
Brakhage, Vaughn, 86
Bride of Critical Mass, 42
Broughton, James, 100
Buñuel, Luis, 23; *Un Chien Andalou/The Andalusian Dog*, 23, 100
Burroughs, William, 132

Cage, John, 22, 27, 90, 91, 95, 105, 109, 129
Camper, Fred, 110
Chikiris, Michael, 51, 116
Chodorov, Pip, *A Visit to Stan Brakhage*, 145
Cinema 16, 100, 101
Cocteau, Jean, 3, 39, 85, 98; *Beauty and the Beast*, 98; *Blood of a Poet*, 100; *Orphée/Orpheus*, 3, 85, 97, 98, 100, 126, 130
Cornell, Joseph, *A Legend for Fountains*, 94
Corner, Philip, 72; *Through the Mysterious Barricades (After Couperin)*, 93
Corrigan, Rick, 93
Creeley, Robert, 130

Dante Alighieri, 83, 84; *The Divine Comedy*, 83
Davenport, Guy, 124, 127
Davis, Jim, 121, 122
De Sica, Vittorio, 98
Debussy, Claude, *La Mer/The Sea*, 103

Deren, Maya, 82; *Meshes of the Afternoon*, 100
Die Tödliche Doris, 93
Dixon, Sally, 116
Dorn, Ed, 130
Dorsky, Nathaniel "Nick," 126
Dreyer, Carl, 40, 73
Duncan, Robert, 29, 44, 98, 130
Durrell, Lawrence, 9; *Justine*, 9

Eddington, Arthur, *The Nature of the Physical World*, 108
Edison, Thomas Alva, 40, 51, 58
Eggeling, Viking, 84, 142
Eisenstein, Sergei, 28, 29–30, 32–33, 34, 35, 38, 39, 40, 41, 48, 67, 73, 80; *Battleship Potemkin*, 35; *Ivan the Terrible*, 28
Erigena, Johannes Scotus, 45, 56

Feldman, Morton, 27
Fischinger, Oskar, 84
Ford, John, 100
Foster, Stephen, 93
Frampton, Hollis, 78, 147, 149, 156
Freud, Sigmund, 9, 22, 115; *Civilization and Its Discontents*, 36; *The Psychopathology of Everyday Life*, 8
Freudfilm, 22

Gamow, Igor, 111
German Expressionist painting, 32, 51
Gilgamesh, 108
Graves, Robert, 18; *The Greek Myths*, 18; *The White Goddess*, 24
Gregorian chant, 12
Griffith, D. W., 38, 39, 67, 73

Haertling, Joel, 86, 93
Hafler Trio, 93
Hammer, Barbara, 78

Hammurabi, 70
Handel, George Frederick, *Messiah*, 129
Hemholtz, Hermann von, 55
hieroglyphs, 70, 71, 131, 132
Hubka, Janis, 44

Impressionism, 139
Impressionists, 143
Invisible Man, The, 61
Irma la Douce, 83
Isou, Isidore, *Venom and Eternity* (aka *Treatise on Drivel and Eternity*), 100
Italian neorealists, 153
Ives, Charles, 72

Jacobs, Ken, 158
James, Henry, 127
James, William, 130
Joe Faust, 86
Johnson, Ronald: *ARK*, 125, 128; "Foundations," 128; "Hurrah for Euphony," 126; *RADI OS*, 126, 129
Joyce, James, 108

Kandinsky, Wassily, 68
Kelly, Ellsworth, 138
Kelman, Ken, 35
Kenner, Hugh, *The Pound Era*, 46, 59
Kline, Franz, 68
Kubelka, Peter, 157
Kurosawa, Akira, 100

Laughton, Charles, 147, 148
Leacock, Ricky, 118
Lewis, C. S., 157
Lumière brothers, 40
Lye, Len, 84

Mackay, Kathryn, 127
MacLane, Chris, *The End*, 100
Malraux, André, *The Voices of Silence*, 77

Matisse, Henri, 132, 133
Méliès, 38, 39–40, 73, 109; *The Dreyfus Affair*, 40
Menken, Marie, 84
Merleau-Ponty, Maurice, 53, 62, 63; *Phenomenology of Perception*, 65
Messiaen, Olivier, 92
Metaphors on Vision, 63, 79, 99, 122, 132, 145
McClure, Michael, 24, 25, 46, 98, 130
Michelangelo di Lodovico Buonarroti Simoni, 95; *David*, 95; *Moses*, 95; unfinished sculptures, 95
Milton, John, 126, 129; *Paradise Regained*, 126
Modernism, 127
Mummy, The, 97
musique concrète, 90

Nelson, Gunvor, 84; *Field Study #2*, 84; *Frame Line*, 84
Night of the Hunter, The, 147
Noh drama, 26
Nurse with Wound, 93
Nutcracker Suite, The, 92

Olson, Charles, 28, 53, 99, 118, 130, 140, 153; *Proprioception*, 28
Oppenheimer, Frank, 49

Patchen, Kenneth, 98
Peterson, Sidney, 100
Phillips, Stan, 96
Plato, 56, 58, 136
Pollock, Jackson, 68, 91, 143
Pound, Ezra, 26, 45, 71, 102, 108, 111, 127; *The Cantos*, 59; *Gaudier-Brezska: A Memoir*, 26
Presley, Elvis, "Blue Suede Shoes," 92

Rameau, Jean-Philippe, *The Conversation of the Muses*, 38

Reed, Mary Beth, 156
Reich, Wilhelm, 49, 58
Rembrandt, Rijn van, 42
Renaissance, 127
Rexroth, Kenneth, 98, 130
Richter, Hans, 142
Rilke, Rainer Maria, 84, 141
Romanticism, 101, 128
Rosenblum, Gordon, 119, 121
Rossellini, Roberto, 98
Rothko, Mark, 68, 73
Rothko Chapel, 72
Rouault, Georges, 133
Ruttmann, Walter, 84

Schlegel, Karl Wilhelm Friedrich, 131
Schneemann, Carolee, 8, 84; *Fuses*, 84
Schumann, Robert, 115
Shakespeare, William, 158; *Macbeth*, 150
Sharits, Paul 38; *S:TREAM:SS:ECTION:S:ECTION:S:SECTIONED*, 38
Sisyphus, 108, 109
Sitney, P. Adams, 4, 49, 50, 119
Smith, Harry, 84, 85
Snow White and the Seven Dwarfs, 97
Solomon, Phil, 103, 158; *Seasons*, 159
Spicer, Jack, 98
Stein, Gertrude, 12, 13, 23, 49, 53, 57, 87, 101, 106, 142, 149–51, 154; *Stanzas in Meditation*, 135, 143; *The World Is Round*, 150
Still, Clyfford, 122
Stroheim, Erich von, 2; *Greed*, 100
Sullivan, Louis, 132
Sunday Associates, The, 87
Surrealism, 22

Tenney, James, 8, 84, 92, 105; *Blue Suede*, 92
Tolstoy, Leo, 143
Turner, J. M. W., 68, 127
Tyler, Parker, 11

VanDerBeek, Stan, 48
Varèse, Edgard, 90, 91, 92; *Deserts*, 91, 92, 105; *Poème électronique*, 91
Victory of Samothrace, 47
Vogel, Amos, 101

Webern, Anton, 12
Weegee, 81
Welles, Orson, 98, 155
Williams, William Carlos, 126
Wittgenstein, Ludwig, 19; *Tractatus Logico-Philosophicus*, 19
Wordsworth, William, 81

Zappa, Frank, 92
Zoviet, France, 93
Zukofsky, Louis, 98, 130

www.ingramcontent.com/pod-product-compliance
Lightning Source LLC
Chambersburg PA
CBHW021842220426
43663CB00005B/366